ASIAN DEFENCE REVIEW 2011

ASIAN DEFENCE REVIEW 2011

Air Commodore
Jasjit Singh
AVSM, VrC, VM (Retd)
Editor

KNOWLEDGE WORLD
KW Publishers Pvt Ltd
New Delhi

Centre for Air Power Studies
New Delhi

The Centre for Air Power Studies is an independent, non-profit, academic research institution established in 2002 under a registered Trust to undertake and promote policy-related research, study and discussion on the trends and developments in defence and military issues, especially air power and the aerospace arena, for civil and military purposes. Its publications seek to expand and deepen the understanding of defence, military power, air power and aerospace issues without necessarily reflecting the views of any institution or individuals except those of the authors.

Jasjit Singh
Director
Centre for Air Power Studies
P-284, Arjan Path
Subroto Park
New Delhi 110010

Tele: (91-11) 25699131
E-mail: diroffice@aerospaceindia.org

Published in India by
Kalpana Shukla
KW Publishers Pvt Ltd
4676/21, First Floor, Ansari Road, Daryaganj, New Delhi 110002
T: +91.11.23263498 / 43528107 **E:** knowledgeworld@vsnl.net
www.kwpub.com

ISBN 978-93-81904-00-8

Printed and bound in India

Contents

Contributors

Mr. **Anand V.** is a Research Associate at the Centre for Air Power Studies, New Delhi.

Ms **Shalini Chawla** is a Senior Fellow at the Centre for Air Power Studies, New Delhi.

Wing Commander **Vishal Nigam** is a Research Fellow at the Centre for Air Power Studies, New Delhi.

Mr. **Winston P. Nagan** is Sam T. Dell Research Scholar, Professor of Law, Affiliate Professor of Anthropology, Affiliate Professor of Latin American Studies and Founding Director, Institute for Human Rights, Peace and Development.

Mr. **Sitakanta Mishra** is a Research Fellow at the Centre for Air Power Studies, New Delhi.

Group Captain **Arun K. Singh** is a Senior Fellow at the Centre for Air Power Studies, New Delhi.

Group Captain **A. V. Chandrasekaran** is a Senior Fellow at the Centre for Air Power Studies, New Delhi.

Wing Commander **Nishant Gupta** is a Research Fellow at the Centre for Air Power Studies, New Delhi.

Group Captain **A. K. Chordia** is a Senior Fellow at the Centre for Air Power Studies, New Delhi.

Dr **Manpreet Sethi** is a Senior Fellow at the Centre for Air Power Studies, New Delhi.

1

China's Space Capabilities: The Satellite Programme

Anand V.

> If it were not for the atomic bomb, the hydrogen bomb and the satellites we have launched since the 1960s, China would not have its present international standing as a great, influential country.
>
> – Deng Xiaoping

Introduction

The space programme in China evolved over the years by achieving significant milestones since its inception in the mid-1950s. At the core of China's space programme is the satellite programme, which has made possible China's telecommunication and broadcasting as well as geo-informatics related applications, and given it the required capability to carry out socio-economic, industrial as well as technological development. Since the launch of the first satellite in 1970, various types of satellites have been developed to cater to diverse applications, both civilian and military.

Recently, China took the world by surprise by launching 15 satellites in a single year in 2010, for the first time matching the US. Such an achievement, through a largely indigenous programme, reflects systematic planning and execution and a strong emphasis on space-faring infrastructure development, while adhering to a definite timeframe. In this context, this paper would attempt to understand in greater detail the space capabilities that China possesses with respect to its satellite programme. The paper would initially trace the origin of China's space programme and its evolution through the years. The key to transporting satellites into orbit, maintaining their positions and controlling their operations in space are the infrastructure facilities, including the launch and telemetry, tracking and control facilities and the launch vehicles, which, would, therefore, be assessed. A detailed study and analysis of the existing active satellites in orbit would then be carried out in each of the different areas of application. The paper would conclude with an attempt to estimate the future trajectory of China's satellite programme, taking into account its current trends as well as future goals.

The Origin and Evolution of China's Space Programme

Civilisational Roots of China's Space-Faring Ambitions

The origins of not only the Chinese, but also the whole of humanity's space-faring efforts can be traced back to ancient China because it was here that the rocket, the indispensible vehicle for space launches, was conceived. Rockets or "flying arrows" in Chinese were invented by Feng Jishen in the year 970 and were powered with gunpowder, yet another Chinese invention. The first Chinese attempt to reach the heavens was made by a 16th century inventor named Wan Hu who used a rocket propelled chair for the purpose, although ending in a fatal accident.[1] Thus, the Chinese ambitions of venturing into the domain of outer space have very old civilisational roots.

Origin of China's Space Programme

These ambitions reemerged centuries later in the People's Republic of China (PRC), established by the Communist Party of China (CPC) in 1949 under Chairman Mao Zedong. China's space programme basically emerged out of its ballistic missile programme. Since the establishment of the PRC, Washington emerged as a foe to Beijing because they found themselves on opposing sides of various geo-political developments like the formation of Cold War blocs, the Taiwan issue and the Korean and Vietnam Wars. The US further intimidated the Chinese with "nuclear blackmail" three times, provoking Mao to plan the establishment of a nuclear weapons programme.[2] Beijing's relationship with Moscow also soured through the end of the 1950s because of political and ideological reasons, especially the widening gap between Mao and Khrushchev, which resulted in the development of the Sino-Soviet schism which came to a head in the 1960s. The deteriorating geo-political and regional security situation with respect to China, thus, demanded the setting up of an effective nuclear deterrence for which developing a robust and reliable ballistic missile capability as part of its delivery system was essential. The ballistic missile programme, thus, established in 1956, also included within it a satellite programme, which initiated China's space activities. During its inception, the space programme was viewed as a medium for the larger ballistic missile programme rather than as a goal in itself.[3] It came to the forefront only after the launch of the Sputnik in 1957, when the military as well as civilian benefits of space and satellite applications became clear for the Chinese government, including gaining technological prowess and international prestige for the nascent nation emerging after a century of backwardness and humiliation.[4] All these reasons contributed to the establishment of the satellite programme in 1958.

Establishment of the Programme

China's space programme was kick-started by Qian Xuesen, widely acknowledged as the father of the nation's ballistic missile as well as space programme. Qian had studied in the US, in prestigious technical institutes like the Massachusetts Institute of Technology (MIT) and the California Institute of Technology (Caltech). He had worked in the field of rocketry and had helped in setting up the Jet Propulsion Laboratories in the US. His proposals inspired the 1950's Dyna-Soar project which ultimately led to the design of the Space Shuttle.[5] However, during the height of the McCarthy witchhunts, Qian was accused of being a Communist and was, thus, deported to China in 1955.

Beijing was quick to welcome Qian and others like Chen Fangyun (electronics expert), Sun Jiadong (rocket and satellite expert), Chen Kuanneng (metal physicist), Yang Jiaxi (automation specialist), Guo Yonghuai (aerodynamicist) and Wang Xiji (recoverable satellite specialist) returning from the US, at a time when it badly required the technical resources required for setting up a robust science and technology base. Moreover, the initiation of the nuclear programme by Mao in 1955 created a pressing demand for the development of delivery systems. Qian himself made a proposal to the CPC Central Committee for establishing a national defence aeronautics industry in 1956. A Scientific Planning Commission was set up under Premier Zhou Enlai after Mao's 1956 proposal to develop science and technology. It drew up a "long range planning essential for science and technology development, 1956-1957" for atomic energy, rockets, jet technology and computers. This led to the establishment of the 5th Research Academy of the Ministry of National Defence by the CPC Central Committee for the nation's space efforts on October 8, 1956, laying the official foundation of China's ballistic missile programme as well as its space programme. Qian was made the first Director of the Rocket Research Institute established under the academy.[6]

Since China was lagging behind countries like the US and USSR in rocketry, it badly required outside technical assistance. This much needed help was obtained from the Soviet Union through the "New Defence Technical Accord" in October 1957 .[7] However, this cooperation did not last long as the Sino-Soviet schism developed due to which the Soviets stopped all technical assistance in 1960. This resulted in China choosing a path towards indigenously developing its space programme with the initial Soviet technical knowhow and the expertise of the US returned team of scientists and engineers. The establishment and further growth of the programme would not have been possible without state as well as military support when it came to technological and economic constraints.[8]

Table 1: Evolutionary Timeline of China's Space Programme

Year / Date	Event
1958	Formation of group 581, initiating the satellite programme*
February19, 1960	Launch of the first indigenous liquid fuelled rocket (T-7M)
1965	Restarting of the satellite programme
April 24, 1970	Launch of the first satellite (Dong Fang Hong-1) through the first Chang Zheng rocket (CZ-1)
1975	Launch and recovery of the first recoverable satellite (Fanhui Shi Weixing)
1979	The first ocean-going tracking ship (Yuanwang-1) commissioned
September 20, 1981	Three satellites launched on a single rocket for the first time (Shin Jian-2, 2A, and 2B)
1986	Entry into the commercial launch programme
April 7, 1990	First commercial satellite launched (AsiaSat-1)
1992	Start of the manned space programme (Project 921 or the Shen Zhou programme)
November 20, 1999	Launch of Shen Zhou-1 (unmanned test flight)
October 14, 1999	Launch of the first China-Brazil Earth Resource Satellite (CBERS-1)
June 28, 2000	Launch of the first micro satellite (Tsinghua-1)
October 31, 2000	Launch of the first Beidou navigation satellite (Beidou-1)
October 15, 2003	Launch of the first manned spacecraft (Shen Zhou-5)
April 18, 2004	Launch of the first nano satellite (nano satellite-1)
September 27, 2008	First extra vehicular activity in outer space (Shen Zhou-7)
January 11, 2007	First ASAT test (on an own weather satellite)
October 24, 2007	Launch of the first unmanned lunar orbiter (Chang'e-1)
September 24, 2008	Launch of Tian Lian-1, the first Data Relay Satellite (DRS)

* The programme was shelved due to economic problems following the great famine in 1959.

The Infrastructure of China's Satellite Programme

Launch Facilities

China started setting up facilities for launching rockets into space from 1958. Up to now, three major space launch centres have been constructed for both domestic and international requirements. The locations have been selected based on the geographical factors affecting launch effectiveness and economy, convenience of transportation as well as national security concerns; and all three of them are located inland. These facilities are claimed to have state-of-the-art facilities for launch vehicle and spacecraft testing, preparation, launch and in-flight tracking and safety control, as well as for orbit predictions.[9]

The first facility is the **Jiuquan Satellite Launch Centre (JSLC)** in the Gobi desert in Gansu province from where the manned missions, recoverable reconnaissance and earth resource satellites and sounding rockets are launched. It was established in 1958 as the first launch site for China's space programme.[10] The geographical coordinates of this launch site are 100°E and 41°N. Its location deep inland which reduced its vulnerability from a US naval offensive was a key security factor which figured in the selection of this site. The dry climate and extended hours of daylight which are characteristic of this arid region are highly favourable for space launches. The first rocket launch in 1960 and also the first satellite launch in 1970 took place from this centre.[11] It is used for launches into low and medium orbits, with large orbital inclination angles ranging from 40-56°. It now has the capability to assemble the rockets vertically.[12] This launch centre has so far carried out 44 launches out of which all except one were successful.

The second facility is the **Taiyuan Satellite Launch Centre (TSLC)** in the northern Shanxi province from where low earth orbit, polar and sun-synchronous orbit launches take place, especially the weather, earth observation and scientific satellites.[13] This centre could be used for launching satellites in both medium and low orbits.[14] The geographical coordinates of this launch site are 37°30'N 112°36'E. The dry climate here too, facilitates launches. It was established in 1966 and was made operational in 1968 and was used as a missile launch base. The initial space launch was carried out here in 1988 when the first meteorological satellite was launched. This launch centre has so far carried out 32 successful launches.

The third facility is the **Xichang Satellite Launch Centre (XSLC)** in the southern Sichuan province near Chengdu, which was established in 1970 and made operational in 1984. The geographical coordinates of this launch site are 28°12'N 102°02'E and are, thus, located closest to the equator. Its location was also preferred as it was far from the coast and the northern borders, which reduced the risk of a possible attack from the US and the USSR respectively.[15] XSLC is China's only low-latitude launch site, capable of launching at inclinations ranging from 28-36.° It is, therefore, used for geo-stationary launches, primarily for communication, broadcasting and meteorological satellites. It is also used for launching powerful thrust rockets, and is the only site in China for launching international commercial missions. Launches are done ideally during the period from October to May when the weather conditions are favourable.[16] This launch centre has so far carried out 64 launches out of which 6 have failed.

Telemetry, Tracking and Control (TT&C) Facilities

An integrated Telemetry Tracking and Control (TT&C) network has been developed by China for controlling its assets in space as well as for assisting the launch and recovery process. This network, along with the launch centres, is managed by an organisation called the **China Satellite Launch and Tracking Control General (CLTC)** working under the Commission of Science, Technology and Industry for National Defence (COSTIND).[17] China's first TT&C network was established in the late 1960s and became operational in the early 1970s. It was further expanded to cover both the domestic as well as international space operations since the establishment of the commercial launch programme in the 1980s.[18] This network is also used for the ballistic missile programme and, therefore, forms a vital part of the national defence infrastructure. The TT&C network comprises ground command and control centres and tracking stations, tracking ships and a Data Relay Satellite (DRS) system in orbit.

The ground facilities consist of the **Beijing Aerospace Command and Control Centre (BACC)** in Beijing Aerospace City, the **Xi'an Satellite Control Centre (XSCC)** in Shaanxi province and 14 land-based space tracking stations out of which 10 are within and 4 outside China. The BACC is the primary command and control centre for the manned as well as the lunar and deep space exploration missions.[19] The XSCC located at Weinan, near Xi'an is the primary satellite control facility in China. The tracking stations within the Chinese territory are at **Weinan** in Shaanxi province, **Changchun** in Jilin province, **Qingdao** in Shandong province, **Zhanyi** in Yunnan province, **Nanhai** in Hainan island, **Kashi** in Xinjiang autonomous region, **Xiamen** in Fujian province, **Lushan** in Jianxi province, Jiamusi in Heilongjiang province, and **Dongfeng** in Inner Mongolia autonomous region, along with mobile tracking stations in the Xinjiang and Inner Mongolia Autonomous Regions. The overseas tracking stations are located at **Karachi** in Pakistan, **Tarawa** in Kiribati, **Malindi** in Kenya and **Swakopmund** in Namibia which came up primarily to support the manned space programme. In addition to these, agreements have been made with France, Brazil, Sweden and Australia for the sharing of space tracking facilities. China has also deployed six **Yuanwang** (or Long View) class space tracking ships starting from the late 1970s for supplementing the land-based tracking systems. They are positioned at the Western Pacific, the Southern

Pacific, the Southern Atlantic and the Indian Oceans.[20] To complement these land and sea facilities, two **Tian Lian** series of satellites have been launched for tracking and data relay purposes, which would decrease China's reliance on the foreign tracking stations.[21]

Fig 1: Map of the Space Launch and TT&C Facilities Within China

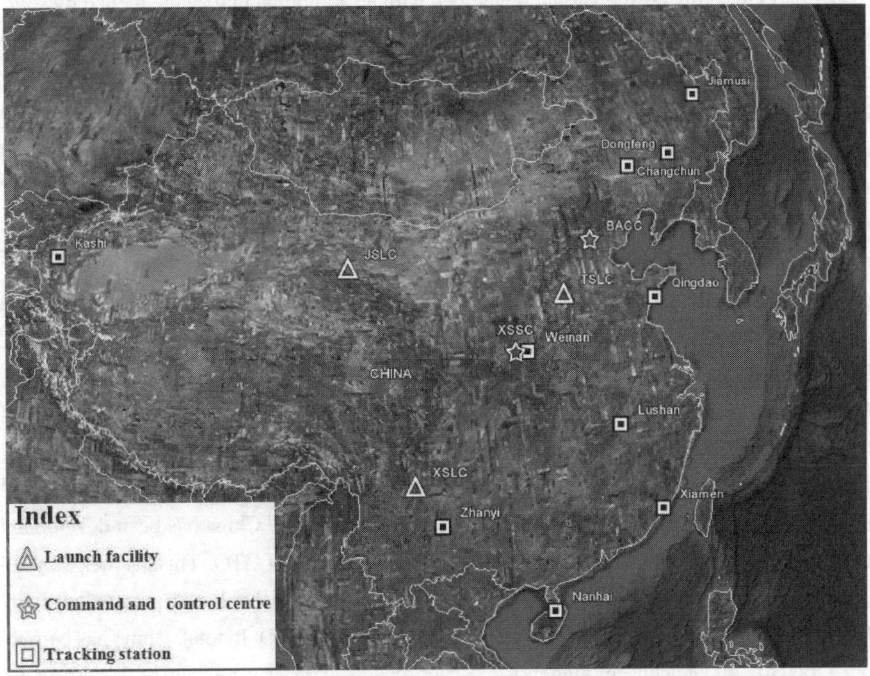

Launch Vehicles

The launch vehicles for China's space applications were derived from its ballistic missiles. During the initial years of China's ballistic missile programme in the late 1950s, China acquired the R-1 and R-2 missiles from the Soviet Union to develop the first Chinese missiles. The Soviets also supplied the necessary technical expertise, design documentation and the tooling for production. Post the Soviet withdrawal from the co-operation agreement in 1960, China went on to develop its own version of the R-2, called the Dong Feng-1 (DF-1) short range missile. It was followed in the 1960s by the first indigenously developed missile, the intermediate range Dong Feng-2 (DF-2) and the DF-3 and DF-4 intermediate range missiles.

The DF-4 missile was modified as China's first launch vehicle to carry the nation's first satellite into the Low Earth Orbit (LEO) in 1970, making China the fifth nation capable of orbital launch.[22] This became the first Chang Zheng (CZ) or Long March carrier rocket, the CZ-1. It was named after Mao's historic Long March of the 1930s and had two liquid propellant stages and a third stage fuelled by solid propellants. Similarly, the first Intercontinental Ballistic Missile (ICBM), the DF-5, which was successfully tested in 1971, was modified into the two stage CZ-2.[23] The CZ series further expanded with many variants of the CZ-2. The CZ-2C/SD (Smart Dispenser) was a variant developed with an additional third stage fuelled by solid propellants for launching the Iridium global wireless communications satellite network. The CZ-2F version was developed especially for the manned space programme and was fitted with four strap-on boosters and an emergency escape system. The CZ-2 series is now primarily used for Low Earth Orbit (LEO) and Geo-stationary Transfer Orbit (GTO) missions. This was followed by the development of the three-stage CZ-3 in which a cryogenic engine was introduced at the upper stage providing re-start capability, which allows heavier payloads to be launched to GTO, its intended destination. The CZ-3B in this category is the most powerful among the CZ family and is used for launching heavy satellites, having four strap-on boosters introduced in its first stage. The CZ-3C, which was developed later, had only two boosters, suitable for launching smaller satellites and, therefore, making the launch vehicle family more versatile. In addition to these, the CZ-4 rockets were developed to be used as back-up to the CZ-3 series. However, currently the CZ-4 series launch vehicles are intended for launches to Sun-Synchronous Orbit (SSO). In total, China has developed 12 types of CZ launch vehicles, out of which currently only 8 are operational.[24] China has been developing the capabilities to carry out launches to the key LEO, SSO and GTO. This has helped it to pursue space projects for diverse applications. Upto now, 57 launches have been carried out to LEO, 1 to MEO (Middle Earth Orbit), 26 to SSO and 49 to GTO. In total, China has carried out a total of 140 launches through its CZ carrier rockets, with a success rate of 95 percent, as seven launches were unsuccessful.

Table 2: Currently Operational Launch Vehicles

Launch Vehicle	L/D* Mass Stages	First flight	Missions	Launch sites	Launch capability (kg)			Success
					LEO*	SSO	GTO	
CZ-2C	43 m / 3.35 m 233T 3 stage	1975	Remote Sensing Scientific Communication Commercial	JSLC TSLC XLSC	3,850	2,100	1,250	33/33 (100%)

CZ-2D	41 m / 3.80 m 250 T 2 stage	1992	Communication Remote Sensing	JSLC	4,000	1,150		14/14 (100%)
CZ-2F	58.30 m 498 T 2 stage	1999	Manned spaceflight	JSLC	8,600			7/7 (100%)
CZ-3A	52.52 m / 3.35 m 241 T 3 stage	1994	Communication Navigation Meteorology Lunar probe	XSLC			2,600	20/20 (100%)
CZ-3B	56.33 m / 4.20 m 456 T 3 stage	1996	Communication Commercial	XSLC			5,500	12/14 (85%)
CZ-3C	54.84 m / 4 m 345 T 3 stage	2008	Navigation Lunar probe	XLSC			3,800	7/7 (100%)
CZ-4B	48 m / 3.80 m 250 T 3 stage	1999	Scientific Meteorology Remote Sensing	JSLC TSLC		2,230		13/13 (100%)
CZ-4C	48 m / 3.80 m 250 T 3 stage	2006	Remote Sensing Meteorology	JSLC TSLC		2,950		7/7 (100%)

* L/D – Total length / Maximum faring diameter

Fig 2: The Chang Zheng Family of Launch Vehicles

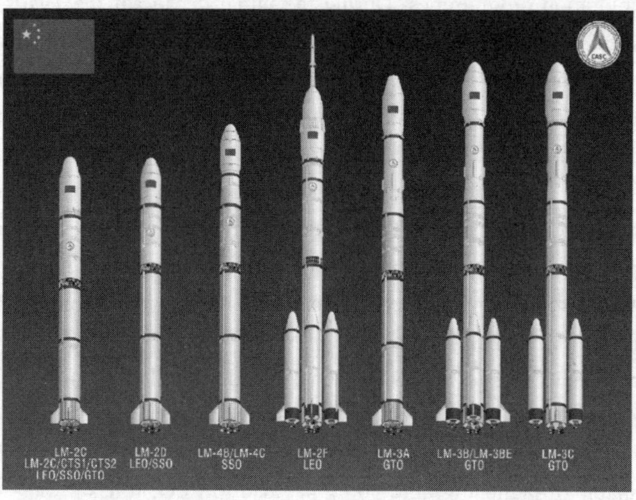

Source: www.cgwic.com

Fig 3: China's Space Launch Trend and its GDP growth (1970-2010)[25]

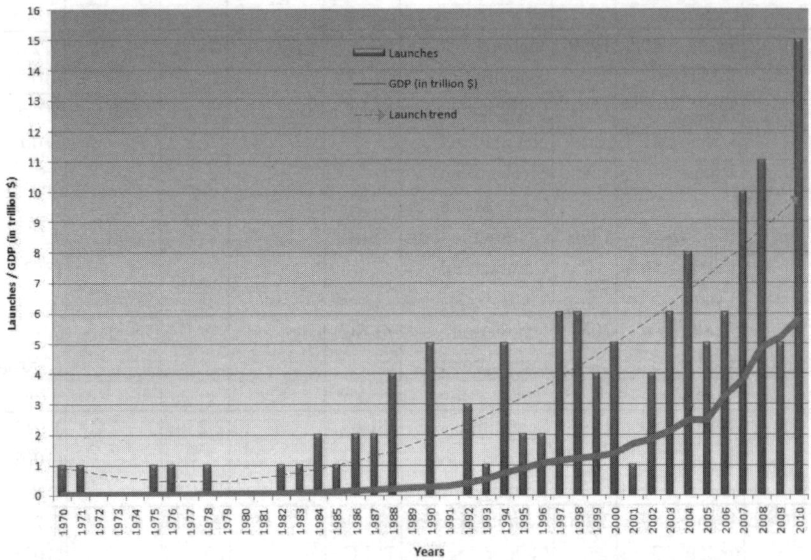

Analysing the launch trend, it could be observed that there had been an initial lull in space launches. Thus, the launch frequency gathered considerable momentum only after the mid-1980s. Further, the launch rate accelerated through the 21st century, with growing diversity in the projects pursued like manned spaceflight, navigation as well as the lunar exploration programmes. During the initial decade of the 1970s, there were only 5 launches. These increased to 13 in the 1980s, to 34 in the 1990s, and to 76 in the 2000s, with the launches doubling every decade. On a long-term average, China has been carrying out a launch every 3 to 4 months, with a rate of about 3 to 4 launches per year. Also, in 2010, China carried out a record number of 15 space launches, matching the US for the first time.[26] These facts reflect the increasing launch capacity and infrastructure of the nation's space programme. This is also a reflection of the level of support and emphasis being given to the space programme by the government. The trend in China's space activity is also very much in consonance with the rise in economic power, as may be observed from Fig 3.

Apart from the CZ series of conventional liquid propellant launch vehicles, China has also developed the Kaituozhe (or Explorer) series of solid propellant launch vehicles since 2000, which are based on the DF-31 solid propellant ICBM.[27] The Kaituozhe-1 (KT-1) is capable of launching upto 50 kg payload to LEO. It has a four-stage design, and can be launched from a mobile launch facility. It is reported that two launches were attempted, in 2002 and 2003, without success. This rocket was supposedly used as a kinetic-kill vehicle in the Anti-Satellite (ASAT) test conducted on January 11, 2007, to bring down the old inactive Feng Yun-1C meteorological satellite. An improved variant called the KT-1A has been developed and is reported to be capable of launching upto 300 kg payload to GTO and polar orbits; and the KT-1B is capable of launching upto 400 kg to polar orbits.[28] These could be used to launch small satellites, an emerging trend in China's satellite programme.

Current Capabilities of China's Satellite Programme

China's first satellite launch took place in 1970, with the Dong Fang Hong-1 (The East is Red) telecommunication satellite, and, thus, it became the fifth nation to do so. It orbited the earth for 26 days, transmitting the revolutionary Chinese song "The East is Red." This marked the first major milestone of China's odyssey into outer space, and established its presence there. Since then, several other types of satellites have been developed by the Chinese for diverse requirements. The four main areas of application of China's satellite programme are remote sensing, telecommunications, navigation, and scientific exploration. Currently, there are 71 active Chinese satellites in orbit. Out of these, 28 are for remote sensing (of which 5 are meteorological), 17 are for telecommunication, 16 are for scientific exploration and 10 are navigation satellites. Of these, 15 satellites are distributed in LEO, 1 in MEO, 28 in SSO, 3 in Inclined Geo-Synchronous Orbit (IGSO), 23 in Geo-stationery Earth Orbit (GEO) and 1 in High Earth Orbit (HEO).[29, 30, 31]

Remote Sensing Satellites

The satellites developed for remote sensing are officially stated to be used for earth monitoring applications, including meteorology, cartography, mining, agriculture, forestry, hydrology, oceanography, seismology, environmental protection, disaster mitigation and urban planning.[32] However, this has given China a space-based image collection capability which could also be used for military reconnaissance purposes.

For meteorological applications, China has developed the Feng Yun (Wind and Cloud / FY) series of satellites. Three categories of these satellites have been launched by China since the first Feng Yun satellite (FY-1) took off in 1988. The FY-1 and FY-3 are meant for conducting global meteorological observations in the SSO, while the FY-2 is a geo-stationary meteorological satellite which monitors China and its neighbouring regions. The FY-1 and the FY-2 satellites are of the optical and infra-red imaging type whereas the FY-3 satellites are of the multi-spectral imaging type. The launches of FY-2D and FY-2E satellites on December 2006 and May 2008 respectively were also intended to cater to the critical weather forecasting requirements during the 2008 Beijing Olympics, and, thus, helped China to organise the major international event. Apart from being part of the China Meteorological Administration (CMA), Feng Yun-1 and 2 satellites are also included in the World Meteorological Organisation's (WMO's) Global Observing System satellites.[33] Currently, five Feng Yun satellites are active in orbit, providing global coverage and having a maximum imaging resolution of 250m.

The **Zi Yuan** (Resources / ZY) satellite series is a much debated satellite series as its details are not disclosed in the public domain except for the officially stated purpose that these are used for land resource monitoring purposes. Therefore, it has been presumed by outside observers that they are dedicated military reconnaissance satellites, part of the military's "**Jian Bing**" class of satellites.[34] Currently, there are two Zi Yuan satellites which are active in orbit, the Zi Yuan-2B and 2C, launched in 2002 and 2004 respectively. These satellites are in the 97.1° and 97.3° SSOs which gives them a global coverage and it could be inferred that they would have the same or even better resolution than the three **CBERS (China-Brazil Earth Resources Satellites)** which preceded them under the same alternative name. The CBERS provided a maximum resolution of 2.5 m.[35] The remote sensing/reconnaissance satellites of the recoverable type, the **Fanhui Shi Weixing** series, appear to have concluded in 2006 as all the satellites launched have been recovered and no further launches have taken place. Since then, China has launched a new family of satellites called the **Yao Gan** (Remote Sensing / YG) series. These are again, as stated by China, remote sensing satellites for civilian applications like land resource observations, whose details are not disclosed, and are, thus, being considered as military oriented satellites. Currently, there are 12 Yao Gan satellites active in orbit, from Yao Gan-2 to Yao Gan 11. The Yao Gan-9A, 9B and 9C operate as a three-satellite constellation in the 63.4° orbit with an individual orbit period of 107.1 minutes. This would reduce the effective orbit period of the constellation to half an hour, and, therefore, changes in very short intervals of time can be monitored. The Yao Gan-3, 6, 8 and 10 are understood to be Synthetic Aperture Radar (SAR) capable satellites.[36] This appears reasonable, considering the fact that only these satellites have been developed by the Shanghai Academy of Spaceflight Technology (SAST), while the others of the electro-optical variety have been developed by the China Academy of Space Technology (CAST). SAR is not included in the officially stated list of payload instruments that CAST has developed,[37] which could be existing in the case of SAST.

China has been increasingly been concentrating on developing small satellites and launching them into SSO for the purposes of remote sensing and possibly reconnaissance. The advantage of small satellites is that they allow rapid expansion as well as replacement of the existing satellite force, especially during instances when there are critical service disruptions.[38] In 1998, the Tsinghua University of China reached a research cooperation agreement with the University of Surrey, UK, on microsatellites. As a result, in May 2000, there was a successful launch of a microsatellite called Tsinghua-1. The Beijing (BJ) satellite (Tsinghua-2), which is currently in orbit, was launched from the Plesetsk mobile launch facility in Russia in 2005 and was meant for disaster monitoring as well as Olympics planning. The two Chuang Xin (Innovation / CX) microsatellites launched in 2003 and 2008 are also meant for environment as well as disaster monitoring purposes. China has extended its remote sensing capability to the oceans by launching the Hai Yang (Ocean / HY) series of small satellites, which are capable of providing a resolution of 250 m.[39] The first satellite was launched in 2002 and the second in 2007, which is currently active in orbit. The launch of these satellites comes at time when China is trying to increase its influence over the seas, not only in the Western Pacific, but also in the Indian Ocean as result of its growing economic and security interests in these regions. Three Tan Suo or Shiyan (Experiment / TS or SY) minisatellites were launched by China since 2004 for land resources and atmospheric observation on an experimental basis. These were jointly developed by the Harbin Polytechnic University, Chinese Research Institute of Space Technology in Changchun, Chinese Academy of Sciences (CAS) and Xi'an Surveys and Designs Institute. The Shiyan-1, which was launched in 2004, is China's first satellite capable of 3D imaging. China has also launched a constellation of two small satellites in 2008, called the Huan Jing (Environment / HJ) series for the purpose of environment and disaster monitoring. These satellites are in the 97.95° SSO which provides global coverage, and also has a maximum resolution of 30m. The latest addition in China's remote sensing satellites in orbit is the Tian Hui (Mapping / TH) satellite. It is a new type of small satellite launched into SSO by China in 2010 which is capable of 3D mapping as well as having a maximum resolution of 5 m. It was developed by the China Spacesat Co. Ltd.

Table 3: Existing Remote Sensing Satellites

Satellite	Purpose	Launch Centre	Launch Vehicle	Launch Date	Orbit	Position	Mass (kg)	Orbit Period (min.)	Remarks
FY-1D	Meteorology	TSLC	CZ-4B	15-05-2002	SSO	98.71°	428	102.20	Optical/IR imaging 1.1 km resolution (2800 km swath)
FY-2D		XSLC	CZ-3A	08-12-2006	GEO	86.5° E	1400	24 hours	Optical/IR imaging 1.25 km resolution
FY-3A		TSLC	CZ-4C	27-05-2008	SSO	98.69°	2295	101.41	Multi-spectral imaging 250 m resolution (2800 km swath)
FY-2E		XSLC	CZ-3A	23-12-2008	GEO	105° E	1390	24 hours	Optical/IR imaging 1.25 km resolution
FY-3B		TSLC	CZ-4C	05-11-2010	SSO	98.72°	2299	101.41	Multi-spectral imaging 250 m resolution (2800 km swath)
YG-2	Earth Observation	JSLC	CZ-2D	25-05-2007	LEO	97.8°		97.60	Electro-optical imagery (CAST)
YG-3		TSLC	CZ-4C	12-11-2007	SSO	97.85°		97.30	SAR imagery (SAST)
YG-4		JSLC	CZ-2D	01-12-2008	LEO	97.83°		97.69	Electro-optical imagery (CAST)
YG-5		TSLC	CZ-4B	15-12-2008	LEO	97.3°		94.12	Electro-optical imagery (CAST)
YG-6		TSLC	CZ-2C	22-04-2009	SSO	97.56°		94.74	SAR imagery (SAST)
YG-7		JSLC	CZ-2D	09-12-2009	LEO	97.92°		97.69	Electro-optical imagery (CAST)
YG-8		TSLC	CZ-4C	15-12-2009	LEO	100.5°		109.40	SAR imagery (SAST)

YG-9A		JSLC	CZ-4C	05-03-2010	LEO	63.4°		107.10	Electro-optical imagery (CAST)
YG-9B		JSLC	CZ-4C	05-03-2010	LEO	63.4°		107.10	Electro-optical imagery (CAST)
YG-9C		JSLC	CZ-4C	05-03-2010	LEO	63.4°		107.10	Electro-optical imagery (CAST)
YG-10		TSLC	CZ-4C	10-08-2010	SSO	97.83°		97.30	SAR imagery (SAST)
YG-11		JSLC	CZ-2D	22-09-2010	SSO	98°		97.70	Electro-optical imagery (CAST)
ZY-2B	Land resource observation	TSLC	CZ-4B	27-10-2002	SSO	97.1°		94.30	Dedicated military satellite
ZY-2C		TSLC	CZ-4B	06-11-2004	SSO	97.3°		96.40	
HJ-1A	Environment and Disaster monitoring	TSLC	CZ-2C	06-09-2008	SSO	97.95°	470	97.56	30 m resolution (700 km swath)
HJ-1B		TSLC	CZ-2C	06-09-2008	SSO	97.95°	470	97.56	
HY-1B	Ocean monitoring	TSLC	CZ-2C	11-04-2007	SSO	98.46°	360	100.70	250 m resolution (500 km swath)
TH-1	Mapping	JSLC	CZ-2D	24-08-2010	SSO	97.37°	2500	94.55	5 m resolution (60 km swath)
BJ-1	Imaging	Plesetsk	Cosmos-3M	27-10-2005	SSO	98°	166	98.60	4 m resolution (24 km swath)
TS-1 (SY-1)	Earth observation	XSLC	CZ-2C	18-04-2004	SSO	97.45°	204	96.71	1st 3D imaging satellite 10 m resolution
TS-2 (SY-2)		XSLC	CZ-2C	18-11-2004	LEO	98.1°	300	98.8	3D imaging satellite
TS-3 (SY-3)		JSLC	CZ-2D	05-11-2008	LEO	98.5°	300	100.8	
CX-1(1)	Environment and disaster monitoring	TSLC	CZ-4B	21-10-2003	SSO	98.5°	100	99.20	Micro satellite
CX-1(2)		JSLC	CZ-2D	05-11-2008	LEO	98.47°	100	100.77	

Telecommunication Satellites

The very first satellite launched into orbit by China in 1970 was a telecommunications satellite. China currently has four types of telecommunications satellites active in orbit. The Zhong Xing (China Star / ZX) series is the state owned telecommunications satellite, AP Star is a commercial satellite of the AP Star Corporation based in Hong Kong, Tian Lian (Sky Link / TL) is a tracking and data relay satellite and Xi Wang (Hope / XW) is an amateur radio microsatellite made for the youth. There are currently 3 AP Star satellites, 10 Zhong Xing and 2 Tian Lian satellites in GEO and one Xi Wang satellite in LEO.

The AP Star satellite is entirely based on the foreign satellite bus, namely the FS1300 and the SB4000C2 of Space Systems/Loral (US) and the Thales Alenia Space (France) respectively. Meanwhile, the Zhong Xing satellite buses are mainly from the indigenous Dong Fang Hong (DFH) series of satellite system – the DFH-3 and the DFH-4. However, they also use foreign made satellite buses like the A2100A from Lockheed Martin (US), SB3000 from Aerospatiale (France) and SB4000 from Thales Alenia Space. The Tian Lian satellite is exclusively based on the DFH-3 bus.

In terms of coverage, the AP Star-2R has the largest area of coverage, including almost the entire Eurasia as well as parts of Africa and Oceania. Among the Zhong Xing satellites, the Zhong Xing 6B has the maximum coverage area, including the whole Asian continent and Oceania, and the Zhong Xing-9 has the least coverage area, limited to China and its immediate neighbourhood. The remaining AP Star satellites and Zhong Xing satellites have regional coverage over the Asia-Pacific.[40] The Tian Lian satellites, which were put into orbit to facilitate communication between the China's spacecraft and ground stations have increased the coverage area of tracking from a mere 15 percent using only the ground facilities to almost half of the spacecraft's trajectory.

Fig 4: Maps Showing Coverage Area of Various Chinese Telecommunication Satellites

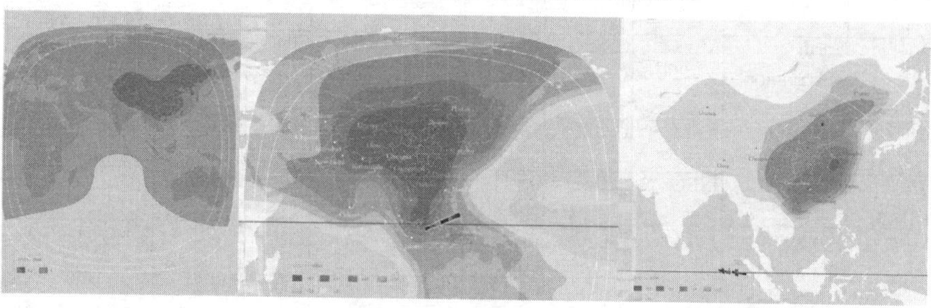

AP Star-2R Zhong Xing-6B Zhong Xing-9

Source: www.chinasatcom.com

There have been speculations about the Zhong Xing-20, 20A and 22A satellites as being dedicated military communication satellites under the names Shen Tong (Zhong Xing-20) and Feng Huo (Zhong Xing-22).[41, 42, 43] This appears to be actually so as there is very little officially declared information on these satellites. Further, these satellites are not mentioned in the list of satellites operated by the state owned China Satellite

Communications Co. Ltd. which operates all the other Zhong Xing satellites.[44] Since all three of these satellites have been based on the indigenous DFH-3 platform, comparing their weight with other DFH-3 satellites of the same series, the number of transponders can be roughly estimated to be around 10 to 11 in each of these satellites. Considering this, the number of existing Chinese transponders could be well over 400.

Table 4: Existing Telecommunication Satellites

Satellite	Launch Centre	Launch Vehicle	Launch Date	Orbit	Position	Mass (kg)	Orbit Period (min.)	Remarks
ZX-5A	XSLC	CZ-3B	30-05-1998	GEO	87.5°E	2984	24 hours	18 C-band and 20 Ku-band transponders Regional coverage
ZX-5B	XSLC	CZ-3B	18-07-1998	GEO	110.5°E	2820	24 hours	24 C-band and 14 Ku-band transponders Regional coverage
ZX-20	XSLC	CZ-3A	15-11-2003	GEO	98.17° E	2300	24 hours	10 transponders
ZX-22A	XSLC	CZ-3A	13-09-2006	GEO	98° E	2300	24 hours	10 transponders
ZX-5C	XSLC	CZ-3A	01-06-2007	GEO	125° E	2200	24 hours	10 C-band transponders Regional coverage
ZX-6B	XSLC	CZ-3B	05-07-2007	GEO	115.5°E	4600	24 hours	38 C-band transponders Continental coverage
ZX-9	XSLC	CZ-3B	09-06-2008	GEO	92.2° E	4500	24 hours	22 Ku-band transponders National coverage
ZX-6A	XSLC	CZ-3B	05-09-2010	GEO	125°E	5000	24 hours	1 S-band, 24 C-band and 8 Ku-band transponders Regional coverage

ZX-20A	XSLC	CZ-3A	25-11-2010	GEO	130°E	2300	24 hours	10 transponders
ZX-10	XSLC	CZ-3B	20-06-2011	GEO	110.5°E	5000	24 hours	30 C-band and 16 Ku-band transponders Regional coverage
Satellite	Launch Centre	Launch Vehicle	Launch Date	Orbit	Position	Mass (kg)	Orbit Period (min.)	Remarks
APStar-2R	XSLC	CZ-3B	17-10-1997	GEO	76.5°E	3700	24 hours	28 C-band and 15 Ku-band transponders Semi-global coverage
APStar-5	Sea Launch Platform (Russia)	Zenit 3SL (Russian)	29-06-2004	GEO	138°E	4640	24 hours	38 C-band and 16 Ku-band transponders Regional coverage
APStar-6	XSLC	CZ-3B	04-12-2005	GEO	134°E	4800	24 hours	38 C-band and 12 Ku-band transponders Regional coverage
TL-1(1)	XSLC	CZ-3C	25-04-2008	GEO	77° E		24 hours	Tracking and data relay service
TL-1(2)	XSLC	CZ-3C	11-07-2011	GEO			24 hours	
XW-1	TSLC	CZ-4C	15-12-2009	LEO	100.4°	50	109.40	Amateur radio microsatellite

Navigation Satellites

China has become the third nation to develop the Bei Dou (Compass / BD), its own global satellite navigation system after the Global Positioning System (GPS) (US) and GLONASS (Russia). It will be the fourth such international project after GPS, GLONASS and Galileo (Europe). This system has its roots in the 1980s, and took on the shape of the Bei Dou experimental satellite navigation system in 2000, when the first geo-stationary satellite for the purpose was launched. It was followed by three more satellites, setting up the first experimental phase of the network. From 2007 onwards, the second phase started under which 5 geo-stationary and 30 non-geo-stationary satellites were to be put into orbit, to establish a regional satellite navigation system by 2012 and further extension into a global system by 2020. It is developed by CAST and offers to provide an accuracy of 10 m for location and 0.2 m/s for velocity. It is also stated to be compatible and interoperable with the other existing satellite navigation systems. With the initial phase of the system in place, China claims to benefit from it as in the case of the 2008 Olympics as well as the disaster relief operations during the Wenchuan and Yushu earthquakes of 2008 and 2010 respectively.[45]

The development of such a programme can be seen as part of China's efforts to achieve self-reliance in high accuracy navigation and positioning, avoiding any kind of dependence on foreign systems. Currently, there are only two active satellites remaining from the first phase and eight active satellites from the second phase out of which four satellites are in GEO and the remaining four are in non-GEO.

Table 5: Existing Navigation Satellites

Satellite	Launch Centre	Launch Vehicle	Launch Date	Orbit	Position	Orbit Period (min.)
BD-1B	XSLC	CZ-3A	21-12-2000	GEO	80.6° E	24 hours
BD-1C	XSLC	CZ-3A	25-05-2003	GEO	110.6° E	24 hours
BD-M1	XSLC	CZ-3A	14-04-2007	MEO	56.5°	13 hours
BD-G2	XSLC	CZ-3C	15-04-2009	GEO	120° E	24 hours
BD-G1	XSLC	CZ-3C	17-01-2010	GEO	141.5° E	24 hours
BD-G3	XSLC	CZ-3C	02-06-2010	GEO	84.6°E	24 hours
BD-IGSO(1)	XSLC	CZ-3A	01-08-2010	IGSO	54.9°	24 hours
BD-G4	XSLC	CZ-3C	01-11-2010	GEO	160.1° E	24 hours
BD-IGSO(2)	XSLC	CZ-3A	18-12-2010	IGSO	55.1°	24 hours
BD-IGSO(3)	XSLC	CZ-3A	09-04-2011	IGSO	55.4°	24 hours

Scientific Exploration Satellites

The Shijian (Practice / SJ) series of satellites are the most prominent among the scientific exploration satellites developed by China meant for studying the space environment and conducting technological tests. Currently, there are 12 active satellites in orbit out of which 9 are in SSO and 3 are in LEO. The types of payload in these satellites mostly include particle detectors and field detectors which study the space environment, and systems dealing with testing new satellite technologies. Launch of these satellites started gaining momentum only during the latter half of the last decade, considering the fact that prior to that, only six such satellites had been launched. Therefore, it could be inferred that during the past five years, a comparatively high amount of testing of new technologies has been taking place. This points to the rapid pace at which the Chinese space research and development capabilities are growing.

China has developed a mini satellite series called the Tan Ce (Probe / TC) jointly with Europe for the first time as part of the "Double Star" project for the purpose of probing and predicting geo-magnetic storms which comprise one of the major factors causing disruptions in satellite operations. The agreement for joint development of these satellites was made in 2001 between the China National Space Agency (CNSA) and the European Space Agency (ESA). According to this, two Chinese satellites will be operating along with four European satellites in regions of space that have not been covered by other satellites. The first satellite launched in 2003 was an equatorial orbiting probe put in a High Earth Orbit (HEO) with an apogee double that of GEO, becoming the highest orbiting satellite China has ever launched. The second satellite, which is still active, is a polar orbiting probe and was launched in 2004.

In addition to these, China has also developed nano and pico satellites, which are active in orbit. The Na Xing (Nano satellite /NX) is the first nano satellite developed by China, for the purpose of testing new satellite technologies. This satellite was developed jointly by the Tsinghua University and the Aerospace Tsinghua Satellite Technologies Co. Ltd. The Zheda Pixing (Zhejiang pico satellite / ZP) series comprises pico satellites developed by the Zhejiang University for microelectronics studies, with two satellites currently operating in orbit.[46]

Table 6: Existing Scientific Exploration Satellites

Satellite	Launch Centre	Launch Vehicle	Launch Date	Orbit	Position	Orbit Period (min.)
SJ-6A	TSLC	CZ-4B	08-09-2004	SSO	97.8°	96.60
SJ-6B	TSLC	CZ-4B	08-09-2004	SSO	97.8°	96.60
SJ-7	JSLC	CZ-2D	06-07-2005	SSO	97.7°	95.20
SJ-6C	TSLC	CZ-4B	24-10-2006	SSO	97.7°	96.60
SJ-6D	TSLC	CZ-4B	24-10-2006	SSO	97.7°	96.60
SJ-6E	TSLC	CZ-4B	25-10-2008	SSO	97.6°	96.50
SJ-6F	TSLC	CZ-4B	25-10-2008	SSO	97.6°	96.50
SJ-11(1)	JSLC	CZ-2C	12-11-2009	SSO	98.2°	98.70
SJ12	JSLC	CZ-2D	15-06-2010	LEO	97.7°	96.60
SJ-6G	TSLC	CZ-4B	06-10-2010	LEO	97.7°	96.60
SJ-6H	TSLC	CZ-4B	06-10-2010	LEO	97.7°	96.60
SJ-11(3)	JSLC	CZ-2C	06-07-2011	SSO	98.2°	98.70
TC-2	TSLC	CZ-2C	25-07-2004	HEO	88.47°	11 hours
NX-1	XSLC	CZ-2C	18-04-2004	SSO	97.5°	96.80
ZP-1B	JSLC	CZ-2D	22-09-2010	SSO	98.0°	97.50
ZP-1C	JSLC	CZ-2D	22-09-2010	SSO	97.9°	97.50

The Future of China's Satellite Programme

It can be seen that China has been expanding its capabilities in all areas of space applications technology through its satellite programme. In the field of remote sensing, China has stopped depending on imagery recovered many days after observation to near real-time imagery transmitted directly from space. China has increased its digital imagery resolution to greater than 2.5 m, has developed 3D imaging ability and has apparently acquired SAR capability which would enable satellites to have day and night coverage and also the ability to see through obstacles like clouds, smoke and fog, and even underwater or underground. In the field of communication, China has acquired semi-global coverage largely on its own. China has indigenously developed its own navigation system which is set to achieve global coverage within a decade, thus, realising complete self-reliance in navigation. The regularity of testing new satellite technologies has increased recently, along with China's experiments with small satellites, enabling it to launch satellites cheaper and with greater frequency, further expanding its satellite fleet.

China is well aware that there still exists a large gap between itself and the advanced countries in areas like space science, technology and applications even after completing 40 years of space-faring. Also, China's contributions in these areas to its own development as well as to the rest of humanity are disproportionate with its status as a nation with the largest population and a growing economy on its way to become the largest in the world.[47] Therefore, China has come up with a development strategy and roadmap for space science, applications and technology up to 2050, as proposed by the Chinese Academy of Sciences in 2009.

A remarkable amount of contribution to space science is one of the goals explicitly highlighted in the roadmap. This could mean an ever greater number of scientific satellite launches being conducted in the coming years, with missions related to the study of the space environment. China lays stress on exploring the unsolved as well as fundamental realms of space science which would be instrumental in creating its own mark in this field. Another likely trend for the future, as could be assessed from the specified goals is the enhancement of earth observation satellite capabilities to provide adequate data for developing a robust earth observation infrastructure capable of modelling and forecasting environmental changes and resource exploration. To realise the aim of global navigational capability by 2020 through the Bei Dou project, 27 more satellites need to be put into orbit in the next nine years (more than three satellites per year on average). Considering the fact that during the initial period of the second phase for the last four years, China has put 8 such satellites in orbit (two satellites per year on average), it appears that it could well be on track to achieving its goal. The advancement of key technologies related to providing strong technical support to space science as well as applications is also one of the stated goals. This involves developing ultra-high resolution imaging capability, ultra-high precision standards, laser communication technology, and light satellites and payloads.[48] This obviously points towards the continuation of the miniaturisation trend, but in an accelerated manner which has already started through the development of small satellites like the Tsinghua, Chuang Xin and the Na Xing satellite series.

Supplementing these plans are critical infrastructure developments, like the new launch site which is currently being built at Wenchang in Hainan Island, which will be operational by 2013.[49] The uniqueness of this launch site will be its proximity to the equator as well as to the eastern sea. The maritime proximity to the east would facilitate launches to orbits having a wide range of inclinations. The equatorial proximity would make launches cheaper due to fuel savings and also facilitate the launch of heavier satellites with more equipment as well as more fuel, especially to the GTO. This would mean that multi-purpose payloads can be launched together and also satellites with longer in-orbit life can be launched as more fuel can be accommodated.

Thus, there are plenty of indicators which predict the future of China's satellite programme to be characterised by advances in cutting-edge technology as well as a high launch rate. In sharp contrast to the China during the formative years of the space programme, today's China has an abundance of technological, material and financial resources as well as skilled manpower. This, along with a highly determined and organised technocracy in command provides a highly facilitating environment for the achievement of the stated strategic goals. One decisive factor which could impede the growth of China's ambitious space programme would be the economic trajectory. A severe economic downturn in the future could lead to a space budget crunch, precariously slowing down the programme. However, this possibility can be considered remote since China has demonstrated its capacity to overcome two such instances in the last two decades. However, one major challenge that China will inevitably face in the near future will be the replacement of existing satellites. It can be observed from the launch data that most of the satellites that are currently in orbit are newly developed ones, launched towards the latter half of the last decade. This could mean that around 2020, a relatively high demand in the need for replacements would arise. This would also coincide with satellite projects like the final launches of the navigational constellation and scientific missions, and projects like the manned lunar programme, the Mars and Venus probes, as well as the regular supply launches to the space station, expected to be completed by 2020. The future of China's satellite programme would then be very much dependent on how well it would be able to increase the capacity of its satellite fleet within the existing constraints.

Notes

1 Brian Harvey, *China's Space Program: From Conception to Manned Spaceflight* (UK: Praxis Publishing, UK: 2004), pp.15-17.
2. Roger Handberg and Zhen Li, *Chinese Space Policy: A Study in Domestic and International Politics* (UK: Routledge, 2006), p. 64.
3. Manu Midha, "Chinese Space Programme: Influence of Chinese Strategic Culture on its Development," *Air Power Journal,* Vol. 6, No. 1 (Spring 2011), p. 79.
4. Ibid., p. 58.
5. Erik Seedhouse, *The New Space Race: China v/s the United States* (UK: Praxis Publishing, 2010), p. 14.
6. Harvey, n. 1, pp. 20-22.
7. Gregory Kulaki and Jeffrey G. Lewis, *A Place for One's Mat: China's Space Program* (USA: American Academy of Arts and Sciences, 2009), p. 5.
8. Midha, n. 3.
9. "CGWIC Launch Sites," see http://www.cgwic.com/LaunchServices/LaunchSite/JSLC.html, accessed on June 14, 2011.
10. Luo Ge and Zhang Yao, "Following an Indigenous Path: China's Space Activities from 1956 to 2006," in P.V. Manoranjan Rao, ed., *50 Years of Space: A Global Perspective* (Hyderabad: Universities Press (India) Private Limited, 2007), p. 186.
11. "China's Three Major Space Launch Bases," October 15, 2003, see http://www.chinadaily.com.cn/en/doc/2003-10/15/content_272334.htm, accessed on June 14, 2011.
12. Lin Zhi, "Backgrounder: China's Four Space Launch Bases," January 10, 2010, see http://news.xinhuanet.com/english2010/database/2010-01/10/c_13131894.htm, accessed on June 14, 2011.
13. Marcia S. Smith, "China's Space Program: An Overview," *CRS Report for Congress*, October 18, 2005, pp. 1-2, see www.fas.org/sgp/crs/space/RS21641.pdf, accessed on February 10, 2011.
14. Zhi, n. 12.
15. Handberg and Li, n. 2, p. 65.
16. "China's Satellite Launch Centers," September 23, 2008, see http://www.chinadaily.com.cn/china/2008-09/23/content_7052063.htm, accessed on June 14, 2011.
17. "China Satellite Launch and Tracking Control General [CLTC]," see http://www.fas.org/nuke/guide/china/contractor/cltc.htm, accessed on June 15, 2011.
18. Wei Long, "China Builds Advanced Spacecraft Tracking and Command Network," May 29, 2000, see http://www.spacedaily.com/news/china-00za.html, accessed on June 15, 2011.
19. "Beijing Aerospace Command & Control Centre," December 1, 2010, see http://www.sinodefence.com/space/facility/bacc.asp, accessed on June 15, 2011.
20. "Tracking, Telemetry & Command (TT&C) Network", see http://www.sinodefence.com/space/facility/space-ttc.asp, accessed on 15 June 2011.
21. Stephen Clark, "Chinese Data Relay Spacecraft put Into Orbit", see http://www.spaceflightnow.com/news/n0804/25tianlian1/, accessed on June 16, 2011.
22. Steven J. Isakowitz, Joshua B. Hopkins and Joseph P. Hopkins Jr., *International Reference Guide to Space Launch Systems* (USA: American Institute of Aeronautics and Astronautics, 2004), pp. 261-262.
23. Kaza Lalitendra, "Dragon in Space: Implications for India," *Air Power Journal,* Vol. 3, No. 3, (Monsoon 2008), p. 68.

24. Launch vehicle details obtained from the China Great Wall Industrial Corporation website, see http://www.cgwic.com , accessed on June 22, 2011.
25. GDP details available at http://www.chinability.com/GDP.htm, accessed on July 24, 2011.
26. David Axe, "China Matches US Space Launches for First Time", see http://www.wired.com/dangerroom/2010/12/china-matches-u-s-space-launches-for-first-time/, accessed on June 30, 2011.
27. Isakowitz et. al, n. 22, p. 204.
28. "Kaituozhe 1 (KT-1) Launch Vehicle," February 20, 2009, see http://www.sinodefence.com/space/launcher/kaituozhe1.asp, accessed on June 23, 2011.
29. Satellite details obtained from NASA National Space Science Data Centre (NSSDC), see http://nssdc.gsfc.nasa.gov/nmc/spacecraftSearch.do, accessed on July 7, 2011.
30. Satellite status obtained from Celestrak website, see http://celestrak.com//, accessed on July 7, 2011.
31. Satellite launch reports obtained from news archives of China Aerospace Science and Technology Corporation (CASC) website, see http://www.spacechina.com/english/news.shtml, accessed on July 13, 2011.
32. "White Paper: China's Space Activities in 2006", see http://www.china.org.cn/english/features/book/183715.htm, accessed on June 25, 2011.
33. B. Bizzari, "Dossier on the Space-based Component of the Global Observing System (GOS-2011)," see ftp://ftp.wmo.int/Documents/PublicWeb/sat/DossierGOS/, accessed on July 16, 2011.
34. "Ziyuan 2," see http://www.sinodefence.com/space/satellite/ziyuan2.asp, accessed on July 16, 2011.
35 See China Centre for Resources Satellite Date and Applications (CRESDA) website, http://www.cresda.com/n16/n92006/index.html, accessed on July16, 2011.
36. "Yaogan," see http://www.sinodefence.com/space/military/yaogan.asp, accessed on July 13, 2011.
37. "Satellite Equipment," China Academy of Space Technology (CAST) website, see http://www.cast.cn/CastEn/Special.asp?SpecialID=17, accessed on July 13, 2011.
38. n. 25, p. 82.
39. Bizzari, n. 33.
40. Satellite details obtained from see China Satellite Communications Co. Ltd. Website, see http://www.chinasatcom.com/en/News_Info.aspx?m=20110329113845577061&n=20110329133705937193, accessed on July 17, 2011.
41. n. 25, pp. 77- 78.
42. "Shentong (ChinaSat 20),"see http://www.sinodefence.com/space/military/st.asp, accessed on July 17, 2011.
43. "Fenghuo (ChinaSat 22)," see http://www.sinodefence.com/space/military/fh.asp, accessed on July 17, 2011.
44. n. 42.
45. Bizzari, n. 33.
46. Ibid.
47. Huadong Guo and Ji Wu, *Space Science and Technology in China: A Roadmap to 2050* (Berlin: Science Press, Beijing and Springer-Verlag, 2010), p. 43.
48. Ibid.
49. Radhakrishna Rao, "China's Space Programme," see http://www.ipcs.org/article/china/chinas-space-programme-2977.html, accessed on April 22, 2011.

2

Pakistan's Nuclear Arsenal: Issues of Security and Safety

Shalini Chawla

Pakistan's nuclear arsenal has undergone a significant expansion in the last ten years. Pakistan has reportedly been building close to 12-15 weapons per year, nearly doubling its warheads in the last three years. Presently, the total number of warheads with Pakistan stands between 90-120.[1] The fissile material production is being expanded through two new reactors. Also, the growth rate of the delivery systems, including the ballistic missiles, aircraft and cruise missiles has been brisk.

The challenge is obviously to guard the nuclear arsenal, including more than 100 weapons and a variety of delivery systems of diverse ranges. The pace at which Pakistan is expanding its arsenal adds to the challenge of securing these weapons. Although, the Pakistani leadership has repeatedly expressed assurance in the security of their nuclear weapons, the United States has expressed its distress rather frequently. In fact, not only abroad but also domestically there has been enough anxiety regarding the safety of the nuclear weapons.

The safety and security of the nuclear arsenal becomes extremely critical in the case of Pakistan mainly due to three factors:

First, the clandestine nature of the nuclear programme and highly controversial proliferation record, which brings out the loopholes in the political and administrative system.

Second, Pakistan's unwritten doctrine believes in first use and there has very often been talk about using nuclear weapons in the initial stages of a war or even merely the threat of a conventional war with India. This enhances the probability of accidental use of weapons or use even through miscalculation.

Third, incompetence and corruption ingrained in the functioning of the Pakistani state system. There is clearly a lack of systematic and structured functioning within the state system where even the simplest affairs of the state are mismanaged, and, hence, the safety of the nuclear arsenal does become questionable. As rightly observed by a Pakistani commentator, "We are unable to efficiently manage simple functions of state, the haphazard traffic on our roads is a reflection of our organisation, how can one expect that the security of our nuclear assets is foolproof?" [2]

Fourth, escalating terrorism within Pakistan, which has expanded to the interiors of Punjab and Sindh, posing a major challenge to the security forces and establishment. The anti-state terrorist organisations like the Tehrik-e-Taliban Pakistan (TTP) (allied with Al Qaeda), high levels of radicalism in the Pakistani society, the insurgencies in Pakistan's periphery and undeniable extremist elements within the Pakistan Army have increased the concerns regarding the safety of the nuclear arsenal in the last 7-8 years. This is greatly bothering the international community, specifically the United States, and according to senior Administration officials, the United States has spent more than $100 million to assist Islamabad to secure its nuclear weapons. Undoubtedly, Barack Obama's worst security nightmare is the possibility of Pakistan's nuclear weapons falling into the hands of Al Qaeda or other non-state actors.

With rising terrorism in Pakistan and frequent attacks on the high security and heavily fortified complexes, the possibility of non-state actors breaking into the nuclear arsenal with insider support is high. In a recent attack on Mehran Naval Base in May 2011, the role of insiders was well demonstrated. Under these circumstances, two aspects need attention: one, the nuclear command and control organisation for employment of the nuclear arsenal; and two, the safety and security of the nuclear arsenal and its components.

Structure of Nuclear Command and Control

The Pakistani leadership started to take some structured measures towards command and control after the nuclear tests in 1998. Not much is known in the public domain regarding Pakistan's nuclear command and control in the initial phases of the nuclear programme. The civilian and military leadership was primarily focussed on building the weapon and, thus, command and control was not given much attention. The nuclear weapon programme was solely controlled by a few and Dr A. Q. Khan was directly reporting to the Prime Minister's office in the 1970s. A. Q. Khan was initially under the Pakistan Atomic Energy Commission but later, in 1976, Prime Minister Zulfiqar Ali Bhutto provided him autonomous control of the uranium enrichment project and Khan became directly answerable to the Prime Minster himself. [3] The Khan Laboratories were officially given a free hand in pursuing research.

Some of the authoritative sources indicate that a nuclear decision-making committee existed since 1975. One source is Mushahid Hussain, a Senator close to Musharraf, who stated that from 1975 to 1991, the nuclear programme had been controlled by committee under the supervision of a body headed by Ghulam Ishaq Khan who became the President in 1988. [4] There is not much clarity regarding the nature of this committee. It could be the body created in 1976 to monitor the activities of the Kahuta Research Laboratories (KRL) and the Pakistan Atomic Energy Commission (PAEC) or it could be the troika of three to oversee the entire nuclear programme: the President, the Prime Minister and the Army Chief.[5] This, in practice, implied that essentially Ghulam Ishaq Khan, Gen Aslam Beg and Benazir Bhutto were tracking the nuclear activities in the later 1980s. Khan shared a close relationship with A. Q. Khan and Ghulam Ishaq, and according to him, he guarded the nuclear programme "like a rock."[6] But undoubtedly, the army remained the most powerful institution, fully dominating the nuclear command and control, leave alone the total power structure of Pakistan. Bhutto commanded little influence in the nuclear decision-making. [7] Benazir had, in fact, 'famously' complained that she was never allowed to visit the nuclear facility. However, senior military officers serving during Benazir's period have refuted this allegation and stated that she never expressed a desire to visit the nuclear facility.[8] The fact is that lack of a clear formal command and control structure controlled by the army benefitted Khan and provided him a free hand with the programme. [9]

In 1996, Gen Jehangir Karamat established a think-tank in the General Headquarters (GHQ), working directly for the Army Chief's Secretariat, basically to provide analytical input and conduct studies in strategic affairs. [10] In early 1998, there were discussions regarding some arrangement on command and control, and former Army Chief Gen Aslam Beg did talk about some arrangement which was more of a nuclear decision-making body comprising the Army Chief, the President and senior scientists. But this arrangement was not meant for the operational aspect. According to Brig Naeem Salik, serious efforts in the direction of streamlined command and control were initiated in 1998 before the tests. [11] After the nuclear tests in 1998, the then Army Chief Gen Jehangir Karamat appointed Maj Gen Khalid Kidwai to oversee an Evaluation and Research Cell (E&R). The recommendations of the E&R cell would, by and large, form the basic guidelines for the command and control system. The E&R recommendations were complete by the fall of 1998 but the unexpected resignation of Gen Karamat and the appointment of Gen Musharraf as the new Chief delayed the proceedings.[12] In 1999, the command and control structure was formalised and approved by Gen Musharraf who was prompt in getting the approval of the Cabinet and the National Security Council in February 2000 after the military coup in Pakistan. Khalid Kidwai was appointed as the Director General of the Strategic Plans Division (SPD) – the most critical tier of the command and control assigned to formulate the nuclear doctrine and strategy and development of the nuclear arsenal, and he has retained the position even after he retired from the army in 2007.

Pakistan claims that its nuclear weapons are completely secure and its command and control over its nuclear weapons is compartmentalised and includes strict operational security. Pakistan's command and control system is based on "C4I2SR" (Command, Control, Communication, Computers, Intelligence, Information, Surveillance and Reconnaissance).[13] The system is a three-tiered one consisting of the National Command Authority (NCA), the Strategic Plans Division (SPD) and the Strategic Forces Command (SFC).

National Command Authority

The NCA, which is the first tier in command and control was created in 2000. It supervises the functions and administration of all the organisations within Pakistan working on the research, development and employment of the nuclear weapons and the military Services that operate the strategic forces.[14] The NCA is the highest decision-making body in Pakistan's nuclear command and control infrastructure. It is a ten-member body and has a mix of civilians and military representatives. The membership includes the Prime Minister as the Chairman, the Ministers of Defence, Interior and Finance, the Director General of the SPD, the commanders of the army, navy and the air force and the Chairman of the Joint Chiefs of Staff. [15] The final authority to take the decision for a nuclear strike requires consensus within the NCA, and the Chairperson, the Prime Minister of Pakistan, casts the final vote. [16]

The NCA is responsible for policy formulation, development and employment of control over all strategic nuclear forces, negotiating arms control/disarmament, overseeing implementation of export controls and safeguarding nuclear assets and sites.[17] The NCA consists of the Development Control Committee (DCC) and Employment Control Committee (ECC) (Fig 1). The two committees function independently for operational and developmental aspects. The Director General of the SPD is a member and Secretary of both committees.[18]

Fig 1: Organisation of the National Command Authority

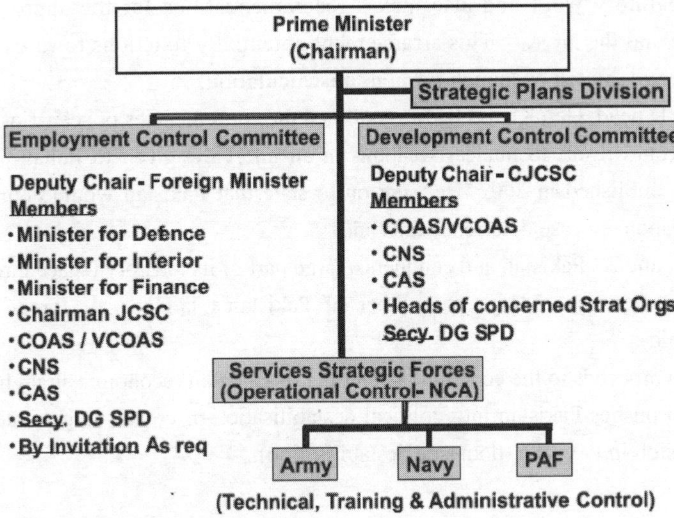

Source: Christopher Clary, Thinking about Pakistan's Security in Peacetime, Crisis and War, IDSA Occasional Paper, No. 12, New Delhi, IDSA, 2010, p. 12.

Employment Control Committee

The ECC is the main policy-making organ and functions as a politico-military committee.[19] The ECC is the superior committee and it periodically reviews the latest information on the threats to national security, strategic weapons programme, their developments and deployments. It takes the decision about the responses to the development. It provides the policy direction during peace-time and also controls the employment of the strategic forces command during the war.[20] It plays a significant role in the evolution of the nuclear doctrine and, thus, also supervises the policy for the use of nuclear weapons. It overlooks the command and control system in order to safeguard or prevent any accidental or unauthorised use of the nuclear arsenal.[21] The composition of the ECC involves representatives from both the political and military sides, providing it a good balance in some form (Fig1). It includes the Foreign Minister (as the Deputy Chairman), federal Ministers for Defence, Finance and Interior, the Chairman, Joint Chief of Staff Committee (CJCSC), Chiefs of all the three Services and Director General (DG) SPD. Other officials can be a part of the committee by invitation. The ECC is responsible for employment of the Pakistani deterrent capability; it is responsible for identifying the national security threats which would lead to the use of nuclear weapons. The SPD assists the committee in its preparatory work and also makes recommendations for the approval of the committee and the NCA.[22] This arrangement potentially functions towards avoiding any accidental launch or launch through miscalculation.

The SPD head, Gen Khalid Kidwai outlined the contingencies or scenarios in which Pakistan would resort to nuclear weapons in an interview given to Italian journalists which was published in 2002. He went on to state that Pakistan would definitely use nuclear weapons in case deterrence fails and:

- If India attacks Pakistan and conquers a large part of its territory (space threshold);
- If India destroys a large part either of Pakistan's land or air forces (military threshold);
- If India proceeds to the economic strangling of Pakistan (economic strangling);
- If India pushes Pakistan into political destabilisation or creates large-scale internal subversion in Pakistan (domestic destabilisation). [23]

It can be presumed that these contingencies were talked about only after the approval of the ECC. Eventually, we have had statements by the Pakistani military leaders about using nuclear weapons as a "last resort".[24] But the last resort option has not been quantified and there is nothing available (at least in the public domain) which gives any specific details of the Pakistanis' last resort.

Development Control Committee

The DCC is a subordinate committee which supervises and ensures the implementation of the decisions taken by the ECC. It is a military-technical committee (Fig 1) and consists of the top military leadership: CJCSC, the three Services Chiefs, and heads of various strategic organisations. The DG SPD (who is from the army) acts as the Secretary.[25]

The DCC is responsible for the development of the nuclear capabilities and keeping the deterrent in a state of preparedness. The committee exercises complete control over day-to-day technical, financial and administrative matters of the strategic organisations involved in the nuclear weapon programme, which include the Pakistan Atomic Energy Commission (PAEC), KRL, North-East Social Communication (NESCOM) and Pakistan Space and Upper Atmosphere Research Commission (SUPARCO). The DCC is responsible to ensure that the development of the strategic weapons programme progresses as per the approved development strategy.[26]

Fig 2: Pakistan's Strategic Plans Division

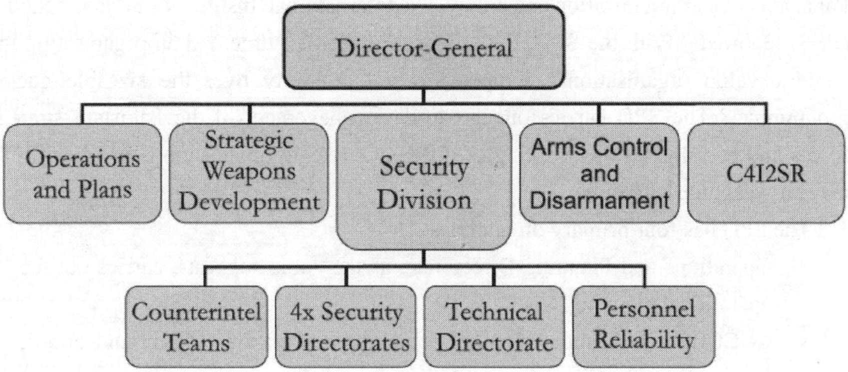

Source: Christopher Clary, p. 12.

Strategic Plans Division

The SPD is the second and most critical tier of command and control and it would not be totally incorrect to state that entire the command and control rests with the decisions, strategy and policies formulated by the SPD which is headed by the DG Army. Created in 1998, the SPD acts as the Secretariat of the NCA, and formulates Islamabad's nuclear policy, doctrine and strategy. The SPD, rightly termed as the true "nuclear enclave," is the key to Pakistan's nuclear management.[27] The SPD reports directly to the Prime Minister. It is headed by a Director General who is appointed from the army and comprises 50-70 officers from all three Services, reflecting the army's dominant position in strategic issues.[28] The DG is entrusted with the responsibility to handle any and everything related to Pakistan's nuclear capability. The SPD is the most crucial component of the command and control structure and, in a way, manages Pakistan's nuclear capability in totality, controlling the policy formulation, operations, plans, weapons development, storage, finances and safety and security. [29] It ensures the safety and security of the nuclear assets in both the short and long terms, and helps the NCA to exercise control over the strategic organisation. According to Khalid Banuri, Director, Arms Control and Disarmament Affairs at the Strategic Plans Division in Pakistan, "On behalf of the NCA, SPD exercises firm control over all strategic organisations and coordinates their financial, technical, developmental and administrative aspects. SPD is also responsible, in collaboration with the Foreign Ministry, for providing military inputs in the formulation of Pakistan's position on disarmament, non-proliferation and arms control issues." [30]

It is observed that the SPD under Gen Khalid Kidwai had taken firm control over Pakistani nuclear organisation and policy. The International Institute of Strategic Studies (IISS) reported, "With the SPD, the military for the first time had an organisation that could develop organisational competency and authority over the sizeable nuclear programme." The SPD carries out day-to-day management of the Pakistani strategic forces and coordinates the working of different strategic organisations involved in the nuclear weapon programme.

The SPD has four primary directorates:

- Operations and Planning Directorate, as the name suggests, carries out the operational planning.
- CCCCIISR (Computerised, Command, Control, Communications, Information, Intelligence, Surveillance and Reconnaissance Directorate) is responsible for developing and maintaining strategic command and communication links.
- The Strategic Weapons Development Directorate carries liaises with the strategic organisations, scrutinises their budgetary demands, and carries out audits of funds.
- The Arms Control and Disarmament Affairs Directorate provides recommendations on all arms control and disarmament issues and participates in relevant bilateral and multilateral non-proliferation discussions. [31]

There are some subsidiary organisations like the Consultancy Directorate, comprising technical experts who provide technical advice on all construction projects, and the Strategic Forces Communications Planning (SFCP) cell, comprising communications experts, to assist the C4I2SR directorate. [32]

The Security Division is the largest component of the SPD and is composed of around 9,000-10,000 personnel reporting to a serving two-star General. This division provides the internal and external security for nuclear-related sites.[33] The other directorates are: Counter-Intelligence Directorate, Technical Directorate, Personnel Reliability Programme Directorate and Security Directorate. The SPD has divisions to carry on various other functions, namely, Security Division, Civil Works Organisation and Strategic Forces Communications Planning Cell.

During peace-time, the SPD has the responsibility of guarding the nuclear programmes from external as well as internal threats. According to Luongo and Brig Salik, at present, there is a multi-layered approach to perimeter security and the SPD plays a crucial role:[34]

- Inner Perimeter: The central responsibility of the security of all the nuclear installations, civilian or military, is with the SPD, and the security division is the coordinating body. Reportedly, some facilities get additional protection by air defence elements.
- Outer Perimeter: This includes security through fencing, electronic sensors and closed circuit television cameras, etc.
- Third Tier: This involves counter-intelligence teams which work towards identifying the external threats.

Protection of nuclear material against theft and preventing infiltration of non-state or, for that matter, illegitimate factions, into the strategic organisations is primarily the responsibility of the SPD. The organisation does go through several programmes related to secrecy, physical security, personal screening programmes, procedural and technical controls in order to strengthen its safeguarding capabilities.[35] It is the SPD which controls the information regarding the location of Pakistan's nuclear warheads and delivery systems and, apparently, the information is not shared with the regular military and intelligence officers.

Peter R. Lavoy, who interacted with the SDP on a regular basis has described the set-up:

> This organisation essentially coordinates with all intelligence agencies about any external threats. The Inter-Services Intelligence Directorate (ISID) forms the outermost ring of security and works closely with the security division. Prior to this, there was no formal role for the ISID in nuclear matters. Even now, the ISID director-general is not a formal member of the NCA. (Reportedly, he is a regularly invited member). [36]

Secrecy is the key to the security of Pakistan's nuclear arsenal and is certainly treated as the most significant safeguard against both internal and external threats.[37] The SPD is also responsible for the Personnel Reliability Programme (PRP). Pakistan has apparently evolved Personal and Human Reliability Programmes to ensure the entry of only authorised and trusted personnel into the nuclear installations. This factor is critical, particularly in the case of Pakistan, given the rise of extremism in the country and the latest attack on Mehran Naval Base in May 2011, which clearly involved insider support. The PRP is administered by the SPD in conjunction with Pakistan's three intelligence agencies – Inter-Services Intelligence (ISI), Military Intelligence, and Intelligence Bureau.[38]

The PRP covers all persons working in the sensitive areas of the nuclear system. The PRP has been strengthened as per Pakistani officials much more after 9/11 and the system is based on the lessons learned and adopted from the US system. The screening involves checking of the complete background, including checks on family, political affiliations and personal inclinations. After the initial screening, there are periodic checks and screenings every two years and also at the time of transfer of an employee from one section/location to another. There is also a procedure of random checks which are carried out whenever required.[39]

The SPD coordinates with the strategic forces command. All the three forces, the army, navy and air force have their respective strategic forces command but the operational planning and control rests with the NCA.[40] The SPD formulates the short-term and long-term force development strategy for the strategic forces. The SPD is also responsible for formulating strategic and operational plans at the joint Services level for the movement, deployment, and employment of strategic forces.[41]

Strategic Forces Command(SFC)

The SFC is at the third tier of the command and control. All the three Services have their respective strategic forces command. The three Services retain training, technical and administrative control over their respective forces, but operational control remains under the jurisdiction of the NCA, which provides military direction through the Chairman of the Joint Chiefs of Staff Committee housed in the National Command Centre.[42] The role of the strategic forces command has been defined by Luongo and Salik:

> The primary responsibility of these commands is to exercise technical, training, and administrative control over the strategic delivery systems. The operational control, however, rests with the NCA. The army strategic force command possesses ballistic and cruise missiles, while the air force strategic command has the aircraft capable of delivering nuclear weapons. The naval strategic force command was the last to be established, and there is no public information as to whether they already have nuclear delivery systems and weapons or whether this capability is still evolving.[43]

Decision-Making in the Command and Control Structure

The NCA and SPD formulate the basic guidelines for the deployment and final use of the nuclear weapons. Obviously, the details of these are highly confidential and one can only draw some broad conclusions in this regard based on the various statements made by responsible military and political leaders. The decision to launch a nuclear strike rests on the consensus within the NCA, and the Prime Minister, the Chairman of the NCA would cast the final vote. Whether, the political leadership is 'actually' in a position to cast the final vote without the approval of the army for the use of nuclear weapons, is debatable.

But, as per the approved command and control structure, the final authority lies with the Prime Minster of Pakistan. The NCA would then communicate the decision and delegate authority to implement the decision to the SPD and down the institutional hierarchy/ structure.[44] Reportedly, Pakistan applies the two or three-man rule to the authorisation of assembly and use of nuclear weapons. [45] While, there is little clarity on the number of people involved at various steps for the deployment of the nuclear weapon, according to Pakistani officials, no single individual at any rung of the nuclear hierarchy is in a position to carry out the strike on his own and at least two or three people authenticate the launch codes for nuclear weapons.

Measures for Safety and Security of the Nuclear Weapons Assets and Sites

Security of the Nuclear Weapons

Pakistan has expanded the size of its nuclear arsenal—both the number of warheads as well as the delivery systems. Pakistan maintains two types of delivery systems–land- based missiles and aircraft. The weapons are believed to be kept separate from their delivery systems, with the nuclear cores removed from their detonators. It is difficult to estimate the number of actual weapon-storage sites, but nuclear weapons would certainly be dispersed at various sites. However, Khalid Kidwai has stated that Pakistan's nuclear weapons can be mated quickly.[46] Originally, Pakistan's nuclear warheads were not equipped with Permissive Action Links (PALs), but now, as declared by Samar Mubarakmand, in an interview with a private TV network in 2004, each Pakistani warhead is fitted with a "code-lock device."[47] Pakistan follows a two-man or three-man rule to authenticate the codes that call for the release of the weapons. In 2002, Khalid Kidwai referred to a "three-man rule."[48] Later, in their writings, Feroz Hasan Khan and Naeem Salik, mentioned the "two-man rule" that in some situations becomes a "three-man rule."[49] Neither Salik nor Feroz Hasan Khan give the details of who would be the authorised personnel for the code. It is also not clear whether these two, or in some cases three, men receive a common set of instructions through the same communication channel or different instructions through varied channels.[50] In 2006, Lt Gen. Kidwai confirmed the employment of the system equivalent to the PAL, a system used to keep a weapon from detonation in 2006, and, while addressing the US Naval Postgraduate School, he stated, "Pakistani nuclear controls include some functional equivalent to the two-man rule and Permissive Action Links (PALs) that the United States and some other nuclear-weapons states rely on."[51]

Pakistan has received assistance on the nuclear weapons security from the US and the Bush Administration reportedly spent almost $100 million on a highly classified programme to help President Musharraf secure his country's nuclear weapons, according to senior Administration officials.[52] But the US assistance does not mention the transfer of PALs, not only because the US was sensitive about sharing the information due to legal restrictions but also because the Pakistanis were suspicious that the American technology could work towards disabling their nuclear weapons.[53]

Safety of the Fissile Material and Spent Fuel

Safety of the fissile material is extremely critical, particularly to avoid the misuse of the fissile material by the non-state actors or even by rogue members within the system. The SPD has been responsible for conducting regular audits on all nuclear inventories since 1998. Any new radioactive or nuclear material which enters the safeguard system comes under the supervision of the International Atomic Energy Agency (IAEA), which monitors the movement of the material till it is disposed.[54]

Four of Pakistan's nuclear facilities, namely, the Karachi and Chashma-1 power reactors and the Pakistan Atomic Research Reactors I and II in Rawalpindi, operate under IAEA safeguards. But the other important Pakistani nuclear facilities which are producing plutonium and weapon grade uranium are not under IAEA safeguards, including the Kahuta Research Laboratories and Khushab research reactor.[55]

A bigger concern for the Pakistani authorities is the safety of the spent nuclear fuel and high-activity radioactive sources which are more difficult to protect. Pakistan is making efforts to acquire specialised vehicles to prevent attempts to target transportation containers.[56] Not many details are available regarding this issue.

Establishment of the Pakistan Nuclear Regulatory Authority (PNRA)

On January 22, 2001, the Pakistan Nuclear Authority Ordinance, was promulgated and consequently the Pakistan Nuclear Regulatory Authority (PNRA) was established as an independent entity to implement nuclear and radiation safety regulations in the country. The PNRA is responsible for controlling and supervising all matters pertaining to the safety of nuclear installations[57]

The PNRA is headed by a Chairman and is assisted by two full-time and seven part- time members. The DG SPD is also a member of the PNRA. The Authority functions as a regulatory and decision-making body.[58] The main functions of the PNRA are as follows:

- It takes licensee decisions for both nuclear and radiation facilities.
- It sets policies and directions on safety and environmental issues that concern the nuclear industry and the public.

- It maintains close liaison with all national organisations involved in any form in the execution of its responsibilities.
- It maintains a computerised inventory of radioactive sources in the country. The safety and security of radioactive sources are given the utmost importance in the PNRA activities.
- It is anticipated to play a significant role in the national arrangements in response to a nuclear accident or radiological emergency. The PNRA has established a National Radiation Emergency Coordination Centre (NRECC) to coordinate various steps during a nuclear emergency.[59]

In 2002, the PNRA announced a series of fresh measures for protecting "the plant and society from hazards that could be man-made or natural"[60], which included "stricter quality control and monitoring for infrastructure and equipment, multiple physical barriers to uncontrolled release of radioactive materials, radiation protection and acceptance criteria, and disaster mitigation equipment and arrangements." [61]

Radiological sources do become an area of concern and these can be misused by the rogue elements much more easily as compared to other nuclear equipment. According to Luongo and Salik, it is difficult to ascertain the total number of radiological sources in Pakistan. However, it is estimated that 65 percent of the sources are claimed to be stored and 34 percent of sources are in use. More than 50 percent of the amount in use is not under the PAEC. [62]

Export Controls

The internal export control guidelines for all the nuclear organisations were issued in 2000 by the SPD. Before this, the organisations were acting independently, thus, leaving numerous opportunities for suspicious transactions. The institutions are now required to follow certain procedures for all exports and seek clearance from the SPD and Ministry of Foreign Affairs. [63]

The Export Control Act was promulgated in 2004 in order to exercise export control on goods, technologies, material and equipment related to nuclear and biological weapons and their delivery systems. The salient elements of the Export Control Act include:

- Control over export, reexport, transhipment and transit of goods, technologies, material and equipment covered. Prohibition of diversion of controlled goods and technologies.
- Wide jurisdiction (also includes Pakistanis visiting or working abroad).
- Envisages an authority to administer rules and regulations framed under this

legislation. Also provides for the establishment of an Oversight Board to monitor the implementation of this legislation.

- Comprehensive control lists and catch-all provisions.
- Licensing and record keeping provisions.
- Penal provisions: up to 14 years imprisonment and Rs. 5 million fine or both, and on conviction, the offender's property and assets, wherever they maybe, shall be forfeited to the federal government. Right of appeal provided for. [64]

Gen Musharraf did try and take certain steps to ensure accurate monitoring of the import of nuclear and biological weapons. But given the more than 2,000 km of Pakistan's permeable border, it is indeed challenging to monitor and control radiological import/export.

US Assistance in Securing Nuclear Weapons

Preventing Pakistan's nuclear weapons from a potentially disastrous possibility of falling into the extremists' hands, or an Islamist coup is certainly on Washington's priority list. The American concerns were evident in the speech of Chairman of the Joint Chiefs of Staff Admiral Michael Mullen on September 22, 2008:

> To the best of my ability to understand it—and this is with some ability—the weapons there are secure. And that even in the change of government, the controls of those weapons haven't changed. That said, they are their weapons. They're not my weapons. And there are limits to what I know. Certainly, in a worst case scenario, with respect to Pakistan, I worry a great deal about those weapons falling into the hands of terrorists and either being proliferated or potentially used. And so, control of those, stability, stable control of those weapons, is a key concern.[65]

Although Pakistan has consistently claimed the infallible security of its arsenal, it is also true that alarming incidents indicating threats to the nuclear weapons have taken place in the past. On American requests, the Pakistani authorities detained Bashiruddin Mahmood and Abdul Majeed, retired Pakistan Atomic Energy Commission (PAEC) officials on October 23, 2001. The British trained scientists had a long career in the Pakistani nuclear programme and had held multiple important positions before they retired in 1999.[66] The officials have been involved in relief work in Afghanistan through a non-governmental organisation, Ummah Tameer-e-Nau (UTN), which they had set up, and had worked on various developmental projects in Kabul and Kandahar. In November

2001, the Coalition forces in Afghanistan discovered documents that indicated the UTN's interest in biological weapons. Under interrogation, the two scientists revealed to the Pakistani authorities that they had a series of meetings with Osama bin Laden and the last meeting took place in August 2001. They reportedly discussed with Al Qaeda about the development of chemical, biological and nuclear weapons.[67] The two men were released and arrested again, and were finally freed in 2001, without any charge. This was despite the fact that they had breached the secrecy oath in their visits to Afghanistan.[68] The United States also wanted the detention of two other nuclear experts, Suleiman Asad and Mohammad Ali Mukhtar, who are believed to have been associated with Pakistan's secret nuclear installations. The Bush Administration was suspicious of their possible links with the militants, but the two experts were never detained. [69]

The US obviously has been concerned, and has offered assistance for the safety of Pakistan's nuclear arsenal. Reportedly, the US did offer nuclear security assistance to Pakistan post September 2001 which included the sharing of best practices and technical measures to prevent unauthorised or accidental use of nuclear weapons, as well as contribute to the physical security of the storage facility and personnel reliability. [70] The issue of offering PAL technology was debated in the US Administration. While many nuclear experts in the federal government favoured the offer given the fact that Pakistan's nuclear arsenal was the most vulnerable arsenal in the world, others felt that sharing of technology would teach Pakistan too much about American weaponry. Apparently, the same logic restricted the Clinton Administration from sharing the technology with China in the early 1990s.[71]

Feroz Hasan Khan in his article in *Arms Control Association* stated:

> In 2001, US Secretary of Sate Colin Powell offered nuclear security assistance to Pakistani President Gen Pervez Musharraf. The SPD carefully examined the offer and accepted training but declined technology transfers, which they perceived as intrusive or likely to compromise programme secrecy. Since then, Pakistan has benefitted from advanced-level training from US national laboratories and has improved its best practices in accordance with its own security culture.[72]

The US assistance was confirmed during Secretary of State Condoleezza Rice's confirmation hearing in January 2005. She responded to Senator John Kerry's query regarding the safety of the Pakistani nuclear weapons in the event of a radical Islamic coup in Islamabad, and stated, "We have noted this problem, and we are prepared to try to deal with it."[73] However, there is great suspicion about the US' intentions in Pakistan which aggravates each time there is a press report or comment about the US authorities taking control of Pakistan's nuclear arsenal in the wake of a breakdown of the governance which remains in constant turmoil or the prospective rise of *jihadi* elements in the leadership positions.[74] Pakistan has maintained its stance on denying any foreign access to its arsenal precisely because it fears that the knowledge might be used to target the weapons. They have also been hesitant in receiving technical assistance for fear the US will install tracking devices to locate the weapons or secret methods of disabling them.[75]

Pakistan has been in a state of denial with respect to receiving any assistance from the US in this regard. As recently as November 8, 2009, a Pakistan Foreign Office spokesperson stated that Pakistan "does not require any foreign assistance in this regard". Pakistan will never "allow any country to have direct or indirect access to its nuclear and strategic facilities," and further added that "no talks have ever taken place on the issue of security of Pakistan's nuclear arsenal with the US officials."[76] Some press reports have indicated that the US provided Pakistan with PAL in 2003, but retired Brig Gen Naeem Salik stated, "Pakistan has developed its own PAL system which obviously ensures that even if an unauthorised person gets hold of a weapon, he cannot activate it unless he also has access to the electronic codes." [77]

The US has provided assistance in securing Pakistan's nuclear weapons, although the efforts have been restricted due to Pakistan's reluctance to provide access to the nuclear facilities. Some American experts say that "they have less ability to look into the nuclear laboratories where highly enriched uranium is produced".[78] A former US official's comment regarding the US assistance was, "Everything has taken far longer than it should….. and you are never sure what you really accomplished."[79] It is unclear as to what extent Pakistan has shared information regarding its arsenal. Also, the Pakistani officials have stated that they have been discreet about accepting assistance and that Pakistan reserves the right to "pick and choose" the nuclear security measures, and will accept only such measures as are "non-intrusive."[80] Reports suggest that the US had spent approximately $100 million on the classified nuclear security programme by 2007, which is not so significant considering the total amount of aid Pakistan has received from the US, starting 2002, which amounts to more than $20 billion.

Risks to the Nuclear Weapons

Pakistan's nuclear weapons are "stored in component form", which implies that the nuclear weapons are stored separately from the delivery vehicles. Reports suggest that Islamabad's nuclear weapons are stored unassembled, with the fissile core separated from the non-nuclear explosives. Khalid Kidwai, the head of the SDP, has said that the nuclear warheads (containing the fissile cores) may be mated with their delivery vehicles. [81]

Kidwai has reportedly also stated that the nuclear weapons "will be ready when required, at the shortest notice; (but) the Pakistani doctrine is not endorsing the US-USSR model with weapons at hair trigger alert". The 2001 Defence Department report suggested that Pakistan can probably assemble its weapons fairly quickly. [82]

Storage of nuclear warheads away from the delivery vehicles could prevent accidental launches, but the political and domestic situations make the nuclear weapons extremely vulnerable. When Pakistan developed its nuclear weapons, its prime concern was an attack by India, and now after 25 years of nuclearisation, Pakistan's biggest nightmare is the safety of its nuclear weapons from the *jihadi* elements on its own soil.

Pakistan has, undoubtedly, evolved a structured command and control system which is impressive. But the danger for Pakistan's weapons does not emerge from the loopholes in the command and control but from the uniquely dangerous environment in which the weapons are placed. At present, hardly a week passes by in Pakistan without a daring terrorist incident, sparing not or even the armed forces, for that matter, the GHQ. However, it will be useful to analyse some of the scenarios in which the unauthorised use of nuclear weapons/material could occur.

Miscalculation

Although the final nuclear decision-making regarding the use of the nuclear weapon requires two or may be three authorised personnel to take the decision, the persistent domestic instability within Pakistan, with constant rifts between the army and the civilian forces, leading to use of nuclear weapons through miscalculation cannot be negated. A. Q. Khan did acknowledged this threat:

> .... there is a real danger of nuclear war by accident due to technical failure or malfunctioning, or due to accidental detonation or launching of a nuclear weapon. Nuclear war can also be started by unauthorised action, human error or sheer madness. There is, moreover, a great danger of a person or a group of persons responsible for launching nuclear weapons going insane and deciding to launch a nuclear attack on the enemy, eliciting immediate retaliation and a real holocaust.[83]

Former Pakistani Foreign Minister Agha Shahi, had raised similar concerns:

> Pakistan may well be confronted with a hair trigger alert situation. Neither country [India and Pakistan] has an effective early warning system against missile attacks to detect intruding aircraft carrying nuclear devices. The flight time of their [India's] nuclear-

> armed short and medium range missiles is only three to less than ten minutes. Hence, a 'launch-on-warning' system [launching missiles before incoming missiles arrive] that existed between the United States and the former Soviet Union—25 minutes of warning time in case of ICBMs [Inter-Continental Ballistic Missiles] and 15 minutes in that of their SLBMs [Submarine Launched Ballistic Missiles] from deployed submarines—would elude Pakistan and India. The risk of a nuclear strike by miscalculation or unauthorised use, therefore, cannot be but high, as the respective command and control systems cannot ensure real-time instructions for alerting and launching nuclear forces.[84]

The danger of miscalculation is more exasperating in the case of Pakistan where the doctrine is unwritten and consistently there has been a tendency of projection of irrationality from the governing elites. Pakistan has often threatened to go nuclear in the case of even the threat of an Indian conventional attack. In fact, the military has tried to exploit its irrational posture rather judiciously on various occasions. Practice of this nature increases the probability of accidental use of nuclear weapons.

Outsider Threat

The threat of the nuclear facilities being attacked by the terrorist/ extremist organisations has been most worrisome and has raised concerns both worldwide and within Pakistan. The rise of extremism in Pakistan has been significant post 9/11. Raging insurgency on the Frontier borders, Al Qaeda's leading associates hiding in the heart of Pakistan and most importantly, the rise of the Tehrik-i-Taliban Pakistan (TTP), with a strict anti-state and anti-military agenda, has made the military and nuclear installations prime targets. The nuclear installations and also the nuclear personnel have been targeted in the past on several occasions.

In 2007, two Pakistan Air Force (PAF) facilities associated with Pakistan's nuclear weapons were attacked. A suicide bomber riding an explosive-laden motocycle blew himself up near a bus carrying the air force personnel on duty to Sargodha Air Base,[85] considered to be the country's most important air base. It is the headquarters of the Central Air Command, and two squadrons of F-16 fighter jets are based there. The F-16s are supposedly Pakistan's prime aerial delivery system. On December 10, 2007, a school bus carrying the children of air force personnel outside was targeted at Kamra Air Base, which is a base for the Mirage Vs which, supposedly, could be used for nuclear missions. On August 21, 2008, twin suicide bombers carried out an attack on the gates of the Pakistan's ordnance factory at Wah, which is reportedy a site for nuclear weapons also.[86] The Pakistani Taliban claimed the responsibility for the attack.

On October 10, 2009, the TTP and Lashkar-i-Jhangvi militants attacked the Army GHQ in Rawalpindi, the most secure military complex in Pakistan. Ten TTP militants dressed in army uniforms attacked the GHQ, killing six people, including a Brigadier and a Lieutenant Colonel. According to Professor Shaun Gregory, Director of the Pakistan Security Research Unit at the University of Bradford, UK, the modalities of this attack add up to a vital blueprint for an attack on a nuclear weapons facility. For example,

- The penetration of several security checkpoints and barriers.
- Use of army uniforms, fake ID cards , a military vehicle to deceive the army.
- Use of a safe house near the GHQ for weeks before the attack.
- Use of maps of the GHQ to allow operational planning. This also projects the possibility of internal involvement in information sharing or poor management of the GHQ.
- Use of tactics that allow final tier barriers to be penetrated: grenades and/or suicide detonations at entry points which then allow penetration by follow-up commando-style groups.[87]

During the attack on the GHQ, the terrorists entered the complex and took nearly 40 people hostage. It took the Pakistan Army Commando's Special Services Group (SSG) more than 20 hours to gain control of the situation and free most of the hostages.[88]

These incidents indicate that the scenario of a militant organisation taking control of a nuclear site or some part of a nuclear site is not a remote possibility. As the number of nuclear weapons grows, the challenge to secure this enhanced number would also intensify. Militant outfits like the TTP clearly adopt an anti-state posture and have ample support from international terror outfits like Al Qaeda, with which it shares an ideological alliance. Thus, the financial and military assistance for these outfits never seems to be problem. Taliban spokesman Ehsanullah Ehsan has openly talked about using the Islamic bomb:

> Pakistan is the only Muslim nuclear power state. Isn't it a shame for us to have the Islamic bomb, and even then, we are bowing down to the pressures of America?[89]

A more likely scenario for terror outfits would be to get hold of the spent fuel which can be converted into a dirty bomb. Bharad Karnad talked about this scenario of nuclear terrorism in his article:

> The much easier route to nuclear terrorism is the 'dirty bomb'—a radiation diffusion device (RDD) that can be configured by terrorists. All that is needed is a bundle of

> spent fuel (featuring radio-isotopes such as cobalt 60, strontium 90 and cesium 137) powering X-ray machines, gamma ray cameras, etc., used extensively in the health and industrial sectors, a smuggled 'pencil' fuel at a time. These can be tied together and fitted into a shoebox, and the entire package blown up with a conventional explosive, such as dynamite.......a small explosion followed by release of radioactivity which, depending on ambient conditions, can spread with the wind and quickly affect an entire city.[90]

Insider Threat

The possibility of an insider conspiracy or insider-outsider collusion, with an objective to takeover nuclear items poses a severe challenge to the command and control set-up in Pakistan. The assassination of Salman Taseer, Governor of Punjab, a critic of the blasphemy law, by his own bodyguard in broad daylight, who was then welcomed by a shower of rose petals in the judiciary, raises serious doubts about the credibility of the personnel guarding the military and nuclear establishments. Although the SPD is extremely confident about the PRP and, according to them, the programmes have a screening process from "cradle to grave," the possibility of extremist motivation leading to a mishap cannot be ruled out.

In May 2011, the Pakistani Taliban attacked the Mehran Naval Base in Karachi, about 15 miles away from a suspected nuclear storage facility in another glaring example of insider collaboration.[91] The Mehran Base attack could not have been possible without insider assistance. As many as 70,000 people in Pakistan have access to knowledge of some element of a nuclear facility or weapon system, given the size of the arsenal and personnel involved in the entire programme. In an environment where the survival of liberal thinking is difficult, the possibility of extremism influencing the personnel is certainly not ruled out. Dr Gregory, in his report, stated:

> As the number of nuclear weapons facilities grows, and the number of those with access to nuclear weapons or related components rises, the complex challenge of assuring the security of nuclear weapons and nuclear weapons components will become even more difficult.[92]

The insider threat may be reflected in various forms like leakage of sensitive information, assisting an outsider to break in, or theft of nuclear material. Feroz Hasan Khan, in his article, talks about misperceptions regarding the safety of nuclear weapons, but he acknowledges the insider threat:

> Western fears about Pakistani nuclear security range from valid to bizarre. The more valid concerns involve theft of material, sabotage, unauthorised use of nuclear weapons, and insider-outside collaboration.[93]
>
> He adds:
>
> The most difficult aspect of measuring effectiveness comes from the unpredictability of human motivations. Motivated individuals can always elude barriers.
>
> Sig Hecker, in his article, states:
>
> Pakistan is also at the top of my list of nuclear risks because it is the most likely place in which fissile materials could find their way out of the hands of government and into those of terrorists. However, it is also the most difficult place to do science diplomacy. The five-nation dialogue facilitated discussion with Pakistani officials on nuclear materials security and the proliferation activities of Pakistani nuclear scientist Abdul Qadeer Khan. But Pakistan's nuclear scientific community is not accessible, and the problems are difficult and extremely sensitive politically….[94]

With the expansion of the arsenal, the nuclear expertise is also expanding within Pakistan and the challenge for the military and the civilian regime is of controlling the nuclear expertise. Although, Pakistan has reemployed the nuclear scientists in various other programmes, dealing with the retired scientists is certainly a problem. Protection of sensitive information is one of the biggest issues in Pakistan where the temptation could not be only ideological but also monetary.

Conclusion

Given the volatile political situation and existing threat of *jihadi* elements within Pakistan, the issue of safety and security of the nuclear weapons is certainly one of the biggest concerns for not only the Pakistani establishment but also the international community, particularly the United States. Post 9/11, Pakistan has worked towards strengthening its nuclear command and control system and has received over $100 million of US assistance for increasing the security of the nuclear weapons. There have been major changes in the NCA, integration of command and control, employment of the permissive action links on nuclear weapons and export control measures. The political crisis in 2007 followed by steadily increasing terrorism and raging insurgency did perk up the issue of safety of the nuclear weapons. Although the Pakistani leadership has repeatedly expressed confidence about the security of the weapons, but with the political instability, deteriorating civil-military relations and declining US-Pakistan relations, the concerns for the safety and security of the world's fastest-growing nuclear stockpile would continue to grow.

Notes

1. See Hans M. Kristensen and Robert S. Norris, "Pakistan's Nuclear Forces, 2011," *Bulletin of Atomic Scientists*, Vol 67 No 4, July/August 2011, pp. 91-99.
2. Maj Gen Muhammad Ali Durrani, "Pakistan's Strategic Thinking and the Role of Nuclear Weapons", Cooperative Monitoring Centre Occasional Paper 37, Sandia National Laboratories, July 2004, p 27.
3. "Nuclear Weapons Research, Development, Testing, Production and Naval Nuclear Propulsion Facilities: Pakistan," NUCLEAR Files.Org, at http://www.nuclearfiles.org/menu/key-issues/nuclear-weapons/issues/facilities/pakistani-nuclear-weapons-facilities.htm.
4. Mushahid Hussain, "Media Off Traget with Pakistan Nuclear Scare", *Asia Times*, November 7, 2001, as cited in "Nuclear Black Markets: Pakistan, A. Q. Khan and the Rise of Proliferation Networks: A Net Assessment," IISS Strategic Dossier (UK, IISS, 2007).
5. Gordon Corera, *Shopping for Bombs: Nuclear Proliferation, Global Insecurity and the Rise and Fall of the A.Q. Khan Network* (London: C.Hurst & Co (Publishers) Ltd, 2006), p.50.
6. Ibid.
7. Bhutto visited Washington in 1989 and according to the intelligence experts, she had no real influence over the programme. The CIA officials acknowledged in a secret paper, written just before the visit, that Bhutto was "unlikely to gain control over nuclear decision-making anytime soon." CIA Internal Report, "CIA Near East and South Asia Review : Prime Minister Bhutto and the Pakistan Nuclear Issue," May 5, 1989, declassified September 1, 2000, at www.cia.gov, as cited in Gordon Corera, n. 5, pp. 50-51.
8. Owen Bennett Jones, *Pakistan: Eye of the Storm* (New Delhi: Viking, 2002), p. 210.
9. Ibid.
10. Naeem Salik, *The Genesis of South Asian Nuclear Deterrence: Pakistan's Perspective* (New York: Oxford University Press, 2010), p. 234.
11. Ibid.
12. Christopher Clary, "Thinking about Pakistan's Security in Peacetime, Crisis and War", IDSA Occasional Paper, No. 12, New Delhi, IDSA, 2010, p. 11.
13. Paul Kerr and Mary Beth Nikitin *CRS Report for Congress*, "Pakistan's Nuclear Weapons: Proliferation and Security Issues," February 23, 2010, p. 8. Updated June 20, 2008.
14. December 2007 Ordinance to provide for the constitution and establishment of the National Command Authority. As cited in Kerr and Nikitin, Ibid., p. 9.
15. Ibid.
16. Ibid.
17. Kenneth Luongo and Naeem Salik, "Building Confidence in Pakistan's Nuclear Security", *Arms Control Today,* December 1, 2007.
18. Rabia Akhtar and Nazir Hussain, "Safety and Security of Pakistan's Nuclear Assets," in Usama

Butt and N.Elahi, eds., *Pakistan's Quagmire: Security, Strategy and the Future of the Islamic-Nuclear Nation* (New York: Continuum, 2010), p. 179.
19. Luongo and Salik, n. 17, pp. 12-13.
20. Zafar Iqbal Cheema, *Indian Nuclear Deterrence* (Oxford Publishers, 2011), p. 181.
21. Ian Bremmer and Maria Kuusisto, "Pakistan's Nuclear Command and Control :Perception Matters," *SASSI Research Report,* August 2008, p.10.
22. Cheema, n. 20, pp.181-182.
23. As cited in Paolo Cotta-Ramusino and Maurizio Martellini, *Nuclear Safety, Nuclear Stability and Nuclear Strategy in Pakistan,* Landau Network – Centro Volta Report, Rome, Italy, January 21, 2001.
24. President Pervez Musharraf, in May 2002, said that if it came to war between the nuclear-armed rivals, he would "respond with full might." Also see, Agha Shahi, Zulfiqar Khan and Abdul Sattar, "Securing Nuclear Peace", *The News* (Islamabad), October 5, 1999.
25. Khalid Banuri and Adil Sultan, "Managing and Securing the Bomb", *Daily Times,* May 30, 2008.
26. Air Commodore Khalid Banuri's lecture on Pakistan's command and control structure at Fatima Jinnah Women University Rawalpindi, in April 2009, as cited in Akhtar and Hussain, n. 18, p. 180.
27. IISS, Strategic Dossier, n. 4.
28. Ibid., p.112.
29. Akhtar , n. 18, p. 181.
30. Ibid.
31. Luongo and Salik, n. 17, p. 13.
32. Ibid.
33. Clary, n. 12, p.12.
34. Luongo and Salik, n. 17, p. 14.
35. Clary, n. 12, p. 13.
36. Peter Lavoy, "Islamabad's Nuclear Posture : Its Premises and Implementation", at kms1.isn.ethz.ch/serviceengine/Files/ISN/47509/.../en/Chapter+5.pdf.
37. Clary, n. 12, p.13.
38. Ibid.
39. Luongo and Salik, n. 17, p.14.
40. Ibid., p.9.
41. Cheema, n. 20, 186.
42. IISS Strategic Dossier, n. 4, p. 112.
43. Luongo and Salik, n. 17, p. 13.
44. Bremmer and Kuusisto, n. 21, p.11.
45. Mahmud Ali Durrani, as cited in Ibid., p. 11.
46. Kerr and Nikitin, n.13, p. 13.
47. Cited in. Luongo and Salik, n. 17, p. 13.
48. Clary, n. 12, p. 15.
49. Ibid., p. 15.
50. Ibid., p.15.
51. Lt Gen Khalid Kidwai's CCC Address, "Pakistan's Evolution as a Nuclear Weapon State", Centre on Contemporary Conflict, Naval Postgraduate School, at http://www.nps.edu/

academics/centers/ccc/news/kidwaiNov06.html
52. David E. Sanger and William J. Board, "US Secretly Aids Pakistan in Guarding Nuclear Arms," *The New York Times,* November 18, 2007.
53. Ibid.
54. Luongo and Salik, n. 17, p. 13.
55. Ibid.
56. Ibid
57. *Country Report on Control of Radiation Protection Practices in Pakistan, Pakistan Nuclear Regulatory Authority (PNRA)* IAEA/RCA MID TERM REVIEW MEETING IAEA MODEL PROJECT RAC/9/026, RAS/9/027 Beijing, June 7-11, 2004 , at http://www.rca.iaea.org/members/Projects/RAS9029/Appendix%20%2018A%20Country%20Report%20Pakistan.doc.
58. Ibid.
59. Ibid.
60. Luongo and Salik, n. 17, p. 15.
61. Ibid.
62. Of the total in use, 49 percent is under the PAEC, of which 26 percent is for medical use and 74 percent for non-medical use, and 51 percent is non-PAEC, of which 12 percent is for medical use and 88 percent is for non-medical use. Cited in Luongo and Salik, n. 17, p. 16.
63. Luongo and Salik, n. 17, p. 15.
64. Pakistan's national legislation entitled: "Export Control of Goods, Technologies, Material and Equipment Related to Nuclear and Biological Weapons and their Delivery Systems Act, 2004" *IAEA*, Information Circular, INFCIRC/636, November 23, 2004.
65. Kerr and Nikitin, n. 13, p. 1.
66. Zahid Hussain, *Frontline Pakistan: The Path to Catastrophe and the Killing of Benazir Bhutto* (London: Penguin Books, 2008), p. 154.
67. "Nuclear Experts Briefed bin Laden, Pakistan says," *Washington Post,* December 12, 2001, as cited in Hussain, n. 66, p. 155.
68. Ibid.
69. Ibid., p.156.
70. Joby Warrick, "US Has Concerns Over Security of Pakistan's Nuclear Weapons," *The Washington Post*, November 11, 2007; David Sanger and William Broad, "US Secretly Aids Pakistan in Guarding Nuclear Arms", *The New York Times,* November 17, 2007, as cited in Kerr and Nikitin, n. 13, p. 13.
71. David E. Sanger and William J. Broad, "US Secretly Aids Pakistan in Guarding Nuclear Arms", *The New York Times,* November 18, 2007.
72. Feroz Hasan Khan, "Nuclear Security in Pakistan: Separating Myth From Reality", *Arms Control Association,* July/August 2009.
73. "The Nomination of Condoleeza Rice to the Secretary of State," Hearings before the Senate Foreign Relations Committee, January 18 and 19, 2005, as cited in Karr and Nikitin, n. 13, p. 13.
74. Michael Krepon "How Safe and Secure are Pakistan Nuclear Weapons?," June 13, 2008, Condensed version of the testimony submitted to the Senate Committee on Homeland Security and Government Affairs on June 12, 2008, at http://beta.stimson.org/pub.cfm?ID=628.
75. Gordon Corera "How Secure is Pakistan's Bomb?" February 4, 2008, BBC News, at http://news.bbc.co.uk/2/hi/south_asia/7225175.stm.

76. "Pakistan Foreign Office Rejects US Media Report on Nuclear Arsenal", *Associated Press of Pakistan*, November 9, 2009, as cited in Kerr and Nikitin, n.13, p13.
77. Corera, n. 20.
78. Sanger and Broad, " n. 71.
79. Ibid.
80. Kerr and Nikitin, n. 13.
81. Maurizio Martellini, "Security and Safety Issues About the Nuclear Complex: Pakistan's Standpoints. A Concise Report of a Visit to Islamabad by Landau Network Centro Volta (LNCV) Mission, carried out on February 9-13 2008" as cited in Kerr and Nikitin, n. 13, p. 10.
82. "Proliferation :Threat and Response : January 2001," US Department of Defence, p. 27.
83. Quoted in Hussain and Kamran, eds., *Dr A. Q Khan,* p.28, as cited in Jones, n. 8, p. 207.
84. Shahi, address to seminar, Islamabad, February 2000, as cited in Jones, n 8, p. 208.
85. "Nine Killed in Suicide Attack on PAF Bus", *Pak Tribune,* November 1, 2007, at http://paktribune.com/news/Nine-killed-in-suicide-attack-on-PAF-bus-193375.html
86. See, Sabir Shah, "40 Major Terror Hits Rock Armed Forces Security Agencies," *The News*, May 24, 2011.
87. "Terrorist Tactics in Pakistan Threaten Nuclear Weapons Safety", *Combating Terrorism Centre,* June 1, 2011.
88. Ibid.
89. Bharat Karnad, "5 Minutes to Nuclear Jihad?," *Asian Age*, May 29, 2011.
90. Ibid.
91. "Insiders Helped Militants Plot PNS Mehran Naval Base Attack: Experts," *The Nations*, May 23, 2011.
92. Peter Goodspeed, "Pakistan's Nuclear Arsenal may be 'Compromised': Report," *National Post*, June 14, 2011, at http://news.nationalpost.com/2011/06/14/pakistans-nuclear-arsenal-may-be-compromised-report/.
93. Feroz Hasan Khan, "Nuclear Security in Pakistan: Separating Myth From Reality," *Arms Control Today*, July/August 2009.
94. Siegfried. S. Hecker, "Adventures in Scientific Nuclear Diplomacy", *Physics Today*, July 2011, at http://www.physicstoday.org/resource/1/phtoad/v64/i7/p31_s1?bypassSSO=1.

3

Transformational Trends in China's Aviation Industry

V. Nigam

China's tryst with history was replete with centuries of foreign intervention, including the Japanese invasion and a prolonged civil war, which have become the soul of its security paradigm. Though the Nationalists, along with the fleeing warlords, had the required military arsenal, the Communists in the Mainland had to start afresh. The Chinese, therefore, had to urgently build their defence infrastructure which, by default, was modelled on the lines of the Soviet Union, but to a great extent, with Chinese characteristics. As a result, the arms industries over the years have been able to produce a wide range of conventional weapon systems like tanks, small arms, armoured vehicles, artillery, missiles, bombers, fighters and naval vessels, which though obsolete when compared with the West, nevertheless, were manufactured primarily for the People's Liberation Army (PLA).

The1950s was an era of consolidation which not only witnessed sharing of technology but also transfer of skilled human resources in the field of aviation as well as other arms sectors from Russia to China. The institutionalisation of the defence industry was marked by the setting up of a military industry commission and an aviation industry commission under the visionary leadership of Zhou en Lai in 1951. The idea of setting up a commission in the early years after the civil war reinforced China's belief in the importance of security requirements. Its obsession with possessing a robust defence infrastructure modelled on the Soviet lines blossomed during the First Five-Year Plan (1953-57)[1]. However, the hard knocks of the Great Leap Forward (1958-61) and the Cultural Revolution of the mid-1960s led to reorganisation and reconsolidation of its industry. The period of the Cultural Revolution paralysed institutions; and created a plethora of uneducated leader who were responsible for slowing down the development of the Military-Industrial Complex (MIC) in the 1970s and 1980s[2].

Legacy

It is a commonly known fact that the factories earlier located in and around the major industrial cities in China were relocated to the remote and primitive interiors of Sichuan and the western parts of Hunan, Hubei, Henan and Shaanxi provinces as a part of Mao's ambitious programme of **strategic dispersion** in 1964. The programme not only added to the huge infrastructural development cost but also led to the employment of poor quality manpower, leading to poor quality output and huge transportation costs, as well as massive operating costs, since a majority of these factories were located in the hinterland of China. The idea of setting up the 'Third Front' was to base industries at locations not only out of the range of US attacks but also with an intention to make them 'legacy' industries and provide technological diffusion as well as employment to the hinterland. As a part of the legacy strategy, **55 percent** of these industries were relocated to remote and internal areas not connected by either the road or rail network.[3] However, the entire model, designed with a typical Stalinist giganticism, even today continues to haunt China with a 'legacy' that plagues China's defence Industry.

The 1960s and 1970s were 'decades of confusion and disarray' in China's contemporary history. Some 41 out of 156 key industrial projects, conceptualised and set up under the guidance of, and with technical assistance from, Russia, happened to be defence industries, focussing primarily on the aviation sector; 60 percent out of the total defence outlay during the period went into the aviation sector[4]. Barry Naughton further estimates that the '**third front**' consumed almost two-third of China's total investment on industry; and only 20 percent of this amount was directly absorbed by the defence industries, while the rest was spent on the development of infrastructure of the '**third front**'; which included construction of railway lines and tunnels in the inhospitable terrain of the Chengdu and Kunming areas. Despite the huge investments, the factories located in the remote areas accounted for less than a quarter of the output compared to the facilities located in the coastal areas. In 1991, the *China Daily* termed the distribution of the third front plants as irrational and the conditions as extremely tough and unattractive for college graduates to travel to the hinterland and work in difficult conditions—conditions which continue to afflict some of the MICs in the 21st century!

Formative Years

Although the 1980s witnessed a revival of China's aviation industry in the aftermath of the Cultural Revolution, the investments in the early years of transition in the defence industry sharply fell to under 4 percent of the state's industrial outlay, trailing China's economy, which was growing at almost 10 percent year on year. This was, however, according to Deng's orchestrated plan, which, in principle, believed that defence development should piggy-ride the economic growth. China's drive to modernise its economy by carrying out path-breaking reforms, overcoming contradictions inherited from the past, and realising the goals for development of a new society, had its roots in its ultimate quest for security. China also believed that defence development should be coordinated with the country's overall economic development, both yardsticks to measure the country's comprehensive national power and transform China into a modern state by the turn of the century. The thrust of the 'four modernisations' set priority on agriculture; industry, followed by science and technology and national defence; but with a strong conviction that finally it will be military power in the backdrop, absolutely essential for China to eventually ascend to 'superpower status.'

Quest for Technology

Until the 1990s, it was no secret that China possessed the most laggard and technologically backward defence industry in the world. Most indigenously developed weapon systems were of poor quality and trailing behind the West by at least a decade and a half, if not more. China had in the past been a victim of the imperialistic mindset and Western arms embargos and, therefore, had been pursuing a development approach summed up by the slogan "walking on two legs"; centred on import of technology by any means and, at the same time, on its quest for self-reliance. China by the 1970s and 1980s had almost become enslaved to foreign technology which in the past had come to it easily from the Russians; and over the years, China had been using the 'Russians' as a 'quick fix' solution during many crisis situations, including as a panacea to the PLA Air Force's (PLAAF's) depleting stock of sophisticated aircraft.[5] In the early years of transition, there was technology flow from the West through the 'peace pearl,' as well as notable assistance from Israel and Italy. The Israel Aerospace Industry (IAI) was instrumental in providing significant exposure to China in the realm of high end technology through the1980s and 1990s and created an uproar in the American establishment primarily over its ramifications on the security across the Taiwan Strait. As a result, Israel was coerced into abandoning the sale of the Phalcon Airborne Warning and Control System (AWACS) to China in 2000. China's growing insecurity was as a result of its overt dependence on Western high end technology, reaffirmed by its belief that there was no substitute for self-reliance and, therefore, China had to quickly transmute from **walking on two legs** to **standing on its own two feet!** It was left with no choice but to develop a robust Research and Development (R&D) infrastructure to counter its seasonal isolations from the West, which had been pursuing a systematic 'on and off' strategy when it came to the business of providing assistance in high end technology to China. As a result, China decided to strengthen its R&D base by churning out huge numbers of graduates and engineers in the mid-1990s and providing them incentives to travel overseas for higher education. The intention was to utilise the qualified human resource which could later be reinjected into the system to augment the capability of some of the strategic industries and, thereby, help build a strong R&D base for China[6]. However, even today, China's defence R&D continues to lag behind in critical areas, which include aeronautics, jet engines, micro electronics, computers, avionics, sensors and seekers, electronic warfare and advanced materials. Hence, other than missiles and a few spikes of excellence, China's defence industries failed to impress the world by their capability to design and produce advanced and conventional weapon systems in the1990s.

Notwithstanding decades of hard work, China's continual reliance on foreign technology in critical areas was due to its incapability to make the necessary breakthroughs in the technology required for the production of arms, and also in the aviation sector. China was confronted with considerable difficulty in moving prototypes into the production stage, resulting in extended developmental phases and delays; like in the case of the J-10, which took more than a decade to move from conception to the first flight and almost two decades before entering operational service with the PLAAF. The quest for an indigenously developed fighter jet engine continues to be an extremely weak area and embarrasses the Chinese no end. One such example which haunts them even today, was their inability to produce a power plant for the JH-7 fighter bomber, leading to programme delays and, as a result, China was forced to knock on the doors of the British in the 1970s. The aircraft designed around the British Rolls Royce Spey Mk-202 engine was unable to enter service until the late 1980s, since the Xian engineers experienced protracted problems as the engine was incompatible with the airframe. David Shambaugh describes his interaction with an extremely frustrated Roll-Royce engineer involved in the development of JH-7, who said that ".......they still can't get the damn thing off the ground."[7]Also, the J-10, outfitted with a Russian engine, once again highlights China's incapability to produce a jet engine and, therefore, its continued to reliance on imported platforms and components in the new millennium as it remains diffident about the quality as well as capability of its indigenously produced weapon systems. This was also evident from the fact that although in the 1990s, China had a series of frontline fighter programmes either in the development or production stage like the J-8 II; JF-

17 and J-10, it preferred to buy several dozen Su-27, and soon after, also acquired more than100 advanced Su-30MKK strike aircraft.

Analysing the technological difficulties of any country cannot be done in isolation and, therefore, has to be done in the larger context encompassing R&D, organisational reforms as well as the cultural deficiencies responsible for holding back design and development to manufacture advanced weapons platforms. A majority of the MICs in China were vertically integrated, highly compartmentalised structures; restricting diffusion of advanced technology and obstructing flow of information between the civilian and defence sectors, which ended in limiting the spin-in and spin-off benefits that could have accrued from the system[8]. The model followed was inefficient and every industrial complex tried 'to do it all,' resulting in exacerbated redundancy and duplication of effort. The defence industry for a long time functioned under a management system which was highly centralised, hierarchical, bureaucratic and risk averse; and the managers, dwarfed by the gargantuan system, did not enjoy the freedom to make adjustments associated with innovations.[9] The entire system turned out to be personality driven where major decisions were taken by one individual and the others in the chain were mere conformists; the overall arms production industry until the 1990s in China was, by and large, inefficient and plagued with overcapacity. At one time, it is estimated that the aviation industry employed 6, 00,000 workers to produce a few dozen vintage aircraft—three times the actual capacity required! The system lacked accountability and quality control; nobody really paid heed to the end user requirement, and cost cutting was the last point on their agenda since there was no competitive bidding for a contract.[10] To summarise, there were too many factories employing far too many workers producing too little, leading to redundancy and, as a result, most of these factories ended up becoming debt ridden.

Cheetah or Gazelle......

By now, it was clear that the Chinese had no choice other than to pursue the 'Cheetah Strategy'—and carry out the huge generation leap. They were running out of time and could not afford to wait and be transformed into a 'gazelle' until their own R&D matured. Therefore, they had to depend on others for technological advancements and incorporate them in their own defence industry. The 2004 defence White Paper mentions the PLA's modernisation strategy of a 'generation leap,' which was to skip and shorten stages of R&D and generations of weapon systems. This strategy worked because of China's latecomer advantage of not only being able to exploit technological innovations but also gain by avoiding the mistakes made by others! The conversion era of the 1980s was premised on Deng's desire to make the third front—burdened with overcapacity—more viable, efficient, productive and self-sustaining. This, according to Deng's belief, could be done by efficiently utilising the overcapacity of the military factories for civilian use[11]. However, the 1990s witnessed an end to the 'conversion era' and a critical shift in policy towards promoting integrated **dual-use industrial systems** capable of developing and manufacturing military and civil goods. The new strategy became a priority and was also incorporated in the defence industry's tenth Five-Year Plan for 2001–05, which emphasised the dual importance of transfer of military technology for commercial use and also transfer of commercial technology for military use. The state not only urged the Chinese arms industry to develop dual-use technologies but also promote **joint civil–military technological cooperation** as a roadmap for overall military modernisation and, consequently, benefit from the spin-in from advanced commercial technologies. The key areas of China's focus on dual-use technological development and subsequent spin-in benefits included microelectronics; space systems; composites and alloys; propulsion; missiles; computer-aided manufacturing, and also information technology. In 2002, the Chinese government created the China Electronics Technology Corporation (CETC) to promote national technological and industrial developments in electronics in areas of defence interest. Under the tenth Five-Year Plan, many technological breakthroughs surfaced under the '863' science and technology programme, initiated in March 1986. Defence enterprises formed partnerships with Chinese universities and civilian research institutes to establish technology incubators and undertake cooperative R&D on dual-use technologies. Additionally, foreign high-technology firms wishing to invest in China, set up joint R&D centres in China. Plan 863, was, therefore, aimed to promote what is now widely termed **'dual-use' industrialisation**: the development of local capacity in sophisticated commercial technologies applicable to both the defence and commercial sectors.

China's policy on Foreign Direct Investment (FDI) after its entry into the World Trade Organisation (WTO) was also instrumental in the development of its strategic industries. As a consequence, many of these industries became foreign-owned, integrated into the global technology value-chain, enabling China to accelerate its technological transformation—otherwise a long drawn process. Beijing, over the years, has been absolutely consistent in its approach of hiding one's weakness and taking advantage of one's strength and, therefore, had no intention to reinvent the technology wheel—its primary weakness. Therefore, it aimed to exploit the progress made elsewhere and utilise that progress to leapfrog the early stages of industrial development. In this regard, the stratagem of fostering FDI as the vehicle for technology transfer was perceived as the most cost-effective way forward, and the world for the first time in history was witnessing a free market system embedded in a centralised structure. Hence, the foreign investment into China's strategic sectors was not coincidental but a deliberate policy by both the foreign investors and the People's Republic of China (PRC). The foreign investors, on the one hand, were convinced that the future growth was located in this region; while, on the other, China's interventionist strategy to short circuit the early stages of industrial development, became the main driver for this stratagem which laid emphasis on liberalisation, competition and globalisation. The American wars of the 1990s and the after-effect of the Taiwan Strait crisis, leading to heavy militarisation, also had a profound impact on the Chinese psyche and its need to alter the security architecture in the region. Post the1996 crisis, Taiwan was aggressively modernising its military and rebuilding its air force with top of the line American fighters; as a result, China too was left with no other choice than to modernise its aviation industry. Post 1998, the defence industry witnessed a number of reforms in the organisational structure and, as a consequence of these reforms, China's aviation industry started forging new business ties with some of the leading aircraft manufacturers in the world, resulting in many MICs turning around from the red.

Civil Way

The aviation industry has come a long way from the loss making relic of the 1970s, to reaping profits and being able to turn around the sector in the new millennium. It would only be fair to assess that the industry is slowly shedding the baggage of its excessive dependence on Russia and fast evolving as an independent entity by developing capabilities to deliver advanced weapon platforms, including a variety of the fourth generation fighter aircraft. It is smartly consolidating by deriving benefits from the reforms and the spin-in from the dual use technology framework. The aviation industry has effectively transformed itself from being a technology dawdler and a drain on the economy in the past, to a contributor, by posting record earnings and revenue growth for the first time in 2003. In 2009, the profits of the Aviation Industry of China (AVIC) jumped to a record high of US $ 1.4 billion; revenue grew to US $ 28 billion; and AVIC barged its way into the Fortune 500 list of companies.[12] Also, as part of a larger strategic vision, Xian Aircraft International (XAI) acquired 91.25 percent of Fischer Advanced Composites Components (FACC),[13] a leading Austrian company specialising in the development, design and manufacture of composite components and systems for major global civil vendors. Some of the major aviation giants like Boeing, Airbus and Embraer started engaging with China to derive benefits from Xian's acquisition of FACC; and China, on the other hand, as a larger part of its strategic vision, encouraged this collaboration to develop capabilities to produce a domestic two-aisle civil aircraft. XAI was also contracted by the Commercial Aircraft Corporation of China (COMAC) to produce components for the indigenously developed C919 aircraft and its alliance with FACC would only become an enabler to this process.

The Chinese are intrinsically guarded as far as their prospective plans for their aviation sector are concerned and not much about these is really available in the open domain. The White Papers too are silent on many facets of this sector, and therefore, the analysis becomes more challenging. However, since the turn of this century, China has been riding high on the success of its aviation sector and the future plan is to forge ahead by propelling itself into the top ranks of the global aviation hierarchy by 2030. The focussed and long-term strategic planning was also included in the 12th five-year defence industrial programme, and the medium and short-term development plans within the timeframe of five to ten years were being monitored and piloted under the Ministry of Industry and Information Technology (MIIT) and AVIC. The highlights of some of the prospective development plans are mentioned below:[14]

- Long-term plan to build a world class airliner—the approach is based on a step by step policy.
- The foundation is based on first developing a single aisle 70-110 seat ARJ 21 followed by a C919; a 150-seat airline is scheduled to make its first flight in 2014; and, finally, this technology is to be developed to build a two-aisle aircraft by 2020.
- The larger goal would probably be to eventually utilise the spin-on from the civil aircraft industry and subsequently absorb it in the military aircraft industry.[15]

Hence, the plan was to open up and diversify the aviation sector through the process of liberalisation, competition and globalisation, under the ambit of foreign ownership, with the broader aim to reduce overt dependence on the state; and invigorate these companies with systems to make them self-sustaining and capable of raising their own capital. The process of financial independence started in 2007 as the regulatory authorities started permitting large numbers of strategic industries to raise investments through initial public offerings, private shares, bond issues and bank loans. AVIC now has almost two dozen companies listed in the stock markets of Shanghai, Shenzhen and Hong Kong with a market capital close to Yuan 200 billion and a future expansion plan to increase revenue to Yuan 1 trillion by 2017.[16] The strategy of AVIC since the last decade, as one sees it unfold, is based on heavy investment in the civil aviation industry which would eventually spin-in the benefit to the military aviation sector. The financial reform in the aviation sector is based on the interventionist strategy to leapfrog and overcome the earlier stage of technological developments and become a global player in the aviation industry by 2030, if not by 2025! The remerger of AVIC I with AVIC II in 2009 was also driven by the goal that with the increased market capital as a result of the merger, AVIC would be able to compete against the big boys in the market: Boeing, Lockheed Martin and EADS.

The strategy for China's **military aviation industry** was also based on a gradual step by step increment by carrying out upgrades on new as well as old platforms like the J-8, J-10, J-11, JH-7 and JF-17s through the benefits accrued as a result of 'spin-in,' effectively reducing the incubation time and the cost of development and design to almost half. The larger philosophy was that the spin-in benefits from a wide array of commercial systems and components like avionics equipment; information technology; Computer Aided Manufacturing (CAM); composite technology; material science and micro electronics would eventually find their way into the next generation fighters, transport, strategic heavy lift and helicopters being indigenously developed and produced in China. Hence, the aviation industry was pursuing an approach which was incremental, planned and, most importantly, based on a long-term strategic vision.

Tai Ming Cheung has described China's aviation policy as one following multiple pathways. Irrespective of the policy, the DNA of China's aviation industry, by and large, has remained unchanged, but over the years, has undergone several stages of mutation. However, the core of the aviation industry continues to be vested in its 'imitation strategy' and, therefore, China can be complimented for using this strategy not only effectively but also consistently. The most recent example of its unswerving determination to effectively put in place the concept was distinctly highlighted in the production of the Su-27, also called the J-11 by the Chinese. Through an **incremental approach,** by updating the existing platforms, AVIC followed the process of step by step upgrades to meet the requirements of the end users, in this case, the PLAAF. Though the step by step upgrades resulted in the production of a number of variants of the same platform, each variant gained from the evolving strategy and the benefits derived from the spin-in of the emerging civil aviation sector, resulting in almost a transformational change in the architecture and the capability of the platform. Hence, the incremental approach strategy being relentlessly pursued by China's aviation industry became an effective tool to leapfrog and offset the earlier stages of technological developments.

The final pathway would, however, have to be the hard technological innovation coming from the advanced R&D and by creating resources through the means of higher education in China and abroad. This would eventually become the big game-changer to invigorate the aviation industry and reduce the gap in technological developments between China and the West in areas of critical technology like avionics, radar and fire control systems. Though AVIC is upbeat about its performance in the last decade; the industry still suffers from a few structural weaknesses that threaten its long-term strategic goals to narrow the technological gap and eventually catch up with the West, and for now its biggest Achilles heel continues to be its inability to produce a state-of-the-art high performance power plant for its frontline fighter aircraft, which, if not addressed, will continue to remain its major impediment to bridging the technological gap.

Strategising Approach

The 1990s marked the end of the Cold War, the break up of the Soviet Union, China's realignment with Russia, and its entry into the WTO. China was quick to grab the opportunity and get into a partnership with the newly formed states of the former Soviet republics, whose economies were solely dependent on their arms industries. China, therefore, effectively planned to derive benefits from disintegration of this gigantic superpower to leverage and transform its own defence industry. Also its entry into the WTO resulted in its integration with the world economy and the aviation industry automatically became a beneficiary of the global network of the arms industry.[17] China, for the first time, was entering a new realm and experiencing the flavours of limited access to dual use technology; however, even today, it largely continues to be a technology starved nation and practically isolated from the rest of the world[18]; evident, as recently as November of 2010 when Hu Jintao informally mentioned to Obama on the sidelines of the G-20 about loosening the restrictions on the export of high-tech products to China.[19]

Channelling private funds into defence R&D and encouraging investments in the defence industry have also been effective measures to provide impetus for the growth of this industry. China employs more than 1,20,000 personnel in aviation related R&D, making it the largest in the world[20]. China can no longer be called a technology straggler and today occupies almost the same position as Japan in the 1960s and South Korea in the 1970s. It is fast evolving and becoming the workshop of the world, manufacturing items ranging from low-end technology like toys to high-end technology products like the '**wing box**' for commercial aircraft and driving its ambition to manufacture a high-tech aeroplane in the future.[21] James Brooke's article in the *New York Times*, "**Tokyo Fears China May put an End to *Made in Japan*** '" was not a figment of Brooke's imagination but is almost a reality in the 21st century!

The reforms in the Chinese aviation industry have been a mixed bag. On the one hand, the restructuring has primarily been superficial at the macro level, with little or no work carried out in creating cross-competing defence conglomerates and, more specifically, horizontally integrated facilities like those found in the West. Although AVIC was broken up into two enterprises for the same reason, the model was flawed since both units consisted of different types of aircraft. AVIC I was involved in fighter aircraft production, while AVIC II concentrated on helicopter and jet trainer production, leaving little or no scope for competition or integration!

However, AVIC in the 21st century, has displayed significant buoyancy by making its presence felt at the various air shows, as a result, enhancing sales and recording profits and substantial growth in revenues. The turn of the century has also witnessed a major sector-related shift in favour of high-tech goods, with China actively participating in the globalisation process. It plans to pursue a development strategy through a process of liberalisation, competition and cooperation in the global framework, which in the opinion of the Chinese would eventually guarantee them national security, a factor absolutely vital in the country's rubric.[22] Hence, the aviation industry, earlier exacerbated by the unwillingness of the conservative leaders to implement path-breaking reforms, reduce inefficiency and redundancy, has, to a great extent, been reversed in this millennium, and the industry is fast consolidating, to be able to rub shoulders with the top ranks in the global aviation sector.[23] It emerges that there has been a definite shift in the guiding principle driving the aviation industry from the earlier obsession for quantity to now quality; from a being technology imitator to eventually becoming an enabler with a major thrust on the sector to transcend and match the global standards, if not by 2020 then at least by 2030!

Notes

1. Herbert Wulf, *Arms Industry Limited* (SIPRI,1993), Ch. 14, p.280.
2. Discussion with Air Cmde Jasjit Singh, Director CAPS, on November 30, 2010, in his chamber.
3. John Frankenstein, "Globalisation of Defence Industries: China", Senior Fellows Publication in February, 2003 at the Atlantic Council of the United States.
4. John Frankenstein, *China's Defence Industries: A New Course*? ch.10, accessed through the website www.rand.org/pubs/conf_proceedings/CF145/CF145.chap10.pdf, on December 01,2010.
5. You Ji,*The Armed Forces of China* (IB Tauris,1999), ch. 5, p.155.
6. n. 2.
7. David Shambaugh, *Modernising China's Military, Progress, Problems, and Prospects* (California Press, 2003), ch. 6, p.260.

8. Ibid.,ch.6,p.240.
9. Richard A Bitzinger and J.D. Kenneth Boutin, "China's Defence Industries :Change and Continuity," in Ron Huisken, ed., *Rising China: Power and Reassurance* (Canberra: ANU E Press,2009) ch.10.
10. Ibid.
11. Shambaugh, n. 7, ch.6, p.251.
12. Xinhua News Agency, "Profits of China's Top Aircraft Maker up 14 Percent Last Year," January 20, 2010.
13. "XAC gets Majority of Austrian Aviation Supplier FACC AG", *China Economic Review*, October 06,2009, as appeared on its website http://www.chinaeconomicreview.com, accessed on December 03,2010.
14. Xinhua News Agency, "China Will Start to Formulate Long-term Aviation Development Plan", June 01, 2009.
15. Discussion with Dr V. Siddhartha, Distinguished Fellow at the Centre for Air Power Studies on November 23, 2010, in his chamber. Dr V. Siddhartha graduated from the Indian Institute of Technology, Chennai, in 1965 and from the Cranfield Institute of Technology and Imperial College, London. He has served in senior positions in the Government of India; Department of Science & Technology as Adviser, Head, Technology Utilisation at the Council of Scientific and Industrial Research and Secretary, Science Advisory Council to the Prime Minister of India.
16. Tai Ming Cheung, "Remaking Cinderella: The Nature and Development of China's Aviation Industry", Associate Research Scientist at the Institute on Global Conflict and Cooperation, University of California, San Diego, Paper presented before the US-China Economic and Security Review Commission on May 20,2010.
17. Gong Chuanzhou and Ai Hua, "Development of China's National Defence Industry in the Globalisation Process," Nanjing Army Command Institute at the Army Institute of the People's Liberation Army on May 15,2001.
18. Ibid.
19. Wu Jiao, "Hu, Obama Set Tone for G20," *China Daily*, November 12, 2010.
20. You Ji, n. 5, ch.5,p.146.
21. Sino Consulting Incorporation, *"China's Civil Aviation,"* September, 2007.
22. Chuanzhou and Hua, n. 17.
23. Tai Ming Cheung, *Fortifying China: The Struggle to Build a Modern Defence Economy* (Ithaca:Cornell University Press, 2009).

4

Nuclear Weapons and International Law

Winston P. Nagan

Nuclear Weapons and the United States' Approach to International Law

The most precise summary of the traditional US position on nuclear weapons under international law is found in the legal arguments presented to the International Court of Justice (ICJ) in the case concerning the legality of the use or threat of use of nuclear weapons. The US position was submitted in a document to the court on June 20, 1995. In principle, the US has not shifted its legal posture radically from the position it took in 1995. Essentially, the US justifies its nuclear capabilities by a theory of deterrence and that theory is in part reliant on the international law of self-defence. It is also useful to summarise this outline of the US position because most nuclear capable states tend to justify their nuclear posture by some version of deterrence which implies an interpretation of the international law of self-defence. The US position, therefore, is one that is directly or indirectly embraced by the other nuclear powers (Russia, the UK, France, China, Israel, North Korea and India).

The position of the United States in 1995 was that there was no explicit prescription containing a general prohibition concerning the threat of use and / or use of nuclear weapons. Additionally, the Law of Armed Conflict does not contain a specific prohibition that generally prohibits the threat of use or use of nuclear weapons. Moreover, the international environmental law instruments contain no specific prohibition on the threat of use or use of nuclear weapons. Finally, the human rights instruments do not contain a specific prohibition on the threat of use or use of nuclear weapons. We quote from the United States Memorial:

In the view of the United States, there is no general threat or use of nuclear weapons. On the contrary, numerous agreements regulating the possession or use of nuclear weapons and other state practices demonstrate that their threat or use is not deemed to be generally unlawful. Moreover, nothing in the body of international humanitarian law of armed conflict indicates that nuclear weapons are prohibited *per se*. As in the case of other weapons, the legality of use depends on the conformity of the particular use with the rules applicable to such weapons. This would, in turn, depend on factors that can only be guessed at, including the characteristics of the particular weapon used and its effects, the military requirements for the destruction of the target in question and the magnitude of the risk to civilians. Judicial speculation about hypothetical future circumstances in a matter of such fundamental importance would, in our view, be inappropriate.

The United States also made several representations which challenged the authority of the ICJ to issue an advisory opinion on the question put before it. We have summarised these points below.

- The request is for an opinion on an abstract question;
- It follows that the abstractness of the question cannot give rise to practical guidance in the matter;
- The abstractness of the question is very general and vague but involves complex legal, technical, political and practical considerations;
- These matters cannot be usefully addressed in the abstract;
- Because of the fundamental importance of the issue, the court's response may be too speculative about unknown future situations;
- The court cannot provide practical guidance in this matter;
- An opinion might create difficulties for the UN and as well as for states conducting negotiations on nuclear matters outside of the UN;
- The nuclear weapons issue is complex and sensitive, and court intervention may undermine progress already made;
- This complexity might generate a fruitless debate about the legal implications of the court's judgment and frustrate the progress that has already been made;
- A court judgment offering advice is essentially an exercise in a political rather than juridical matter.

In addressing the proposition that in international law there is no general prohibition on the use of nuclear weapons, the United States asserts a strong or thick version of sovereignty, drawing on the jurisprudence of the *Lotus Case,* namely, that "it is a fundamental principle of international law that restrictions on states cannot be presumed." This means that there must be a source as binding law in conventional treaty-based international law or in customary international law. The United States was unable to find an authoritative source of either conventional international law or customary international law, indicating the *opinio juris* for such a rule. The US follows the same mode of analysis with regard to the law of armed conflict. The same analysis is provided regarding international environmental treaties as well as the human rights regime of the UN. Indeed, the United States maintains that "the citation of human rights instruments adds nothing to the analysis of the question of whether the use of nuclear weapons is consistent with existing international law."

United States Nuclear Posture Review of 2010

We would submit that the officially stated position of the United States in its presentation to the ICJ in its nuclear weapons case represents broadly the position of the United States regarding the legal status of its nuclear arsenal. It is unclear precisely how its position is officially modified by the actual decision of the ICJ. We must, therefore, consider the US position on the international law aspects of its nuclear posture, taking into account both its argument before the ICJ and the judgment of the ICJ itself. Regrettably, these issues are not squarely confronted in the US 2010 *Nuclear Posture Review* (NPR).

In April 2009, President Obama gave a speech in Prague. In this speech, he stressed on the problems in the 20th century that nuclear arsenals presented. In order to overcome these important threats to world peace and security, he stated that "the United States will seek the peace and security of a world without nuclear weapons." The President noted that such a far-reaching goal was a long-term matter. What Obama stressed was that there were immediate challenges that needed to be confronted. The concrete steps required would include reducing the numbers of nuclear weapons as well as their role in the US security posture. The President also assured his audience that while nuclear weapons continued to be deployed, the United States would maintain a safe, secure and effective arsenal. The central justification he proposed was the idea of deterrence regarding potential adversaries as well as broadened security for US allies and security partners. With this background and with great anticipation, the public awaited the release of the *Nuclear Posture Review (NPR)* Report of 2010. The *NPR* Report is an indication of the President's national security priorities and the articulated defence strategies to promote and defend those priorities. The strategic aspects of the matter were identified in a separate review, the 2010 *Quadrennial Defense Review*. The 2010 NPR covers seven main areas. These are as follows:

- The changing national security environment;
- Preventing nuclear proliferation and terrorism;
- Reducing the role of US nuclear weapons;

- Maintenance of strategic deterrence and nuclear stability at reduced force levels;
- Strengthening regional deterrence and reassuring US allies and partners;
- Sustaining a safe, secure and effective nuclear arsenal; and
- Forecasting in the direction of a world without nuclear weapons.

The timeline of the NPR Report focusses on the practical steps that must be taken in the next 5-10 years while considering as well the longer term prospects for progress in reducing nuclear dangers. The report underscores the changes in the international security environment. The Cold War is over and the nuclear threat which accompanied the balance of terror between the world superpowers is no longer of paramount security importance. On the other hand, the changed environment suggests that the risks of a nuclear attack had increased. These threats are identified with terrorist extremists who will seek to acquire lethal nuclear weapons on the black market and then construct devices of great destruction to advance the terrorist agenda. This is the problem of nuclear proliferation to terrorists and organised crime cartels. The other major element is the problem of the proliferation of nuclear capabilities to states which, in addition, wish to acquire and deploy nuclear arsenals. The two leading problem areas for US and Western security are the North Koreans who have both nuclear weapons and the missiles to deliver them, and Iran. Iran appears to have indicated a great interest in developing its nuclear technologies ostensibly for peaceful purposes but which involve technology that may be converted to the development of nuclear arsenals. If Iran develops a nuclear weapons capability, it would certainly enhance security tensions in the Middle East, and the Israeli policy-makers have been arguing for a justifiable preventive strike against Iran. These issues of nuclear terrorism and proliferation are major factors in shaping the speed with which reliance on nuclear arsenals may be reduced on a global basis. It could be argued that the planet would be more secure in a world without nuclear weapons because such a world would be one in which proliferation is impossible, and in a world without nuclear technologies to sell in the black market, terrorists would be deprived of access to such weapons.

The United States' Force Posture

The Cold War generated the overproduction of nuclear arsenals. Indeed, the volumes of the superpowers' arsenals essentially meant that if they were detonated, the earth could be destroyed multiple times. With the end of the Cold War, there has been an urgent need to reduce these arsenals. The nuclear power states are confronted with the problem that the reductions in their arsenals must be done in such a way as to ensure equilibrium and stability in their security posture and strategy. Moreover, no nuclear power wants to unilaterally disarm. And the only power that has voluntarily given up its nuclear weapons is the Republic of South Africa. From the US perspective, the development of improved conventional military capabilities seems to point to a reduced reliance on nuclear weapons. Additionally, the US is bound by Article VI of the Non-Proliferation Treaty (NPT), that is to say, it is under international law obligation to make tangible progress toward nuclear disarmament. The United States also argues that a credible nuclear threat is a deterrent and useful for strengthening regional security alliances. This, in turn, is an incentive for non-nuclear allies not to develop nuclear weapons of their own. The report also refers to the Stockpile Management Programme which obviates the need to create new nuclear arsenals. The report also sees the importance of furthering strategic stability with Russia and China as necessary for making progress to a nuclear weapon-free world. And, finally, it sees these steps as reducing the importance of nuclear weapons in the global environment and moving slowly to eliminate them.

Strategies for Preventing Nuclear Proliferation and Nuclear Terrorism

The NPR Report notes that the US approach includes three key issues. First, it seeks to strengthen the global regime of non-proliferation. This idea is based on the conventional international law of the NPT. It has as yet not found the strategy in which North Korea or Iran is willing to forego its nuclear ambitions. Additionally, it seeks to strengthen the international legal competence of the International Atomic Energy Agency (IAEA). This could be done by sharpening and broadening its safeguards and forcing compliance with them. The object here is to restrain illicit nuclear trade and promote the peaceful uses of nuclear energy, while reducing the risk of proliferation. Second, the United States wishes to accelerate the effort to implement the Administration's initiative to secure all vulnerable nuclear materials globally within the next four years. Third is the role of the US in aggressively promoting global arms control initiatives. Illustrations include the New START (New Strategic Arms Reduction Treaty). The US supports the ratification and coming into force of the important Comprehensive Test Ban Treaty (CTBT). The treaty was blocked by the Senate during the latter period of the Clinton Administration. This treaty is an important complement to the NPT and as a matter of international law, would take the international community a significant distance in the direction of the abolition of nuclear weapons. The Administration has also promoted a verifiable Fissile Material Cut-off Treaty (FMCT) in order to strengthen the international support to reinforce non-proliferation and to secure nuclear materials globally. The Administration's initiatives include the following:

- Speed up the global threat reduction initiative and the International Nuclear Material Protection and Cooperation Programme;
- Enhance capability to disrupt illicit proliferation;
- Interdict smuggling of nuclear materials; expand nuclear forensics to enhance the ability to identify sources of nuclear material or use or intended for use by terrorists;
- The Administration is also initiating a Comprehensive National Research and Development Programme to support progress to a nuclear weapon-free world. This includes work on verification, technology, and transparency technologies and practices;
- Finally, the US has affirmed its fundamental policy to hold fully accountable the states, terrorists groups, other non-state actors which support and enable terrorists' efforts to acquire Weapons of Mass Destruction (WMDs) and which otherwise facilitate, finance, or provide expertise or safe havens for such activity.

Reduction of the Role of Nuclear Weapons in the US Security Posture

Since the end of the Cold War, there has been a reduction in the role of nuclear weapons in US security and strategy, and this has reflected the fact of reduced arsenals. The Report, however, acknowledges that more should be done. It recognises that at present, US nuclear weapons are still a critical deterrent which will deter a nuclear attack on US allies or partners. The United States has additionally sought to strengthen its negative security assurances by declaring that it will not use or threaten to use nuclear weapons against non-nuclear weapon states that are a party to the NPT. This essentially means that the US has narrowed the meaning of deterrence for security purposes. Indeed, the report stresses as well that the US will only consider the use of nuclear weapons in extreme circumstances to defend the vital interests of the United States or its allies and partners. This is a position that comes close to the position of the majority judgment of the ICJ in the nuclear weapons case. It, of course, depends on whether the concept of survival is clarified by the idea of vital interests or whether vital interests are broader than the interest in survival. Additionally, the idea that vital interests and extreme circumstances cover an indefinite number of US allies and partners may stretch the extreme circumstances beyond the limited exception of the ICJ.

We may summarise the key conclusions of the NPR as follows. Notwithstanding the general commitment to disarmament, the US will strategically strengthen its conventional capabilities while it reduces a reliance on the role of nuclear weapons in deterring non-nuclear attacks. It stresses that it seeks to deter a nuclear attack on the US and its allies as the only justification for its current nuclear arms capacity. Moreover, the United States will only consider the use of nuclear weapons in extreme circumstances in order to defend its own vital interests and those of its allies. Finally, the US will not threaten to use or use nuclear weapons against a non-nuclear weapon state that is a party to the NPT and in compliance with nuclear non-proliferation duties.

Current US Nuclear Policy from the Perspective of the Obama Administration

The current US nuclear arms policy adheres to nuclear deterrence while simultaneously pursuing a path toward complete nuclear disarmament. The 2010 *Nuclear Posture Review* explains how the Obama Administration arrived at such a position. It also explains how the Administration has justified (or will justify in the future) certain inconsistencies necessarily resulting from this position. In anticipating the Obama Administration's NPR, many foresaw a complete overhaul of the US national security doctrine and force considerations. Among the key issues under debate is whether the primary purpose of nuclear weapons is to deter a nuclear attack against the United States or its allies. For example, Senator James M. Inhofe (R Okla.), a senior member of the Senate Armed Services Committee, argued: "United States nuclear weapons must continue to deter not only nuclear attacks but also chemical and biological attacks against the United States and its allies. While some reduction in our nuclear arsenals may be warranted, deep cuts would be destabilizing and would encourage other countries to enter into nuclear competition."

Senator Inhofe correctly judges that in the post-Cold War world there is a need for nuclear deterrence that is broader than a response to nuclear threats, but would see national defence as ultimately resting on a far more flexible and tactical design for nuclear arsenals to meet these new threats. The Obama NPR was one of the most eagerly anticipated documents in the area of national security—in part, because it reflects the challenge of his vision for a world without nuclear weapons. The challenge of the NPR was to develop strategic and tactical responses that might move this agenda purposefully forward. Moreover, it was a prelude to the 2010 *National Security Strategy* (NSS). As instruments of the official policy of the executive, these two policy pieces affirm important international law expectations. They also challenge certain international law expectations and even some aspects of international law, thus, staking a claim to change or modify the relevant international law. Although the NPR and the new NSS are unilateral US undertakings, they are communicated worldwide, and other states (and non-states) will react to them in predictable or unpredictable ways.

In the United States, it is an illustration of the President's vision of the future of nuclear arsenals. For this reason, many expressed disappointment when the NPR was issued, finding little change from the traditional US nuclear posture. We disagree, however, with such a wholly negative assessment. Below, we list some of the significant changes (or decisions to adhere to traditional policies) found in the two policy pieces, and we attempt to address the most pertinent critiques that these points have received. To differing extents, the NPR and NSS examined the following issues:

- The role of nuclear forces in the United States' strategy planning and programming;
- The United States' nuclear deterrence policy (including targeting strategy);
- The policy requirements and objectives for the United States to maintain a safe, reliable, and credible nuclear deterrence posture;
- The role that missile defence capabilities and conventional strike forces play in determining the role and size of nuclear forces;
- The levels and composition of nuclear delivery systems that will be required for implementing the United States' national and military strategy, including any plans for replacing or modifying existing systems;
- The type of active and inactive nuclear weapons stockpile that will be required for implementing the United States' national and military strategy, including any plans for replacing or modifying warheads;
- The nuclear weapons complex that will be required for implementing the United States' national and military strategy, including any plans to modernise or modify the complex;
- The US' arms control objectives;
- The importance of the international legal system in fulfilling US policy goals; and
- The deterrence policy that will reveal President Obama's apparent concern with the inhuman effects of using nuclear weapons.

While these issues do not explicitly account for the importance of international legal processes in the consideration of policy options, they have significantly illuminated the evolving position of the US nuclear arms policy and the ways in which this US position intends to respond to (and even direct) international law standards. The US President's emphasis on international rule of law is a positive method of addressing state outliers who refuse to engage in the regulation of nuclear weapons by international law. The eventual goal of complete nuclear disarmament cannot be achieved without first commanding a globally unified position on nuclear weapons. In both the media and international relations, there have been major responses to the inclusion of Israel among the NPT outliers named in the NPT Review Report. Israel, of course, has nuclear weapons but has not signed the NPT. The change in US position regarding Israel's maintenance of nuclear weapons, signals a comprehensive legal strategy to the Obama Administration's nuclear arms agenda. The move sends the message that even close US allies must conform to international legal standards, lest they come under the shadow of dangerous US nuclear posturing. More distressing to the pursuit of a nuclear abolition agenda, the NPR reaffirms the US dedication to the North Atlantic Treaty Organisation's (NATO's) nuclear planning, which inspires tension with US obligations under Article VI of the NPT to negotiate on "effective measures relating to the cessation of the nuclear arms race at an early date and to nuclear disarmament." As a key possessor of nuclear weapons within NATO's strategic nuclear protective stance, the United States may need to redefine its role within NATO to conform with this provision with the NPT. (Conformity may require merely the elaboration of priorities within standing NATO agreements, making it apparent that the protective strategies of NATO include the paramount strategy of nuclear disarmament). As one journalist effectively points out, "As of 2005, the United States was providing about 180 tactical B61 nuclear bombs for use by Belgium, Germany, Italy, the Netherlands and Turkey under these NATO agreements," despite the fact that Articles I and II of the NPT prohibit the transfer of nuclear weapons to non-nuclear states. That journalist predicts little gain for the cause of nuclear disarmament stemming from the impending redraft of NATO's strategic concept, and noting that the last reformulation (in 1999), stated: "The fundamental purpose of the nuclear forces of the Allies is political.... ....to fulfill an essential role by ensuring uncertainty in the mind of any aggressor . . . . The supreme guarantee of the security of the Allies is provided by the strategic nuclear forces of the Alliance." Thus, the point is made again that the United States must bring obligations under NATO in conformity with obligations under the NPT. From what we now know, the Obama Administration is interested in the developing *lex specialis* of international law relating to nuclear weapons and has placed emphasis on diplomacy, negotiation, and finding the space for common-interest activities in which law still plays an important role. The importance of broadening the relevance of international law via the *lex specialis* (as well as through general international law) is that it broadens the scope of international obligation and creates a normative system of global expectation that is inclusive. It is in the interest of the United States that its strategic and tactical changes in the direction of reduced global nuclear threats should carry the mantle of credibility that is completely consistent with global normative priority. There is strong global support for arms reduction, and in particular, a reduction of nuclear threats to global peace and security. Thus, President Obama's commitment to the vision of a world free of nuclear weapons will have greater force if it is underlined by international law and which carries the strength of global *opinio juris*. In short, the NPR Report seizes upon those aspects of which there is evidence of common interest consistent with the President's declared policy aspiration. In part, the credibility of the President's policy directives in the direction of nuclear disarmament must be tied to the role of science and technology facilitating the task of reducing our nuclear arsenals. This in itself is important for international law because law that is context sensitive will provide us with guidelines that are useful in facilitating these presidential goals.

The American Physical Society (APS) recently outlined a strategy for the role of science and technology in facilitating nuclear disarmament. The APS underlines three essential tasks for the scientific community:

- verifying the process of downsizing and dismantling of stockpiles,
- sustaining nuclear weapons capability and expertise for as long as is necessary; and
- removing the capabilities for reversals through various confidence-building measures, in particular by ensuring the peaceful use of fissile materials.

The APS recommends a number of important steps that it believes the government should embrace. These steps include the declassification of the number of all US nuclear weapons, the establishment of international centres for verification, research and validation, the refurbishment of elements of the US nuclear weapons infrastructure, the support of federal investment in key programmes, and the establishment of information sharing among nuclear related industries. The report concludes as follows:

> We are confident that the development of the technology needed for a safe and secure downsizing program for global nuclear arsenals is within our reach if it is adequately supported. The associated operational and doctrinal measures will require major investments as well. The technology steps are clear; the structure of the overall program requires careful assessment and ongoing support.

Since the nuclear weapons problem is one that deeply implicates science and technology, modern international law must also come to grips with the possibilities and limitations of science and technology in order to provide the goal guidance that is both relevant and steeped in realism. One of the central challenges of effective international law is that it must avoid specious utopianism and focus contextually with realism and discipline. From the brief discussion above, it is clear that the stakeholders of international law must provide a better contextual understanding of world order conditions and current security threats, including the threats of terrorism. Such an approach permits us to get past the doctrinal constraints of a bipolar world order thinking and, at the same time, permits us to focus more clearly on the nature of security threats, which may facilitate or limit the achievement of the goals of nuclear disarmament. In addition, the nuclear weapons problem is one that deeply implicates science and technology. A relevant role of modern international law is to come to grips with the possibilities and limitations of science and technology in order to provide the goal guidance that is both relevant and steeped in realism.

The legal status of nuclear weapons poses a difficult, classical problem of the clash between law and effective power. It was this juxtaposition that J.F. Dulles recognised when he suggested that the sheer power of nuclear weapons represented a reality that transcended the international law of the UN Charter. The control and management of nuclear arsenals and how they are produced and deployed have been matters over which there has been significant contention within the US government. Nuclear weapons are such a high priority for national security matters that the high security issues implicated seem to be more suited to decision-making within the class of national security operatives. The perspective of the national security operative draws on a tradition of intellectual thought that sees international relations as largely a matter of exclusively manipulating the national power posture of a state. Theorists such as Morgenthau and Kennan expressed impatience with international law having any important role in international relations involving important security matters. In their view, international law was a dangerous utopian artifact. Its specialised language, which came packaged with a culture of legalism, was irrelevant and possibly dangerous to the appropriate management of foreign relations in a nuclear age. Regrettably, their target of attack was an older version of international law—one not influenced by functionalism or by context sensitive analysis. It is this latter view of international law that has demonstrated a capacity for realism, a challenge to unreflective policy-making, and a willingness to clarify the appropriate role for law broadly conceived in the control and regulation of nuclear weapons. In this, it has succeeded in seeking to bring reason to bear on the possibly unrestrained exercise of raw power, which could include the destructive force of nuclear arsenals. In this sense, President Obama's decision to look to a world free of the threat of nuclear destruction is in keeping with the tradition of law that insists on the importance of reason as an appropriate limit on the unrestrained exercise of power.

While proceeding along the complex path toward the goal of complete disarmament, confronting a concept of nuclear deterrence infinitely broader than the contours of a bipolar world, the Obama Administration presents an evolved position in the US nuclear arms policy—one that directly engages with, and directs, the standards of international law. Commanding a globally unified position on nuclear weapons (while maintaining the framework of existing international obligations that permits the world's only superpower to act as the key architect for nuclear engagement) signals a comprehensive legal strategy to the Obama Administration's nuclear arms agenda. President Obama might successfully contribute to an outlawing of nuclear arms even as the United States maintains the position of nuclear deterrence that the President's activities aim to establish as unlawful under international law. As a former lawyer and legal scholar, President Obama seems to be using effective strategies of both law and power to build a foundation of international law that will support the process of complete nuclear disarmament, even after he no longer wields power.

Nuclear Policy, International Law and the Strategic Posture of the Russian Federation

Russia is the other major nuclear power. It has a nuclear capacity which it inherited from the USSR. The USSR was the US' chief antagonist during the Cold War. In a sense, the US had its policy tied to its perception of the boundaries of Russian policy. Similarly, Russia has its policies tied to its perception of the boundaries and limitations of US nuclear policy. Thus, during the Bush era, when the Bush Administration moved into what was perceived to be a unilateral direction on nuclear weapons policy, Russia pursued its nuclear posture in the light of what it considered to be a heightened threat factor from the US. The US and the USSR had generally enjoyed a complex level of conflict and accommodation on the issue of the strategic deployment of nuclear arsenals. A large part of the agenda of accommodation involved a reduction in the stockpiling of arsenals on both sides. The most important achievement of the Obama Administration was to restart talks on START. That treaty was set to expire and the US sent signals to Russia that it was developing a new approach to nuclear security and the US relationship with Russia.

The Evolving New Military Doctrine of the Russian Federation

The New Russian Military Doctrine was released in 2010. It was influenced by the Obama approach to US-Russian relations. In 2009, the head of the Russian Security Council, Nicolai Patrushev, gave a preview of what the new doctrine might contain. According to Patrushev, the new doctrine allowed for "preventive nuclear attack." The preview doctrine contemplated the use of nuclear weapons depending on the existential situation and the perceived intention of its adversaries. In situations critical to Russian national security, the preview doctrine did not rule out a preemptive strike "against an aggressor." The changed relationship with the USA resulted in the final doctrine of 2010 as favouring a significant restraint in Russian nuclear policy. Thus, the 2010 Doctrine excludes statements about the use of nuclear weapons preemptively or in regional or local conflicts. The 2010 Doctrine preserves a narrower deterrence role for Russian nuclear capabilities and the maintenance of a reduced arsenal is seen as one among several measures for preventing nuclear war. These measures are diplomatic and other non-military strategies. The 2010 Doctrine, therefore, excludes the use of nuclear weapons for ordinary acts of aggression but reserves the right of nuclear self-defence if the very existence of the state is threatened. This brings the Russian military doctrine in line with the majority opinion of the ICJ in the *nuclear weapons case*. Although the Russian posture seems to be consistent with the majority view in the ICJ decision, the further question that must be addressed is of whether the Russian nuclear arsenal is one that is justified by the idea of nuclear deterrence. The question of whether deterrence is consistent with international law is essentially argued along the lines of the US position which holds that there is no explicit conventional or customary international law limitation on the deterrence use of nuclear arsenals or the threat of deterrence. Additionally, Russia maintains that its obligations to not use nuclear weapons against a non-nuclear weapon state party to the NPT unless "that state acts in association or alliance with a nuclear weapon state" seems to be consistent with the 2010 Doctrine and is another element of constraint regarding nuclear weapons.

It is unclear whether the Russian establishment had generated a posture that is the equivalent of Obama's nuclear-free world declaration. It seems that the Russian policy is gravitating to these objectives. An important element of this momentum should be measured by how Russia views the concerns for the non-proliferation of nuclear arsenals. Russian foreign policy joined the United States sanctions against Iran and stopped the sale of the S-300 air defence system to Iraq. It would be critical for US policy-makers to better understand the fundamental perception of Russian security concerns as tied to US policy, and bilateral communication and agreement on nuclear arsenals as the basis for greater Russian activism on non-proliferation and momentum for a nuclear-free world.

The United Kingdom's Nuclear Policy and International Law

It is possible to isolate three periods which define the scope of the UK's nuclear posture. First, the immediate post-war period which resulted in some coolness between the US policy and the policy of the UK on nuclear cooperation. It was what triggered the drive for the UK to establish its own nuclear capabilities. Second, there was a period of the Cold War, as well as the emergence of NATO, which brought the US and the UK into a closer strategic and tactical relationship regarding nuclear weapons. This meant that the UK could rely in some degree on American deployments which could be shared and would be less costly to the UK. The third phase was the post Cold War phase, werein the nuclear threat of the dominant opponent in the Cold War was significantly diminished.

The current UK position was outlined in the *Strategic Defence Review* of 1998. The review does not appear to significantly change the British nuclear policy. The changes are reflected in the delivery systems. Britain still relies on the long-range Trident missiles, free-fall missiles that are still meant to be delivered by aircraft. There is continued thinking about strategically limited weapon systems which may serve a multitude of tactical functions. The emphasis of nuclear thinking is the idea that the ability to launch a limited strike comprises more believable deterrence than a massive strategic response. Most of the important British leaders, including David Cameron, justified the UK's nuclear posture as "an independent deterrent".

Since the UK has announced its plans to renew the Trident missile system, the White Paper published by the government indicates that the renewal of the system is fully compatible with the UK's treaty obligations and international law. The White Paper argues that the Trident replacement is fully consistent with the UK's obligations under the Non-Proliferation Treaty as well as its commitments to disarmament. A further question is whether specifically the retention of the Trident as a deterrent is not incompatible with NPT Article VI. Here the White Paper argues that the NPT provides no specific time-table for nuclear disarmament. Moreover, the treaty does not prohibit the maintenance or replacement of existing nuclear capability. With regard to the issue of deterrence, this falls under the self-defence prescriptions of Article 51 of the Charter. And a generous reading of the Advisory Opinion of the ICJ in the *nuclear weapons case* creates a self-defence exception.

These views have been challenged in the UK by distinguished international lawyers. These lawyers begin by questioning whether the Trident or its replacement may constitute a breach of customary international law. Specifically, customary law makes a clear distinction between combatants and non-combatants. They submit that undermining this distinction is a transgression of customary international law. However deployed, the Trident cannot effectually distinguish between combatants and non-combatants.

Additionally, critics have stated that the use of the Trident system cannot meet the criterion of proportionality, even if the threat is to the very survival of the state. Moreover, the concepts of vital interests as indicated in the *Strategic Defence Review* are much broader than those whose destruction threatens the survival of the state. Using nuclear weapons to secure these expanded vital interests is probably going to result in disproportionate destruction and, therefore, be unlawful under Article

2(4) of the Charter. With regard to the principles of humanitarian law which prohibit indiscriminate attacks and unnecessary suffering, it seems clear to the lawyers that the use of the Trident would violate these principles. British lawyers had also maintained that the broadening of the concept of deterrence to include preventing non-nuclear attacks as a reason to replace or upgrade the Trident violates Article VI of the NPT, as follows:

- Trident upgrading or replacement as security against unascertainable future threats is too speculative to be justifiable under a self-defence deterrence rationale;
- Enhancing capability and yield flexibility is also incompatible with Article VI;
- The renewal or replacement of the Trident at the same capability is probably also a violation of Article VI;
- In all of the above cases, such incompatibility gives rise to a material breach of the NPT.

There are other concerns about the Trident system and its incompatibility with NPT obligations as well the judgment of the ICJ. Opposition to the Trident system in the UK has led to judicial decisions which appeared to support the legal position of the protestors and the ICJ. In October 21, 1999, a court case in Greenock, Scotland, made a major statement on the legal status within the UK of the ICJ's nuclear weapons decision. Three women activists belonging to the Trident Ploughshares 2000 Non-Violent Direct Action Campaign were standing in trial before a jury because they had damaged laboratory equipment used for the operational support of the British Trident Nuclear-Arm Ballistic Missile Submarine Force. Their defence was that they felt compelled to act to prevent the crime of potential genocide. The trial judge accepted their argument that the deployment of the Trident was illegal and that in their actions they were upholding the Nuremberg Charter. The judge instructed the jury to acquit them. The defence based its case on the advisory opinion of the ICJ and in effect was legally challenging, by way of a defence, the lawfulness of the British "nuclear deterrent." Since the defendants were acquitted, that finding could not be challenged on appeal. However, the Lord Advocate of Scotland, proceeding under the Scottish Criminal Procedure Act of 1995, petitioned the High Court to decide points of law that had arisen in the trial. Although the acquittal stood, the High Court tried to find an international legal rationale to justify as lawful Britain's deterrence policy.

France's Nuclear Policy and International Law

President Chirac publicly stated in 2006 that nuclear deterrence was the foundation of the French defence policy; "[Our] defense policy relies on the certainty that, whatever happens, our vital interests will be protected. That is the role assigned to nuclear deterrence, which is directly in keeping with the continuity of our strategy of prevention. It continues its ultimate expression." The critical question is the scope of French vital interests which might trigger a nuclear response under the policy of deterrence. French policy-makers include in that "the integrity of the national territory, including the mainland as well as the overseas departments and territories, the free exercise of our sovereignty, and the protection of the population constitute the core [of these interests] today." President Chirac expanded the idea of vital interest to include "the defense of allied countries". The question here is: how many allies around the world would be included within the framework of a French vital interest? It is being suggested that what was implicit in Chirac's statement was the problem of France's economic security values. For example, would a cut-off of oil and gas to France—something that might result in economic strangulation—be a vital interest that might trigger a French deterrence response? It is possible that here Chirac was following a suggestion from Senator Richard Lugar: "[A]n attack using energy as a weapon can devastate a nation's economy and yield hundreds of casualties.... the [Atlantic] alliance must avow that defending against such attacks is an Article V commitment."

The French idea of vital interest also includes the problem of threats from state sponsored terrorism. According to Chirac: "Leaders of states resorting to terrorist means against us, as those who might consider, one way or the other, weapons of mass destruction, must understand that they risk a firm adapted response from us. And this response can be of a conventional nature. It can also be of another nature."

The French suggest two primary justifications for an up-to-date nuclear capability. The first is that it serves a "life insurance function." Given the unpredictability of global conditions, and France's role as a global power, potential threats will always be an omnipresent reality. The French nuclear deterrent is designed to counter any threat, "even a distant one." A second justification is to assure French policy-makers that no regional power is able to pressure or blackmail France with weapons of mass destruction. Thus, France's nuclear capability could be called counter-deterrence or counter-blackmail.

France's approach to the lawfulness of its nuclear deterrent posture is to insist that it is consistent with international law and in particular with obligations, specifically Article VI, of the NPT. This Article requires that nuclear enabled states move toward total nuclear disarmament. France represented in the NPT Review Conference that it was reaffirming its commitment under Article VI. It insisted that it had significantly reduced its nuclear arsenal since the Cold War ended. It also added that it had reduced its nuclear budget by 50 percent. It also claimed that it had reduced the number of nuclear delivery vehicles by two-thirds and had also abandoned its ground launched ballistic missiles and dismantled its testing site and fissile material production facilities. It declared that its force was now a minimum deterrent.

France has approached the question of the meaning of Article VI from a strict interpretation perspective. It had stressed that Article VI is multi-dimensional and this includes the goal of ending the arms race, the goal of general and complete disarmament. It also considers its actions towards biological, chemical and conventional disarmament to be a part of its record under Article VI. Included here, as well, is its assistance to nuclear threat reduction in Russia. France has also conditioned its nuclear capability reductions on reductions by US and Russian forces. Additionally, apart from France's dismantling of its test site and fissile production facilities, it was the first NPT nuclear power to support the "zero option" for the CTBT. This meant the complete abolition of nuclear testing, no matter how small the yield. The slow progress on international agreements, such as the CTBT and FMCT, and increasing concerns about the continuance of the NPT, has made French policy-makers cautious about the issue of nuclear disarmament. According to Chirac: "It is obvious that we will only be able to go forward on the road toward disarmament in the event that conditions of our overall security are maintained and if the will to make progress is unanimously shared."

Notwithstanding the refinements and justifications that France provides for its distinctive nuclear deterrence posture, in the broad outline, it is not fundamentally at variance with the 1999 NATO strategic concept which reflects a trans-Atlantic consensus. That strategic concept is as follows:

> The fundamental purpose of the nuclear forces of the Allies is political: to preserve peace and prevent coercion and any kind of war. They will continue to fulfill an essential role by ensuring uncertainty in the mind of any aggressor about the nature of the Allies' response to military aggression. They demonstrate that aggression of any kind is not a rational option. The supreme guarantee of the security of the Allies provided by the strategic nuclear forces of the Alliance, particularly those of the United States; the independent nuclear forces of the United Kingdom and France, which have a deterrent role of their own, contribute to the overall deterrence and security of the Allies.

There are three distinctive elements in the French nuclear posture that are somewhat different to those of their British and American allies. France has built into its deterrent idea the concept of "a final warning." The conceptual basis of this idea is to convey a threat to an adversary who has underestimated the intent of French policy-makers to defend their vital interest or where the adversary has misjudged the limits of those interests with a single limited strike on military targets. The final warning would be final and would be followed by a massive strike if the adversary persisted.

The second difference is the way in which France understands the legal position of its nuclear deterrent. Since the end of the Cold War, the US and the UK considered the use of nuclear weapons concerning regional WMD threats by using a threat of unspecified retaliation. France chooses to focus its declaratory policy regarding WMD threats by promising to provide a nuclear response to any aggression that compromises its vital interests. The difference here is that the US and the UK are clear about the conditions that constitute a WMD threshold threat. But the precise response is not clear. The French are unclear about the exact threshold (vital interests) but are clear about how they will respond.

Critics maintained that the US-UK position is reflected in the construction of their doctrines and their understanding of what international law requires. France has read into Article 51 of the UN Charter the idea of thick French sovereignty underlying the interpretation of a self-defence provision in this Article. Implicit in the US-UK position is the concern that a deterrent response should at least have some element of nominal proportionality. The French position does not emphasise this. It should be kept in mind that a central problem with whatever use is made of a nuclear weapon is that there is a great difficulty as Hiroshima and Nagasaki amply demonstrate in the notion that somehow nuclear self-defence meets the criterion of proportionality, let alone the principle of necessity and the principle of humanitarianism. In this sense, the uses of deterrence still carry an infirmity whether justified by a thick or thin version of sovereignty and self-defence.

The third point of difference may be reflected in the scope of deterrence. Clearly, the French do not see deterrence as confined to the territorial boundaries of France. France has indicated that its deterrence is extended not only to national but to European vital interests. How far beyond that does the French deterrence doctrine extend—and that would seem to be an important difference between the US, the UK and France. NATO provides a clearer understanding of the strategy of an extended deterrence:

> The Allies concerned [author's note: i.e. excluding France] consider that, with the radical changes in the security situation, including reduced conventional force levels in Europe and increased reaction times, NATO's ability to defuse a crisis through diplomatic and other means or, should it be necessary, to amount a successful

> conventional defense has significantly improved. The circumstances in which any use of nuclear weapons might have to be contemplated by them are, therefore, extremely remote. Since 1991, therefore, the Allies have taken a series of steps which reflect the post-Cold War security environment. These include a dramatic reduction of the types and numbers of NATO's sub-strategic forces including the elimination of all nuclear artillery and ground-launched short-range nuclear missiles: a significant relaxation of the readiness criteria for nuclear-roled forces; and the termination of standing peacetime nuclear contingency plans. NATO's nuclear forces no longer target any country. Nonetheless, NATO will maintain, at the minimum level consistent with the prevailing security environment, adequate sub-strategic forces based in Europe which will provide an essential link with strategic nuclear forces, reinforcing the transatlantic link. These will consist of dual capable aircraft and a small number of United Kingdom Trident warheads. Sub-strategic nuclear weapons will, however, not be deployed in normal circumstances on surface vessels and attack submarines.

Notwithstanding the differences regarding the scope of deterrence and differences in understanding the precise restraints of international law, French nuclear capability is in large measure founded on the principle of deterrence. We have seen that the scope of deterrence may be somewhat undetermined. However, it would not be inappropriate to insist that the reliance on nuclear deterrence as a form of self-defence be tightly constrained by the ruling of the ICJ that requires an appreciation of a threat to the survival of the state as the only justification for the possible threat of use or use of nuclear weapons. Additionally, even if such a threshold were established, the rules covering the *jus in bello* which require establishing necessity, proportionality and humanitarianism are likely to be violated. This, therefore provides a much broader and important restraint on the deterrence justification for current stockpiles of nuclear arsenals.

Israel's Nuclear Policy and International Law

The state of Israel has recognised that it has in operation a nuclear facility (Dimona). Official recognition was given in Prime Minister Ben-Gurion's speech to the Knesset in December 1960. However, Israel has not officially acknowledged that it has constructed and has in its possession an arsenal of nuclear weapons. In the NPT meeting of 2010, the Arab states were able to get adopted a resolution that in a meeting in 2012, the NPT regime should include the consideration of a nuclear-free Middle East. This resolution, therefore, provides pressure that Israel, which is not a party to the NPT, should join the regime. This would require an acknowledgement that it is a state with a nuclear arsenal and that it would have to disclose important information about its nuclear arsenal. This has been resisted by Israel and although the United States was sympathetic to the Israeli position, it permitted the resolution in the 2010 conference to go forward in order to preserve the institutional integrity of the NPT process. It is unclear how this will evolve. However, it would be worthwhile providing a brief overview of the evolution of Israeli nuclear capability in order to better understand its doctrine and its compatibility with international law.

Israel as a state generated an interest in nuclear technology soon after 1948. With the support of the French, it began a secret programme of building a nuclear reactor and a nuclear reprocessing plant. There is indirect evidence that Israel built its first nuclear weapon in the late 1960s. This was confirmed by the disclosures of Mordechai Vanunu, an Israeli nuclear technician and whistleblower. Vanunu revealed facts about Israel's nuclear weapons programme and delivery systems to the British press in 1986. Reports indicate that Prime Minister Ben Gurion was "obsessed with the new Israeli state acquiring nuclear weapons capability, as a defense to the recurrence of a second Holocaust." According to Ben Gurion "what Einstein, Oppenheimer and Teller, the three of them are Jews, made for the United States, could also be done by scientists in Israel, for their own people." As Israel and France created close ties, Israeli scientists were given access to France's nuclear development programmes. Cooperation between France and Israel continued and, Ben Gurion indicated to an aide about French Prime Minister Guy Mollet, "I owe the bomb to them." Israeli-French relations cooled when de Gaulle became French President in 1958. De Gaulle would not supply Israel with uranium unless its facilities were open to international inspection, declared peaceful, and no plutonium was reprocessed. After compromises, some French cooperation continued and additionally some modest assistance was given by Britain which sent restricted materials to Israel. These included chemicals for reprocessing as well as samples of fissile materials. During the 1960s, Israel also reached a covert understanding with the apartheid regime in South Africa. The importance of South Africa was that it had extensive uranium resources. The cooperation led to South Africa becoming a nuclear power as well. There is circumstantial evidence that both states conducted a test in the South Indian Ocean in an incident known as *The Vela Incident*. A US satellite detected a flash which resembled a nuclear explosion in the South Indian Ocean. The test was conducted on a South African controlled island. The Central Intelligence Agency (CIA) insisted that the flash was a nuclear explosion while for political reasons, the Department of State maintained it was sun spot, a natural phenomenon. According to Richard Rodes and Seymour Hersh, the explosion was a joint Israeli-South Africa nuclear test. According to Hersh, the explosion was the "third joint Israeli-South African nuclear test in the South Indian Ocean." The extent of close collaboration between South Africa and Israel is not a disclosed matter and its full implication is difficult to appreciate. Most recently, for example, the English newspaper, *The Guardian*, disclosed (based on released documents) evidence that Israel had a nuclear arsenal. The same report claimed that Israel offered to sell nuclear weapons to apartheid South Africa. This latter claim is vigorously disputed.

The nuclear doctrine that informs about the development of the Israel nuclear arsenal was initially influenced by the insecurity of the proximity in time to the Holocaust. In this sense, a nuclear capability was an insurance, giving strength to the principle of *Never Again*. Israel has significant strategic and tactical vulnerabilities. Its nuclear doctrine is shaped by its geography. Its geography lacks strategic depth. A jet fighter could cross Israel from the Jordan river to the Mediterranean in four minutes. Additionally, the Israel Defence Force (IDF) is based on reserves so that military losses tend to be magnified because of its small population. Given its geographic and demographic deficits, the Israeli defence doctrine is designed to minimise its weaknesses. Hence, there is great reliance on intelligence capability, military flexibility of movement and deployment as well as overwhelming firepower. The central underlined security value that determines the Israeli doctrine is that the loss of a single war could mean the destruction of the state. Therefore, Israel must prevent wars by a powerful deterrence supplemented by the option of preemption as a form of enhanced deterrence. If these strategies fail, it will have to rely on its second level of capability to prevent escalation and to ensure a war that is fought is quick and decisive, and fought outside its borders. From a strategic point of view, the Israeli nuclear capability, tied to its missiles and aircraft capacities as well as its nuclear armed submarines, represents its effective second level of deterrence. If this defensive strategy does not work and Israeli population centres are under threat, then its deterrence posture of last resort "The Samson Option" which envisions an all out attack on its enemy, may be used. Part of The Samson Option will be the use of the tactical nuclear arsenal. According to historian Avner Cohen, the Israeli doctrine revolves around the four so-called "red lines." These are as follows:

- A successful Arab military penetration into populated areas within Israel's post-1949 (pre-1967) borders:
- The destruction of the Israeli Air Force;
- The exposure of Israeli cities to massive and devastating air attacks or to possible chemical or biological attacks;
- The use of nuclear weapons against Israeli territory.

Israel's nuclear arsenal is estimated to be between 75 and 200 nuclear warheads, which include thermonuclear weapons. Because the Middle East is a region of instability and a flashpoint for violent conflict, the presence of such a significant arsenal is viewed as a threat to the Arab states in the region. These states have embraced two options. First, find the means to acquire nuclear technologies, ostensibly for peaceful purposes, a policy that could take a state rapidly on the road to acquiring nuclear arsenals. This may be a motivation that moved Saddam Hussein's Iraq. It may also be a motivation for the nuclear programme of Iran. It may have been the reason that Gadaffi's Libya also sought to acquire a nuclear capability. There is evidence that Syria has similar ambitions. There is also the pressure generated by Egypt and like-minded regional powers that there should be an agreement to create a nuclear-free Middle East. In principle, Israel does not oppose this. It insists, however, that there must be peace agreements with all states in the region, and that all the states must accept the idea of a legitimate, Jewish, national sovereign state.

Although Israel still maintains a posture of ambiguity, along with an official denial that it has a nuclear capability, it has long been accepted that it is indeed a nuclear weapon state. The US policy, which seeks to retain the posture of ambiguity, appears to undermine its effort to universalise the NPT. What its policy amounts to is that everyone except Israel should be under the authority of the treaty. Leading American experts such as McGeorge Bundy, William Crowe, Jr. and Sidney Drell, maintain that Israeli policy, rooted in ambiguity, compromises the force of the Non-Proliferation Treaty. Moreover, the denial or ambiguity of Israel as a nuclear weapon state essentially means that Israel cannot make an important international argument that no state need fear a nuclear Israel unless it seeks to destroy the Jewish state. In short, it is virtually impossible to discuss appropriate procedures and strategies, including the restraining force of international law, on the Israeli arsenal, if there is no acknowledgement that it exists.

Notwithstanding the lack of official acknowledgement of Israel's nuclear capability there would appear to be enough evidence for which some tentative legal conclusions may be presented concerning the threat of use and or use of the Israeli nuclear arsenal. In the context of Israel, given its strategic deficits in terms of geography and demographics, it would seem that the idea of whether the Israeli strategic deterrence posture is compatible with international law does generate important interpretative questions on the scope of the right of self-defence. In general, it would be implicit in the international legal defence of the deployment of the Israeli nuclear capabilities that they would at least have to be justified by some principle of reasonableness. This means that the claim to preemptive self-defence must at least require strict standards suggesting the imminence of an attack and that preemption is the last resort. This requires a more strict consideration of the threats to Israeli security, based on the non-existence of nuclear arsenals with its potential adversaries. Additionally, the question of the absence of a specific peace treaty between Israel and its neighbours constitutes the ground for deterrence based on weapons of mass destruction, such as nuclear arsenals. An implicit claim made by the Israeli government during the 1973 War was that it could deploy and possibly use nuclear weapons to repel attacks using only conventional forces. This was a posture that generated great concern in the US, and the US policy of providing Israel a fulfillment of its needs in conventional weapons was sought to be the price of Israel not using its nuclear arsenal. The US interest here was also triggered by the unforeseen consequences of such an act which could have triggered a response by other nuclear power states, triggering an uncontainable global catastrophe. It would seem as well that the claim that Israel may make for the threat of use or use of its nuclear arsenal may be justified by the International Court of Justice ruling that such a position may be lawful as a matter of self-defence if the survival of the state is at issue. But this requires a more rigorous appraisal of the conditions which precipitate an ostensible threat to the survival of the state. That decision should not simply be a subjective one; it should be one that may be objectively justified by a third party appraiser.

China's Nuclear Policy and International Law

In view of the diminished threats to China from nuclear capable states, it would be important to consider the nature and character of the Chinese deterrence strategy. The People's Liberation Army (PLA) has produced a National Defence University book which provides detailed analysis of China's thinking about the deterrence doctrine. This book notes that deterrence has been a part of the Chinese military doctrine for 2,000 years. For example, Sun Zi advocated a strategy of "overwhelming the enemy without fighting." China sees deterrence as a strategy for the protection of its national interests and resisting threats to the nation. The Chinese view of deterrence, therefore, is limited to self-defence; this is different from some states that use the idea of deterrence as an aspect of offensive military strategy with the option of a first use of nuclear weapons in any conflict. The Chinese approach appears to be more complex and nuanced. For example, the Chinese distinguish between different situational contexts in which different forms of deterrence might be deployed. For example, there is conventional deterrence, nuclear deterrence, out of space deterrence, regional deterrence, etc. In the context of nuclear deterrence, the Chinese see deterrence as a second strike option which would retaliate against limited targets of the enemy. For the Chinese deterrence includes both violent and non-violent forms. Violent deterrence would be mainly deployed to use force to deter the outbreak of war or the escalation of war. Non-violent deterrence includes using diplomacy, economics, science, technology, trade and military assistance to head off military and political conflicts that could lead to war.

Regarding the Chinese nuclear policy, China is a member of the International Atomic Energy Agency; it signed on the Non-Proliferation Treaty in 1992; it supported the extension of the treaty in 1995; and it announced a moratorium on its own nuclear tests in July 1996. In September 1996, it signed onto the Comprehensive Test Ban Treaty. It is also a member of the Zangger Committee which sets standards for exporting nuclear materials to non-nuclear states for peaceful purposes. China has generously supplied Pakistan with missile technology, weapons grade uranium and assisted Pakistan in the enrichment of weapons grade uranium. Apart from its nuclear cooperation with Pakistan, China has been a progressive force in urging the superpowers to abandon their nuclear deterrence policies and to reduce their nuclear stockpiles.

China has been forceful in suggesting that nuclear weapon states commit themselves to a "no first use policy." China also has called on states that had deployed nuclear weapons outside of their borders to move them inside their own territories. China has agreed with Russia and the US that they will not target each other with nuclear weapons. Moreover, China has pledged that it would unconditionally not use nuclear weapons against non-nuclear weapon states. China also supports the development of nuclear free zones, such as in the South Pacific, Latin America, Africa and the Caribbean. It has also made a commitment to unconditionally provide non-nuclear states and nuclear weapon-free zones with security assurances. China has also for long advanced a policy for the complete prohibition and destruction of nuclear weapons. It has long opposed the development and deployment of nuclear weapons in outer space or missile defence. China supports an early conclusion of the convention banning the production of fissile materials for nuclear weapons or other nuclear explosive devices. Overall, the Chinese record for supporting policies and practices that seek to diminish the global threat of nuclear weapons is a positive one and comes closer to the mandate of international law concerning the outlawing of the threat of use or use of nuclear weapons. As a nuclear power, China's justification as a matter of self-defence may be reconciled with the narrow ruling of the ICJ that "the threat or use of nuclear weapons, in a current state of knowledge, may represent a form of permissible self-defense, if the very survival of the state was as stake." Given the diminished nuclear threat to China, the self-defence justification, is considerably weakened, as with the British deployment of its nuclear capabilities. Notwithstanding China's nuanced and constrained definition of deterrence, it is difficult to see a Chinese justification that deterrence is a justified form of hypothetical self-defence interests. Moreover, the use of nuclear weapons, even if limited to a retaliatory strike, will still not meet the principle of military necessity, proportionality or, indeed, because of the destructive nature of nuclear weapons, the principle of humanitarianism. Such arsenals, whether used offensively or defensively, do not distinguish between combatants and non-combatants, and the victims are civilians.

India's Nuclear Policy and International Law

India has an arsenal of nuclear weapons. It has become an important nuclear weapons capable state. India was attacked by China in 1962. The Chinese attack came as a complete surprise to Nehru's government. Nehru had promoted a policy toward China which was encapsulated in the phrase *"Hindi-Chini Bhai Bhai."* This in rough translation means that the policy was based on the brotherly fraternity of the Indians and Chinese. The attack was a Chinese repudiation of Nehru's pacifist leaning policy towards China. Two years later, in 1964, China detonated its first nuclear weapon. The Chinese attack and later the Chinese nuclear weapon provided a significant incentive for India to improve upon its self-defence capability. India embarked on a programme to improve its military training and leadership capabilities in the military field. It also invested in science and technology for the improvement of its defence posture. India tested a nuclear explosive device in 1974. From the Indian perspective, it needed a nuclear defence capability in the light of China's development of its nuclear arsenal and the fact that China had unilaterally invaded India in 1962. The development of India's nuclear weapons capability was the outcome of its extensive civil and military nuclear programmes. India has at least 10 nuclear reactors, uranium mining and milling sites, heavy water production facilities, uranium enrichment facilities, fuel fabrication facilities and it has extensive nuclear research capabilities. Currently, it is estimated that India has a stockpile of some 80-100 nuclear weapons.

India's nuclear policy is based on the principle of creating a credible minimum deterrence. It also includes in the meaning of this phrase a policy of no first use of nuclear weapons. The Indian government has released a statement indicating that its nuclear weapons will be for retaliation only. The Indian policy-makers maintain that while they will not be the first to initiate a nuclear first strike, they will respond with punitive retaliation should deterrence fail. A decision to authorise the use of nuclear weapons is confined to the highest political authority in the state. Although India has a long history regarding global disarmament, its security realities have required it to be more circumspect. For example, in the nuclear context, India has not signed the NPT or the CTBT. It is a member of the IAEA. To provide for the strategic deployment of India's nuclear arsenal, it has developed a wide range of nuclear missiles – short, intermediate and long range. In addition, India is working on submarine delivery systems which have cruise missile capabilities. India also has nuclear capable aircraft to complement its strategic nuclear capability. These developments should be seen against the backdrop of Indian concerns about the proliferation of, and global threat posed by, nuclear arsenals. For example, in 1988, Prime Minister Rajiv Gandhi said:

> [h]umanity is at a crossroads. One road will take us like lemmings to our suicide. That is the path indicated by doctrines of nuclear deterrence, deriving from traditional concepts of the balance of power. The other road will give us another chance. That is the path signposted by the doctrine of peaceful coexistence, deriving from the imperative values of non-violence, tolerance and compassion.

With this background, it is unsurprising that the principal treaties pointing in the direction of nuclear disarmament such as the Partial Test Ban Treaty (PTBT), NPT and CTBT were all treaties which had been proposed by India to further the cause of nuclear disarmament. And, indeed, India still introduces a resolution before the UN General Assembly titled "Reducing Nuclear Dangers." Indian leaders and, indeed, India's representative at the UN continue to reiterate India's strong commitment to global disarmament. They have listed the seven following steps as a pathway to secure these objectives;

- Reaffirmation of the unequivocal commitment of all nuclear weapon states to the goal of complete elimination of nuclear weapons;
- Reduction of the salience of nuclear weapons in security doctrines;
- Adoption of measures by nuclear weapon states to reduce nuclear danger, including the risks of accidental use of nuclear weapons;
- Negotiation of a global agreement among nuclear weapon states on 'no first use' of nuclear weapons;
- Negotiation of a universal and legally binding agreement on non-use of nuclear weapons against non-nuclear weapon states;
- Negotiation of a convention on the complete prohibition of the use or threat of use of nuclear weapons; and
- Negotiation of a nuclear weapons convention prohibiting the development, production, stockpiling and use of nuclear weapons, and on their destruction, leading to the global, non-discriminatory and verifiable elimination of nuclear weapons within a specified timeframe.

Regrettably, these eminently sensible proposals by the Indian government did not succeed in shaping global public opinion in order to influence policy-makers. Until acceptance recently, with the declaration of President Obama of a goal for a world free of nuclear weapons, we have had no major political figure endorse the Indian proposal. There are those within the Indian establishment who claim that the Indian position was more a case of sour grapes. India did not possess nuclear weapons, thus, it advocated the elimination of nuclear weapons from the states that had them. It would now appear that India as a nuclear weapon state may be taken more seriously should these views be resurrected as a major diplomatic initiative.

The Indian scholar Manpreet Sethi suggests a number of strategies that the Government of India might promote to further the course of nuclear disarmament. For example, she stresses the importance of restricting the ostensible role that nuclear weapons can play in the strategy of self-defence. She notes that the US *Nuclear Posture Review* understands the use of nuclear weapons "only in extreme circumstances." She believes that there is an important task in the reappraisal of nuclear security doctrines so as to make them less attractive by restriction, eventually obviating the role completely. She also advocates the adoption of "comprehensive security assurances." To further this end, she promotes the idea of negative security assurances to non-nuclear weapon states. This essentially means that nuclear weapon states will guarantee not to use or threaten to use nuclear weapons against a non-nuclear weapon state. She, in addition, recommends the wide acceptance of no first use of nuclear weapons. Finally, she would encourage the adoption of an international convention prohibiting the use or threat of use of nuclear weapons. India has annually tabled such a resolution before the UN General Assembly since 1982. A convention along these lines will send a powerful signal to all the important nuclear constituencies. A final lesson from the Indian experience may be indicated in the statement of Prime Minister Nehru in 1962; "Time is limited. If you do not put an end to it soon enough, it may later on be beyond the capacity of human beings or nations to stop it."

North Korea's Nuclear Policy and International Law

North Korea was a party to the Non-Proliferation Treaty; it ratified the Non-Proliferation Treaty on December 12, 1985. The development of a nuclear weapon was a violation of the treaty. North Korea first announced withdrawal from the treaty on January 10, 2003. The withdrawal was triggered by the exposure by the United States that North Korean was secretly developing a nuclear weapon. The withdrawal was specifically the result of the US claim that North Korea had started an illegal enriched uranium weapons programme. The withdrawal became effective three months later, on April 10, 2003. North Korea became the first state to ever withdraw from the treaty.

If North Korea was in breach of its treaty obligations, its withdrawal from the treaty created greater problems, in the sense of seeking to constrain or reverse the North Korean nuclear arms programme. Outside of the treaty, there is a legal base, essentially predicated on the arguments of the US and other nuclear powers that there are no rules of conventional or customary international law that constrain the development of the

North Korean nuclear arsenal, at least for defensive/deterrence purposes. Moreover, apart from developing nuclear arsenals, there are no ostensible restrains on marketing such weapons or technologies and related materials to other states as well as international terrorist groups. The emergence of the Bush Doctrine and its claim to preemptive self-defence has strengthened the North Korean resolve. Therefore, it now has a justification for a nuclear weapon to constrain the prospect of a preemptive strike. The attack on Iraq was justified initially on the basis that Saddam Hussein had a secret stockpile of nuclear weapons and delivery systems. Regrettably for the Bush Administration, no such stockpiles were found and the justification for preemptive action fell away. It is hardly likely that the international community would sanction preemptive action against North Korea in the light of the failure of the Bush Administration to create a new reality and new norms for international law and the use of force. This means that international law must examine other strategies of action to secure compliance with its mandate to prevent proliferation, to reduce or eliminate nuclear arsenals as important milestones in moving the international community to purposefully realise a world free of nuclear weapons.

This still leaves open the question of whether the threat posed by the North Korean nuclear capability is existentially sufficiently real and compelling to pose a threat of the use of nuclear weapons against South Korea. Since there is an armistice which secures the peace between South and North Korea, the question is whether an armistice without a peace treaty is an element that enhances the concern for the maintenance of international peace and security. Second, since South Korea is a democratic state, governed by the rule of law, and has a record of peaceful coexistence, the question is whether North Korea, which is a dictatorship and which has nuclear weapons, is an entity that constitutes an existential threat to South Korean peace and security. Short of intervention involving the military instrument, the question is: what is the scope of the strategies available using the economic instrument, the ideological instrument and the diplomatic instrument. All these strategies have indeed been invoked but the full scope of the possibilities has not been fully deployed. However, the ability to deploy these strategies of international action with collective unanimity would be an important step forward for the entire international community. We would suggest that North Korea does not meet the international minimum required for deterrence for which there is no real threat which might invoke the self-defence exception of the ICJ. And the idea of deterrence should be construed so as to be validated by a real and imminent threat to the survival of the state. The North Korean threats concerning its survival are self-made deficits. In any event, in the broader view of international law, the threat or use of the North Korea nuclear arsenal is clearly a violation of international law.

5

Securing India's Nuclear Facilities: Defence by Design and Beyond

Sitakanta Mishra

REPLYING to the question in the Lok Sabha on March 15, 2011 on "whether ... the atomic power plants in the country are under threat from various terrorist groups and outfits," the Minister of State for Home Affairs, Mullappally Ramachandran said, "In view of the prevailing security scenario, the atomic power plants continue to remain targets of terrorist groups and outfits."[1] However, the Minister assured that the "Central Security Agencies review the security of atomic power plants periodically and make specific recommendations to enhance the security wherever required."[2] This deliberation is, in fact, symptomatic of the dyadic nuclear security debate in vogue in India. For critics, Nuclear Power Plants (NPPs) are the top targets of terrorists because they could cause mass casualties. On the other hand, the nuclear power industry proclaims that nuclear facilities are well fortified with many redundant back-up systems and there is little probability of mass casualty. Given the complexity involved in both security and insecurity of nuclear technology, it is pertinent to examine how secure India's nuclear facilities are, and what measures are taken to ensure their security, especially in the light of the threats anticipated.

Nuclear as Critical Infrastructure

Undoubtedly, security of *critical infrastructure* has been a major global concern, especially since 9/11. "Critical infrastructure" comprises systems and assets, whether physical or virtual, so vital to a state that the incapacity or destruction of such systems and assets would have a debilitating impact on security, national economic security, national public health or safety, or any combination of these matters.[3] In addition, the vulnerability of these interlinked and interdependent infrastructures spanning continents that contributes to the "strategic fragility" of nations is growing perceptibly.[4] A common reason is the emergence of new threats that did not exist a few decades ago. The nuclear establishment that involves highly complex technological systems is a unique critical infrastructure feared amenable to the designs of the non-state actors. If this takes place, it would certainly create havoc in the society as public perception on anything nuclear is negative. Though there is no precedent of a successful nuclear terror attack as yet, the spectre of 9/11 reinforces the notion that every unprecedented event happens for the first time only.

Therefore, security affects the nuclear sector in a way that it does not affect any other form of industry. This is partly because of the legacy of the highly secretive nuclear weapon programmes that thrive under the veil of civil nuclear programmes, and partly also due to the strategic nature of the facilities and nuclear material involved. Though nuclear infrastructure is secluded from the society at large, the ramifications of any nuclear disaster would affect the entire society, both adjacent and far away, as witnessed in the recent Fukushima nuclear disaster in Japan that affected not only the Japanese people, but also the neighbouring countries and the rest of the world as well. Destruction of the nuclear infrastructure has a "debilitating impact on national security, the economic and social well-being of a nation."[5]

However, the difficulty is to quantify the security threats because of "intelligent adversaries" and their tactics, and the paucity of data, as few attacks on nuclear facilities have occurred.[6] The international nuclear security regime was nowhere near as extensive, advanced or entrenched as is the case with nuclear safety regime. A few years ago, there were fewer treaties, less widely accepted set of security principles and practices, and little collaboration between nuclear plant operators worldwide, unlike the World Association of Nuclear Operators (WANO) for nuclear security matters. Rather, there was "an abiding sense that nuclear security is too sensitive an issue to be subject to global governance."[7] Gradually, nuclear security issues have started to draw the attention of the international community and the United Nation Security Council (UNSC) Resolution 1540[8] and the Nuclear Security Summit[9] initiative are among some attempts to strengthen nuclear security across the globe. In fact, the concerns and awareness generated in the wake of 9/11 has brought this issue to the centre-stage.

In a way, therefore, the 9/11 incident seems to have accomplished the job in the 'nuclear security' domain in the coming decades like the Chernobyl disaster did for the 'nuclear safety' regime.[10] The "guns, guards and gates" system as the primary means of achieving the security of nuclear installations has been given a second thought as the scope and nature of current threats transcend the *design basis security system.*[11] Even "the oversimplified assertion that only the state is accountable for nuclear security is increasingly felt unhelpful in defining how the myriad tasks of protecting nuclear materials and facilities are to be managed."[12]

India's Nuclear Infrastructure: India has a sizeable nuclear infrastructure spread across the country. India currently has 20 operational reactors, six are under construction and around three dozen more have been proposed. There is a network of supporting research laboratories, heavy water plants, and nuclear fuel complexes whose security is crucial. Concern for nuclear security, in fact, includes security or safe-keep of uranium/thorium mines and milling plants, transport network, fuel fabrication facilities, research reactors, nuclear power plants, plutonium reprocessing plants, spent fuel pools, breeder reactors, waste immobilisation plants, nuclear waste storage ponds, and above all, the personnel involved.

Moreover, radiological materials are used in numerous institutions like cancer treatment centres, food processing units, oil and gas exploration industry, road construction, steel manufacturing and academic/research centres, etc. located in various parts of the country. The use of ionising radiation sources for various applications in all these areas has registered phenomenal growth. Radioactive materials used for industrial and medical applications are estimated at over 12,000 units which include 300 telecobalt therapy units, 100 accelerators, over 2,000 Computed Tomography (CT) scan units, 150 nuclear medicine centres, 1,400 industrial radiography cameras, 8,000 nucleonic gauges and 14 gamma radiation processing plants.[13] The security of all these units, though important, has not been a matter of as grave concern as that of nuclear facilities that include both civilian and strategic nuclear plants.

Real Concerns or False Alarms?

During the past one decade, the security of nuclear materials and technology seems to have drawn unprecedented political attention of many countries, including India. While the 9/11 tragedy cautioned the Western countries (also all other countries) about the urgency of strengthening the containment design of their nuclear facilities, the Indo-US civil nuclear deal is viewed to have rendered the Indian atomic power plants more vulnerable to terrorist strikes.[14] So India's domestic debate over the apprehension of threats to nuclear installations emanates mainly from four consequent developments. First, the global debate on nuclear terrorism, especially in the post-9/11, period has markedly been reflected in the Indian national security discourse. Second, the Indo-US strategic partnership has led to the fear of threats from Al Qaeda because anybody who is seen as a friend of the US becomes Al Qaeda's target. Third, the political instability in Pakistan and fear of its nuclear arsenal falling into the hands of extremist-terrorist groups has attracted much attention as also the fact that Pakistan is a hotbed of terrorism and has targeted India. Lastly, over the past few decades, sporadic incidents of radiological material smuggling have been reported and terrorist outfits like Al Qaeda have expressed a desire to acquire nuclear materials.[15]

On April 27, 2011, the Department of Atomic Energy (DAE) and the Central Industrial Security Force (CISF) in a meeting, chaired by the CISF Director-General N.R. Das and attended by top officials of 14 atomic energy plants, reviewed the security of the major nuclear power plants in view of the constant threat to India's sensitive installations.[16] In the meeting it was decided to strengthen the water front security of all nuclear installations and fortify these areas with the help of additional security personnel and deployment of security gadgets. For the last couple of years, such official concerns have been frequently reported. The former Union Home Minister Shivraj Patil, in November 2006, informed the police and intelligence brass about the conspiracy by terrorist groups operating from Pakistan to target oil and gas installations, the Information Technology (IT) sector, nuclear installations, communications network and defence installations.[17] Also, the former National Security Adviser M.K. Narayanan disclosed during the same time that nuclear plants like the Bhabha Atomic Research Centre (BARC), Trombay, and the Kaiga plant in Karnataka are on the hit list of terrorists.

A series of intelligence reports on different occasions have revealed that terrorists could target India's nuclear infrastructure. As a result, on the eve of Independence Day, 2006, security was stepped up at BARC with deployment of the National Security Guards (NSG) for the first time, following inputs of a possible terrorist attack.[18] Also, sporadic incidents of uranium and radiological material smuggling have been reported in India. According to a report, in 2001, smuggled uranium, confiscated from suspected terrorists in Balurghat, northern West Bengal, had been removed from the Jaduguda uranium mines in Jharkhand, and was planned to be smuggled across the Bangladeshi border.[19] Five people were arrested in Meghalaya for allegedly trying to smuggle uranium on September 10, 2008.[20] Though the authenticity of these reports can be questioned, the possibility of such incidents is hardly surprising given the location of South Asia between two well-established drug trafficking routes – the Golden Crescent and Golden Triangle.

Also, incidents of occasional malpractices and events within India's nuclear establishment have given rise to speculations about the threat from insiders. One such incident took place in November 2009 when employees of a maintenance unit of the Kaiga atomic plant were treated for radiation poisoning after drinking water containing tritium. Authorities say the source of the contamination, which affected 55 workers, was traced to a drinking water cooler at the government facility. In a clarification then, India's Minister for Science and Technology, Prithviraj Chavan, said that an insider at the plant was suspected of spiking the cooler with "heavy water".[21]

Despite such apprehensions, no big security breach or incident has ever taken place in India during the last six decades. Rather, India has 300 reactor years experience of safe operation. However, no complacency can be allowed when India is preparing for an ambitious nuclear energy expansion programme. It is pertinent, therefore, to analyse how prepared the Indian nuclear establishment is to deal with such an eventuality, if one was ever to take place. Especially, what are security strategy and organisational arrangements that are in place? India's nuclear establishment proclaims that it follows a "defence in depth" strategy based on "root cause analysis" of probable threats.

Patterns and Types of Threats

Nuclear power programmes are sensitive, starting from mining operations to all the way through the final stages of disposing of the by-products safely. Threats to nuclear security, therefore, involve criminals or terrorists penetrating at any stage of the nuclear fuel cycle and using them for malicious purposes. They might seek (a) nuclear weapons; (b) nuclear material to build improvised nuclear explosive devices; and/or (c) radioactive material to cause harm to individuals or the environment, including construction of Radiological Dispersal Devices (RDDs) and Radiological Exposure Devices (REDs). Such threats also include: (d) the dispersal of radioactive material through sabotage of facilities or material in transit.[22] Any such form of these activities is, in fact, related to the design basis threats to the facilities and may be attempted by terrorists with the help of insiders. After 9/11, the threat to nuclear plants has also been perceived from beyond the design basis, like the crashing of an aircraft on a facility or the confiscating of nuclear materials enroute.

India being located in a volatile region, known as the epicentre of terrorism and proliferation, there are chances of non-state actors laying their hands on nuclear technology or orchestrating sabotage of India's nuclear facilities. Evidence of terrorist organisations like Al Qaeda's interest in nuclear weapons is well-known. Also, sporadic incidents of malpractices inside the nuclear establishment generate the apprehension of a probable conjunction between terrorists and disgruntled personnel within the establishment. On the other hand, given the fragile political situation in the neighbourhood, the nuclear weapons or fissile material of neighbouring countries like Pakistan may fall into the hands of extremist-terrorist groups, and, in that case, India would be their foremost target.

Therefore, the physical protection system in and around nuclear facilities in India (and of any other country for that matter) theoretically faces the dual threat: 'insiders' and 'outsiders.' Technically, on the basis of the nature and nomenclature of probable threats, they can be categorised as Design Basis Threats (DBTs) and Beyond Design Basis Threats (BDBTs).

Threat from Insiders: The 'human' factor generally is a contributor to all nuclear security related incidents. Theoretically, nuclear facility officials with access to radioactive materials and knowledge about the set-up could "open the doors to the vault" to provide these materials to terrorists for ideological or mercenary reasons.[23] The range of other possible threats includes theft of materials; support to outsiders by disrupting alarm systems; sabotage of facilities or specific processes (such as cooling systems); and simple acts such as providing building layouts or access codes to terrorists.[24] Disgruntled employees may express their anger by tampering with electrical cables, lighting fires, destroying security cameras, etc. In some situations, either the officials may be blackmailed, coerced or lured to provide these materials or knowhow to terrorist groups. Since insiders have the knowledge of the security layouts, access codes, and knowhow to handle highly radioactive materials, and can find an opportune time for the act, the success rate for such acts would be high. Having both access and authority, insiders could be potential cyber-security threats[25] – especially, leakage of data, introducing a virus to corrupt the network, etc.

So far, no major insider threat event has been noticed except a few reported incidents of mysterious deaths and missing of nuclear facility personnel and material. In February 2004, the theft of 29 aluminium alloy titanium rings (used in rocket engines) from the the Indian Space Research Organisation's (ISRO's) Liquid Propulsion Systems Centre was reported. In June 2009, the mysterious death of Loknath Mahalingam, who was working in the Kaiga Atomic Power Station (KAPS), raised questions about the safety and security of the personnel.[26] Relatively serious was the incident in November 2009 of spiking a water cooler with heavy water by an insider in the Kaiga plant which affected 55 workers.[27] A mechanical engineer, Mahadevan Padmanabhan Iyer of BARC's design and development division reactor group, was found murdered in February 2010.[28] Ten days after this incident, a 27-year old woman scientist of the radio chemistry and isotope group of BARC allegedly committed suicide in her official residence.[29] Though the full truth of these reported incidents is not known, they certainly instigate the public and critics to apprehend that all is not well in India's nuclear establishment.

Moreover, India has a record of betrayal by insiders even at the highest level security arrangements, for example, the assassination of national leaders by their own security guards. Corruption is also rampant in every sector. However, the Indian nuclear establishment seems to have maintained its integrity through elaborate Personnel Reliability Programmes (PRP) and stringent Material Protection Control and Accounting (MPC&A) procedures (discussed in the subsequent sections).

Threat from Outsiders: The possibility that armed individuals or groups from outside may gain access, and sabotage the facility, steal components or fissile material comprises the threat from outsiders. The outsiders' objective is to gain control of these items for their own use or to transfer them to another state or to other non-state actors. Terrorists may attempt to capture such components or fissile material during transportation. To boost the chances of causing devastating damage, terrorist or attackers would devote significant effort to recruit insiders, as they would know about the detailed operations and vulnerabilities at these places. Thereby, "insider collusion would serve as a multiplier effect for outside attackers."[30] Skilled and highly trained insiders, such as nuclear engineers would know how to disable emergency cooling systems and emergency sources of power. Such disablement would increase the likelihood of a reactor meltdown and radiation release.[31] Insiders could sabotage other vital plant systems while outside attackers hold the security guard forces under siege.

India is situated in a region of political turbulence and militancy characterised by the ubiquitous presence of terrorism and porous borders. For the last few decades, radical and terrorist movements have flourished in neighbouring Afghanistan, Pakistan, Nepal, Myanmar, Bangladesh, and Sri Lanka. Within India, terrorists have periodically penetrated zones of high-level military security. Between April 2000 and May 2001, major fires occurred at Army ammunition dumps, some of them very large ones, such as the enormous fire that destroyed some 10,000 tons of ammunition in Bharatpur on April 28, 2000.[32] It is presumed, in some cases, that sabotage was involved.

However, not a single nuclear facility of India has so far faced such an event. The Narora fire incident of 1993 was due to technical failures in the turbine, and was not a sabotage incident. However, unavailability of a precedent is not in itself reassuring. Instances of negligence can be noticed. For example, when India's nuclear tests were being carried out in 1998, an unauthorised individual – an Army washerman who had jumped into a military truck with other soldiers because he wanted to help – was discovered at the test site, that too by accident, because he had been bitten by a scorpion.[33]

Sources and Scenarios of the Threats

If all these hypothetical scenarios are plausible, we need to consider who or which groups would be the potential threats? While terrorists from across the border have penetrated and spread their network all over the country, internal dissident groups like the Naxalites have, on many occasions, attacked public officials and destroyed public utilities. The question is: do these groups really have the motivation and capability to undertake a nuclear terror plan?

There is no precedent of nuclear terror in India yet, nor have any of the terrorist outfits or extremist entities operating in and around India overtly shown interest in resorting to the nuclear path. Al Qaeda is known to have contacted A.Q. Khan, and documents recovered from Afghanistan show that Osama bin Laden was initially considering the designing of a nuclear explosive device, but later gave it up. The reason may be that it is too difficult to materialise such a design owing to the requirement of sophisticated technology and expertise. Also, it can be assumed that terrorist entities may be preparing for such a plan, but have not yet achieved the required capabilities. But considering the way terrorism has spread to every nook and corner of the country, and the sporadic instances of smuggling of small quantities of radioactive materials, if the terrorists were to get hold of the required capabilities, it could be the beginning of a nuclear terror plan.

Terrorist outfits operating in India or in the subcontinent could be expected to have the basic knowledge of the Indian security arrangements, vulnerable areas and topography. In this context, it would be prudent to think about the kinds of nuclear terrorism that could take place in India and the types of entities that might resort to such acts. Broadly, nuclear terrorism is of two types: (1) terrorism using nuclear weapons/materials which is of low probability, but high consequences; (2) terrorism using non-nuclear strikes on nuclear installations/facilities whose occurrence is more probable but would have lower consequences.

An anticipated scenario of nuclear terrorism in India would be the misappropriation of a small radioactive source, a few grams of Co-60 from a cancer radiotherapy unit, and its dispersal by mixing it with conventional explosive (dirty bomb). This would contaminate an area of about 2 sq km, or about 33 city blocks to a level that would require clean-up.[34] Though such an extreme situation may not take place as it involves expertise to appropriate and handle nuclear materials, false news of the acquisition of nuclear material or device by terrorists would create massive disruption, throwing life in any mega city into chaos. Such a hoax would raise a false alarm among the public, causing many road accidents and horrible traffic jams. Entry into, and exit from, the city would be difficult; many patients on their way to hospitals would die, rescue operations would be difficult, and normal life would be disrupted. In any such incident, "public hysteria would overwhelm local authorities, the economic consequences would be long lasting, and government agencies responsible for public safety would come under severe scrutiny."[35]

Even a small amount of Highly Enriched Uranium (HEU), which is odourless, kept in a crowded place, subway of a city, market or railway station would cause radiation without being detected, as radiation detection devices are not widely used in India. A dirty bomb may not be a weapon of mass destruction but "its disturbing consequences qualify it as a 'weapon of mass disruption'."[36]

Assessing Capability and Motivation

Though terrorism is a major challenge before India and modern-day terrorists intelligently leverage communication and financial networks, the probability of a nuclear terror incident may be determined by factors like: (1) location of nuclear facilities (source of the radioactive material); (2) area of operation of the terrorist groups; and (3) their capabilities and motivations. For instance, the threat to the nuclear infrastructure in the northern and northwestern parts of India may emanate from the terrorist and extremist groups active in Jammu and Kashmir (J&K), Al Qaeda operatives, insurgents in the northeastern states, terrorists active in the Indo-Bangladesh border region, and attack from across the border, etc. Nuclear infrastructure in the eastern, central and southern parts of India could be vulnerable to the activities of the Naxalites. The facilities of southwestern India might be prone to religious-chauvinistic elements and terrorist attacks from the sea. However, a realistic assessment of the intent of these sources of threat would provide a picture completely contrary to these apprehensions.

Threat from Terrorist Groups: With the killing of Osama bin Laden, the fate of Al Qaeda is in question. However, it is the only terrorist organisation believed to have the capacity to resort to nuclear terrorism, if it so desires. The 9/11 incident is a demonstration of its intent and reach. While no direct act of terrorism in India by Al Qaeda has been reported yet, its members and many pro-Al Qaeda, Pakistani pan-Islamic *jihadi* organisations have been active in India, especially in J&K, since the 1990s. These are the Harkat-ul-Mujahideen (HuM), the Harkat-ul-Jihad-al-Islami (HUJI), the Lashkar-e-Tayyeba (LeT), and Jaish-e-Mohammad (JeM). The HUJI of Bangladesh, known as HUJI (B), believes in Osama bin Laden's religious call to consider it a duty to acquire WMD but other indigenous Kashmiri separatist groups like the Jammu and Kashmir Liberation Front (JKLF), and All-Party Hurriyat Conference (APHC) have not shown interest in WMD.[37]

Before 9/11, Al Qaeda's attitude towards India or even Kashmir hardly figured in its statements. Since 9/11, and with the evolution of the Indo-US strategic partnership, references of threats to India have been more frequent. The US support to India on Kashmir, and India's relations with Israel are other major reasons for this. In an audio message disseminated in April 2006 in the wake of the visit of President George Bush to Afghanistan,

India and Pakistan in March 2006, Bin Laden projected global *jihad* as directed against the "anti-Islam conspiracy of the Crusaders (Christians), the Jewish people and the Hindus."[38] Previously, there had never been a reference to Hinduism in his pronouncements. But, surprisingly, the reference to Hindus has not figured in subsequent statements. Though the exact interest of Al Qaeda in nuclear terrorism is not known, documents found in Afghanistan reveal that while Al Qaeda's efforts to make nuclear weapons are less than adequate, it is determined to get them and willing to use them.[39] One report says that the idea of attacks on nuclear power stations by Al Qaeda, perceived to be raised in the early stages of the planning of the 9/11 attacks, was vetoed, apparently by Bin Laden himself, perhaps because of the enormous resources and sophisticated technology required.[40] But this does not discount the probability of Al Qaeda acquiring such capability in the future. In any case, with the level of technological expertise it has, it may able to fabricate an RDD or Intermediate Nuclear Device (IND). The same is the case of other smaller *jihadi* groups. Therefore, the northern part of India is vulnerable to the designs of Al Qaeda and its associate groups. They can attempt sabotage of a facility, fire rockets or throw hand grenades into a facility. At the extreme, they can attempt a suicidal attack, similar to 9/11—hijacking an aircraft and crashing it on the premises of a nuclear facility.

Threat from Naxalites: The second grave threat to Indian nuclear facilities would be from the Naxalites. In 2006, Prime Minister Manmohan Singh called the Naxalites "the single biggest internal security challenge ever faced by our country."[41] In 2009, he said the country was "losing the battle against Maoist rebels."[42]

The Naxalites are active in states like Chhattisgarh, Uttar Pradesh, Bihar, Karnataka, Kerala, Uttaranchal, Tamil Nadu, and Andhra Pradesh where many of India's nuclear facilities are located. By 2006, their strength was at 15,000, and, reportedly, the guerrillas control an estimated one-fifth of India's forests, and are active in 160 of the country's 604 administrative districts.[43] As of 2009, Naxalites are active across approximately 220 districts in twenty states of India[44] accounting for about 40 percent of India's geographical area.[45] They are especially concentrated in an area known as the "Red Corridor," where they control 92,000 sq km.[46]

Considering their tactics, motivation and capabilities, one can assume that they may be capable of sabotaging a nuclear facility in their area of activity if they wish to. They can cause harm to uranium mines located in their area of operation by simply destroying the infrastructure and capturing and diverting the raw materials to smugglers. They are known for targeting government offices, police stations, railroad tracks, jails and government officials, but no such attempt has been made on nuclear facilities. Map 1 shows the distribution of nuclear facilities and the Naxal affected states in India.

Map 1: Naxal Affected States and Distribution of Nuclear Facilities

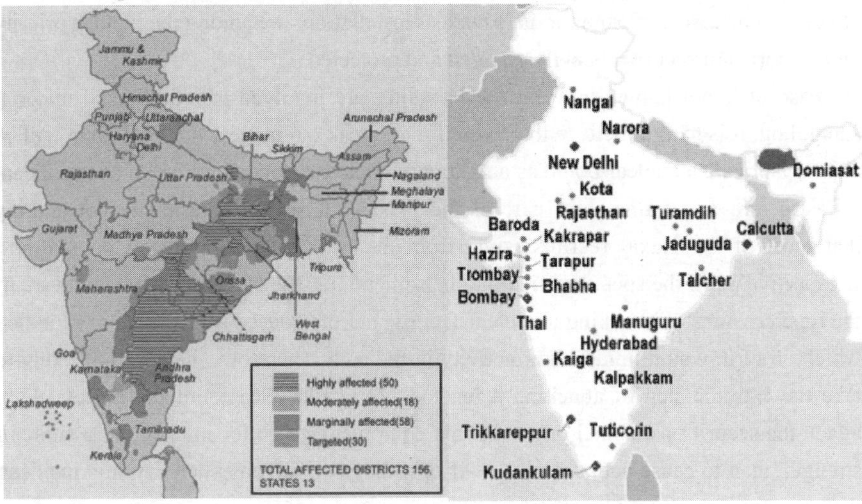

Source: http://pacificempire.org.nz; http://images.google.co.in

The Jaduguda uranium mine, located in Jharkhand state, is frequently in the news for alleged radiological material smuggling and is known to be the hotbed of Naxalites. The Kaiga nuclear power plant in Karnataka was in the news when former Union Home Minister Shivaraj Patil reportedly stated in July 2007 that there was a grave threat from the Naxalites and terrorists to the facility. The police conducted repeated combing operations in the forest region near Kaiga and in nearby Joida *taluk* to check possible intrusions of the Naxalites.[47] According to media reports, the Naxals are quietly expanding their base in states like J&K, Gujarat, Rajasthan, Himachal Pradesh and Meghalaya.[48]

Though it is difficult to assess the level of awareness of the Naxalites about nuclear technology and radiation effects, today, they do not seem to be a threat to India's nuclear facilities. One of the reasons is that Naxalites primarily operate in the tribal, forested areas that are significantly far away from the major nuclear installations. Though they have also attacked outside the strictly forest areas, it is doubtful if they would risk leaving the safety of their hideouts to steal nuclear material sufficient in quantity to cause harm. Not to mention the heightened counter-operations against the Naxalites in the recent months. Considering their fighting methods, nuclear attacks do not seem to fit their *modus operandi*.[49] Conventional weapons, smaller quick killing machines, easy to carry, seem their favoured idea of weapons. The Naxalites mostly operate using guerrilla tactics within a restricted area. To carry out a nuclear attack, they would have to leave their safety zones and venture out far enough so that they themselves are shielded from the effects of a nuclear explosion. India's nuclear installations are among the highest priority units in terms of security, heavily guarded and protected.

Also, it is not known how far the Naxalites are involved in radiological material smuggling. It is hard to believe that even if they sneak out nuclear material, they will be able to fabricate a nuclear bomb as any kind of nuclear device would require significant infrastructure and training on part of the Naxals. It seems improbable considering that most of the Naxal recruits come from the tribal, underprivileged populations. Irrespective of all the speculation about their intentions, the Naxalites must be aware of the repercussions of attacking a nuclear facility and the consequent release of radiation which, in turn, would hinder their activity in the area. Therefore, they are not likely to take the extreme step of attacking a reactor that would release radiation; they might attack the security personnel or steal some equipment, more for impact and a show of strength, than to cause actual damage. Also, if they commit any such extreme incident, their own survival would be at stake.

Threat from Across the Border: The third category of threat that the Indian nuclear facilities might face is the possibility of an attack from across the border. Many of India's neighbours are politically unstable and the extremist groups have a strong hold in these countries. Theoretically, during a time of domestic turmoil, terrorist groups may get hold of nuclear or radiological devices and use them against India. Also the nexus between the state and extremist groups in neighbouring Pakistan is well known; therefore, the chances of state-sponsored nuclear terrorism cannot be ruled out.

The first country in this context that attracts attention is Pakistan. The political situation in Pakistan is in a state of flux. Though the leadership proclaims that the nuclear arsenals are safe and well protected, owing to the disturbed political situation, their safety and security is bound to raise apprehensions. Since 9/11, terrorist incidents like suicide bombings, assassinations and political strife have increased phenomenally in Pakistan. The influence of extremist forces on the Pakistan Army is an undisputed fact. Since the assassination of Benazir Bhutto, violence has flared up across the country. Mark Thompson, while branding Pakistan as the "least stable nuclear state," warns that "if Pakistan slides into total chaos and its military seems on the verge of losing control of its nuclear stockpiles, US troops will dash in to secure them. The trouble is, US officials say they don't know all the secret locations ...."[50]

The other neighbouring country that can be a cause of concern for India in terms of nuclear terrorism is Bangladesh which is developing a "peaceful" and "transparent" nuclear energy programme.[51] Though Bangladesh is relatively less unstable than Pakistan, many extremist groups are active there and may pose serious threats to India. There are many instances of smuggling of radiological materials across the Indo-Bangladesh border by the terrorist groups in Bangladesh.

Threat from Fundamentalist Groups: Fourth is the threat from the religious fundamentalist and apocalyptic groups. But, in India, most of these groups are deeply nationalistic and consider nuclear weapons or facilities as national wealth, and a matter of national pride. Therefore, they would not cause any harm to the nation's nuclear infrastructure. In fact, these nationalistic forces had for long been demanding that New Delhi acquire nuclear weapons. Even sectarian violence may not be directed against nuclear facilities as was seen during the Godhra incident in Gujarat. Gujarat has a history of sectarian (communal) violence, going back decades, even before India's independence in 1947, but there is no evidence of a single incident ever being aimed at the nuclear infrastructure in the state. During the visit of US President Bush to India in March 2006, Muslims staged anti-US demonstrations in Lucknow, Mumbai and Hyderabad. There were reports that sections of the Muslims – particularly in Mumbai – shouted pro-Bin Laden slogans.[52] But beyond that, they do not have the means or motivation to cause any grave harm to the infrastructure. Student activist organisations that are opposing nuclear weapons and India's relations with the US might, at best, go to the extent of staging demonstrations, but not beyond that.

Types of Threats: Design Basis and Beyond Design Basis

The specific objective of the physical protection system of nuclear facilities is to prevent adversaries from successfully carrying out a malicious act. A clear description of the anticipated threat and an efficient assessment process are essential prerequisites for assured and effective physical protection.[53] Ideally, intelligence would provide sufficient information for the specification of design and performance requirements for a physical protection system to help ensure that this objective is met. However, intelligence is often limited, and threats are inherently dynamic. A physical protection system designed only for today's threat may not be effective against tomorrow's threat. The saboteurs can not only manipulate the design of the facility and the arrangements in place but can also cause harm to other nuclear activities beyond the design basis arrangements.

Design Basis Threats: A Design Basis Threat (DBT) assessment is derived on the basis of the probable risks arising out of exploitation of existing vulnerable areas by the enemies. DBT is the threat against which nuclear assets must be protected and upon which the protective systems design is based – primarily the paramilitary type threats. It is the baseline type and size of threat that buildings or other structures are designed to withstand.[54] Analysis of the DBT provides a general description of the attributes of potential adversaries who might attempt to commit radiological sabotage or theft or diversion against which the operator's physical protection systems must defend. It also includes the tactics that aggressors will use against the assets and the tools, weapons, and the explosives employed in these tactics.

To determine the DBT, the threats described in the state's threat assessment are refined to take account of other issues (for example, technical, economic, and political issues) and the particular requirements of planning for system design.[55] For this, rigorous analysis and decision-making are essential. Though specific details of the DBT are classified, in general, it considers the physical protection system required to protect against diversion and theft of fissile material; assumed capabilities of adversaries to operate as one or more teams, and attacks from multiple entry points; assumed target selection that terrorists might attack; vehicles and their movements; and, the threat posed by an insider.[56] Normally, the DBT calculation excludes aircraft attack and rocket propelled grenade attack as beyond the reasonable responsibility of a private security force.

Charles D. Ferguson has conducted a comprehensive study on the military and terrorist threats against Indian civilian nuclear facilities wherein he argues that the sheer complexity of the Indian "three-pronged plan could complicate management of ensuring adequate security throughout the programme." The differential reactor designs "would require detailed attention to differences in vulnerability to various modes of attack."[57] In his assessment:

- The VVER-1000 has some inherent weaknesses. Vulnerabilities include: steam lines and isolation valves too close together, which a single blast could knock out; the control room is located at the lower level of the reactor building, potentially prompting quick evacuation if the containment is breached, thus, minimising the amount of time operators have to control the reactor; and relatively weak containment structures that an airplane might penetrate.
- Many research reactors in India do not use containment buildings, and if they do, the containments tend to be not as strong as those surrounding commercial reactors. Research reactors, especially those at universities, also tend to have less security forces than commercial power plants. Also, most of the Indian research reactors are usually located within institutions and terrorist attackers might find it attractive to strike such facilities.
- The decommissioned reactors, while not operating, could still present potential targets because of the possible presence of radioactive materials on-site. At the BARC at

Trombay, there are two operating research reactors, three decommissioned reactors [Purnima-1, critical assembly, Purnima-2 Light Water Reactor (LWR), and Zerlina Pressurised Heavy Water Reactor (PHWR)].

- An expanding stockpile of weapon-usable plutonium can increase the risk of terrorists building an improvised nuclear explosive.
- The pool at Tarapur-1 was initially designed to store at most 72 metric tonnes of spent fuel. But it now contains more than twice that amount. Storing more than the originally designed amount of spent fuel can increase the risk of the spent fuel catching fire in the event of a loss of coolant incident. Also, the majority of Indian spent fuel pools at PHWRs most likely follow the CANDU design. The typical CANDU plant has its spent fuel pool outside the containment building, thus, it is more exposed to attack than a Boiling Water Reactor (BWR) pool.
- Presently, India uses the PUREX reprocessing method, which is considered to be proliferation-prone because it completely separates plutonium from the self-protecting highly radioactive materials in spent fuel. Thieves or terrorists can carry separated plutonium without suffering near-term harm to health.
- As India reprocess plutonium in bulk at Tarapur and Kalpakkam, there is likely to be loss of Material Unaccounted For (MUF). MUF can add up to many kilograms of plutonium not properly tracked, especially in a bulk handling facility. As India's rate of reprocessing and production of plutonium-based fuel increases, the likelihood of large amounts of MUF will increase.
- The high level radioactive waste storage areas also pose danger to an attack. India has developed the capability to immobilise the liquid waste in glass. Such immobilisation would create hard to disperse radioactive materials and would provide significant protection against radioactivity release from an attack on a high-level waste storage facility. To make effective use of this protection, India would have to operate the immobilisation at a rate commensurate with the production of waste.

On the other hand, according to a study by Rajesh M. Basrur and Friedrich Steinhäusler, Indian Nuclear Power Plants (NPPs) in themselves are characterised by a high level of built-in safety, which makes them relatively less vulnerable to sabotage. Several of the accident-related safety features of the CANDU reactor design used in India are also relevant to terrorist acts. For instance, the subdivision of the core into two thermal-hydraulic loops in most CANDU designs and hundreds of individual pressure tubes within each loop localises a loss-of-coolant incident. The large-volume, low-pressure, low-temperature moderator surrounding the pressure tubes keeps the risk of a fuel meltdown low. The steam generators are positioned well above the core, which promotes natural thermosyphoning (heat movement) in case shutdown cooling is lost. In addition, CANDU plants are enclosed by heavy concrete walls, including a reactor vault of minimum four feet thickness surrounding the nuclear core itself.[58] The CIRUS, a heavy water research reactor supplied by Canada in the 1950s, has been successfully shutdown permanently in 2010.[59] On the issue of MUF, as raised by Ferguson, India has been reprocessing plutonium successfully in bulk for many years now.

Beyond Design Basis Threats (BDB)

Every nuclear plant is designed and equipped to withstand some external threats. However, during the design and construction process, some event sequences are considered so unlikely that complete safeguards against the accident sequence are not built in. Forecasting the location and magnitude of the next earthquake or the size of the next tsunami is difficult. Nuclear plants situated outside of known geological danger zones "could pose greater accident threats in the event of an earthquake than those inside, as the former could have weaker protection built in".[60] The Fukushima I plant in Japan, for example, was "located in an area designated on Japan's seismic risk map as having a relatively low chance of a large earthquake and tsunami; when the 2011 tsunami arrived, it was in excess of anything its engineers had planned for."[61]

A nuclear 9/11 was not thought of until 2001 when terrorists razed the twin towers of the World Trade Centre. The degree of vulnerability of an NPP to air attacks is subject of intense investigation in the aftermath of 9/11. Preliminary results range from affirming that aircraft crashes may result in multiple-failure initiating events,[62] to negating that a commercial, fully fuelled large airliner could penetrate an NPP and release radioactivity,[63] or cause a major disaster. However, future terror designs would not follow the same tactics so far been followed. So, nuclear facilities and their safety and security arrangements must be prepared to deal with unforeseen eventualities.

In the Indian context, it is not known what effect an aircraft loaded with high explosives might have if it crashes into a reactor building. To assess whether Indian nuclear plants can withstand an aircraft crash, one needs to know how strong the containment buildings are. The containment buildings have concrete walls with a minimum thickness of four feet. Reactors like the Kaiga-1 and 2, Rajasthan-3 and 4 and Tarapur-3 and 4 are housed in double-domed structures. The domes of these PHWRs are constructed using the microsilica-based high performance concrete. They have also other added safety features like automatic, quick acting poison injection system to shut down the reactor in an emergency, and micro-processor-based systems for reactor protection and control.[64] However, the containment structures of the old commercial reactors like Tarapur are believed not as robust as those of modern reactors. Though Indian scientists have made extensive modifications in the safety structure of the reactor, its weak containment building might not withstand a large airplane crash.

According to Helmut Hirsch, the two VVER-1000 type plants being built by Russia at Kundankulam in the southern Indian state of Tamil Nadu may be inherently vulnerable to an airliner crash. Weaknesses of existing plants of this type include the inadequate strength of walls and roof, the location of the control room at the lower levels of the reactor building (necessitating early evacuation in case of melt-through of the containment), and close proximity of steam lines and isolation valves, creating vulnerability to a single blast.[65]

While the issue of crashing a hijacked aircraft on the facility seems a simple one, the chances of it crashing on the exact location depend upon the expertise of the hijacker. Even the degree of destruction of the facility depends upon the quantum of fuel in the aircraft. For instance, a civilian aircraft hijacked soon after the take-off stage would cause more damage to the facility as it would be carrying a large amount of fuel. Thus, the probability and consequences of an aircraft crashing into an Indian nuclear facility depend upon factors like the design of the containment building, the distance of the facility from the air base, the kind of aircraft used, and the technical expertise of the terrorists.

Besides an attack on the reactor building of an NPP, it is necessary to consider also the consequences of an aerial terrorist attack on the spent fuel storage pool. In India, these facilities typically have strong concrete walls with steel liners to protect against leaks. However, usually the roof structure may be vulnerable to an aircraft crashing into the storage area. Such pools hold on average up to ten times more long-lived radioactivity than a reactor core.[66] If the aircraft crash results in a loss of coolant from the pool and cannot be replaced in time, this would expose the fuel elements to the ambient environment, i.e. a mixture of burning jet fuel, air and steam. If the cooling water dropped to about 1 metre above the spent fuel rods, this would result in an excessively high radiation dose for an intervention team to replenish the coolant in time.[67] Once the fuel rods are exposed to steam and air, the zirconium cladding of the fuel elements would react exothermically resulting in a fire and releasing large amounts of radioactivity.

During transit of radioactive materials, unintentional opening of packages may occur in normal handling and transport conditions, and radiological damage may occur in severe accident or sabotaging conditions. Though the safe packaging of these materials for transport is a design basis threat consideration, their physical protection against wilful acts such as theft, sabotage, or unlawful removal and use of nuclear materials is beyond design basis planning. The transport of nuclear materials is probably the most vulnerable to hostile acts: the need for ensuring their physical protection has long been recognised but the responsibility rests entirely with the government of a state.[68]

According to the Uranium Corporation of India Ltd (UCIL) figures, the Jaduguda mines, India's primary source of indigenously produced uranium, have an approximate daily capacity of 1,000 tonnes. The mill processes yellow cake, which is transported to Hyderabad via trucks.[69] The Turamdih Uranium Mill can process up to 170 metric tonnes of yellow cake per year, and is currently being expanded to 230 metric tonnes per year in order to handle additional uranium from the Narwapahar mine.[70] The mill processes mined uranium, most of which is then shipped to the Nuclear Fuel Complex (NFC) in Hyderabad. The NFC caters to all nuclear facilities for a vast array of imported and domestically produced nuclear-related machinery and fuel. The vast domestic network of transit of nuclear materials and machinery can be targeted by the terrorists or insurgent groups active in respective areas.

However, the above hypothetical threat scenarios have been in the public domain and the nuclear establishment seems to have not overlooked them. Though absolute nuclear security is a misnomer, keeping in mind the probable security threats encompassing both design basis and beyond design basis threats, a 'defence indepth' safety and security framework is in place in and around India's nuclear facilities.

Defence by Design and Beyond: The Framework

The fact that the nuclear industry is vulnerable to both insider and outsider threats, therefore, demands a unique security arrangement. India seems to practise a layered nuclear security culture comprising a long-term policy, clear-cut organisation and personnel attitude at each level. A *nuclear security culture* that the nuclear community in India strives to establish is based on the foundation and belief that a "credible threat exists and that nuclear security is important." Therefore, the goal set is to achieve effective nuclear security by prioritising the security and management system, also by streamlining organisational and individual behaviour within a clear set of principles to be adhered to. India seems to have adopted a three-layer model for achieving nuclear security, similar to the chart below (Fig 1).

Fig 1: Three-Layer Model

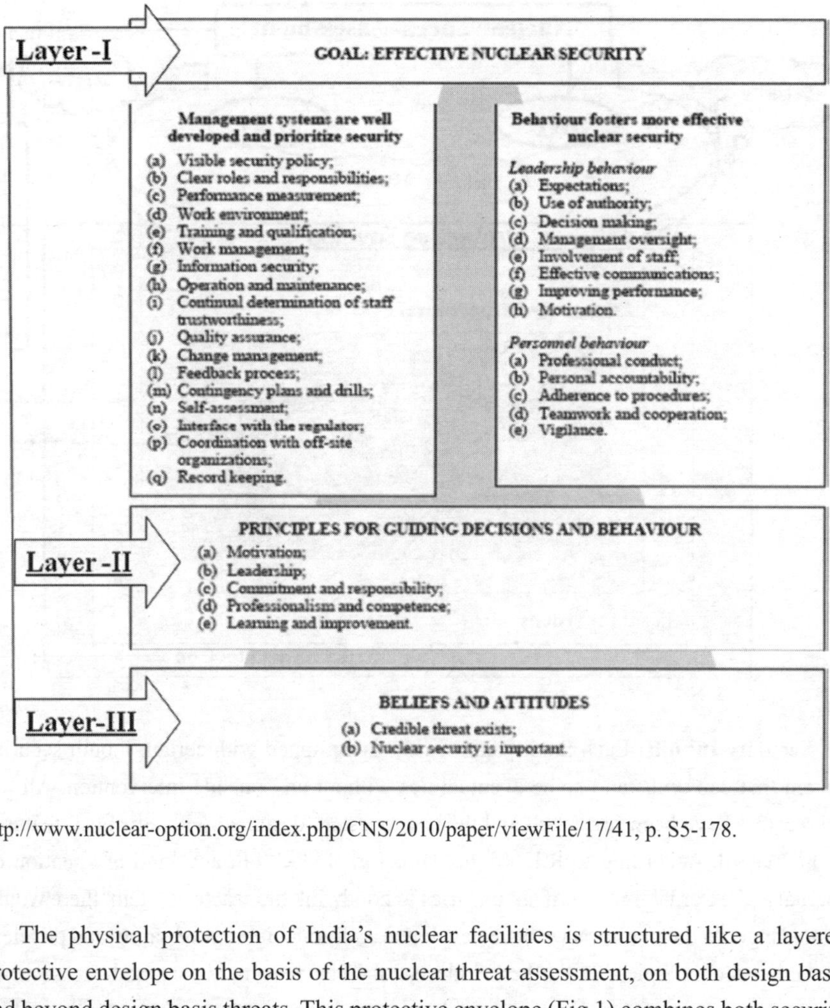

http://www.nuclear-option.org/index.php/CNS/2010/paper/viewFile/17/41, p. S5-178.

The physical protection of India's nuclear facilities is structured like a layered protective envelope on the basis of the nuclear threat assessment, on both design basis and beyond design basis threats. This protective envelope (Fig 1) combines both security and safety measures as nuclear safety and nuclear security have a common objective: the protection of people and the environment, and this can better be achieved through integration of both approaches. Therefore, India has adopted an in-depth and integrated approach to nuclear safety and security best suited to "ensure optimal solutions" to mitigate the threats and manage the emergencies.[71] Each protective layer sends feedback to the threat assessment apparatus to evaluate what additional or corrective arrangements are required. Each concentric square addresses specific security-safety threats, as shown in Fig 2.

Fig 2: Protective Security-Safety Envelope

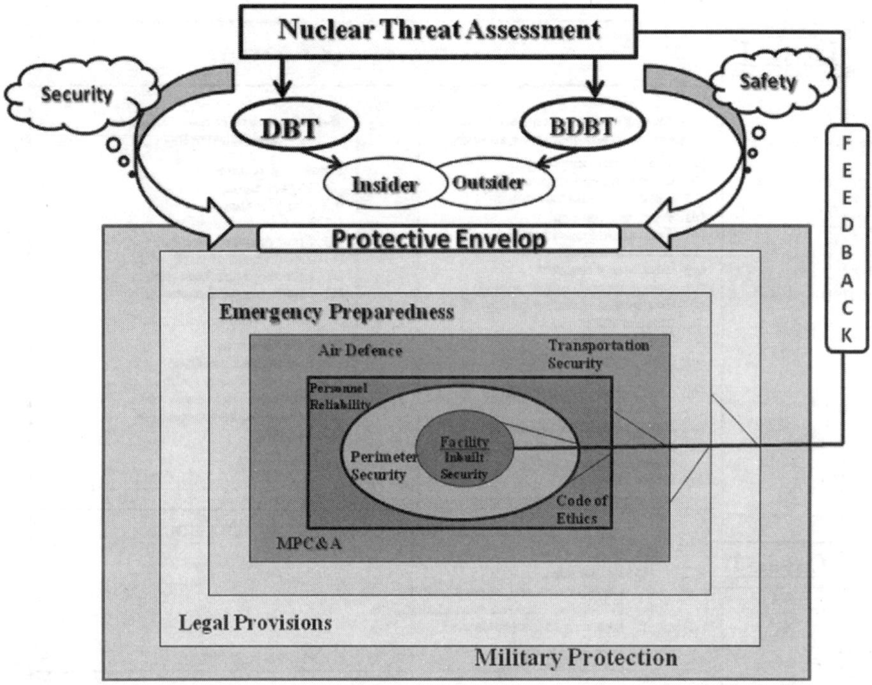

Security Inbuilt: Each facility and reactor is equipped with certain inbuilt security system that can withstand some eventualities without any outside intervention. All the old reactors have been revamped and the new ones are designed with advanced features in this regard. According to R.K. Sinha, Director, BARC, "In any kind of situation of internal and external threat or if anyone tries to hoodwink the reactor system, there would be no danger to the public as we have developed additional integrated safety and physical protection technologies."[72] Further, Sinha said, "The new hardware and the security system developed by BARC which have been already demonstrated successfully will be an additional feature to shut down the reactor automatically in case of any emergency".

The Indian PHWRs are designed with a double containment dome. The primary inner containment of pre-stressed concrete construction is designed to withstand the design basis accidents due to postulated loss of coolant accident and mainstream line break along with the earthquake load. The secondary containment barrier of reinforced concrete envelops the primary containment barrier and the annulus between the two containment walls is maintained under vacuum with a provision of continuous monitoring for any accidental release of radioactivity in the annulus space from the inner primary containment. This double containment ensures zero ground release to the environment.[73] The double barrier also serves to resist the external and internal missile impact loads effectively. Accidents due to an external missile such as aircraft impact has a probability of ~1E-07[74] and adequate care is taken to exclude this event, with proper siting criteria and selecting a safe Screen Distance Value (SDV) as per the standard international safety and design code guidelines. During site selection, if the site falls within SDV for different types of airfields, a probabilistic study of an aircraft crashing on the installation, considering flight frequencies, is carried out. If this probability is not acceptably low, the site is considered unsuitable for establishing an NPP.[75]

However, as part of the safety evaluation programme, Indian containment structures have also been assessed for beyond design basis accidents such as aircraft impact load. Non-linear transient dynamic analysis of the 500MWe Indian PHWR nuclear containment has been carried out for the impact of Boeing and Airbus categories of aircraft operated in India. The impulsive load time history is generated based on the momentum transfer of the crushable aircraft (soft missiles) of the Boeing and Airbus families on the containment structure. A study conducted by Mukesh Kukreja, R.K. Singh, K.K. Vaze and H.S. Kushwaha of the Reactor Safety Division, BARC, on the damage evaluation of 500 MWe PHWRs containment for aircraft impact concludes that this kind of event would cause "local deformation" but the containment is "capable of absorbing the full impulsive load."[76]

The study included the analyses of the Outer Containment Wall (OCW) single model and the combined model with OCW and Inner Containment Wall (ICW) for impulsive loading due to aircraft impact. Initially, the load is applied on the OCW single model and subsequently the load is transferred to the ICW after the local perforation of the OCW is noticed in the transient simulation. In the first stage of the analysis, it is demonstrated that the OCW would suffer local perforation with a peak local deformation of 117 mm for the impact due to the B707-320 and 196 mm due to the impact of the A300B4, without loss of the overall integrity. However, this first barrier (OCW) cannot absorb the full impulsive load. In the second stage of the analysis of the combined model, the ICW is subjected to lower impulse duration as the load is transferred after 0.19 sec for the B707-320 and 0.24 sec for the A300B4 due to the local perforation of the OCW. This results in the local deformation of the ~115 mm for the B707-320 and 124mm for the A300B4 in the ICW, and together both the structures (OCW and ICW) are capable of absorbing the full impulsive load.[77]

India's AHWR300-LEU, with an estimated design life of 100 years, requires no exclusion zone beyond the plant boundary. The reactor will use "natural circulation" to remove heat from its core under both operating and shutdown conditions. In case primary and secondary shutdown systems are not available due to failure of all active systems or malicious employee action, passive injection of a "poison" – a high neutron absorbing liquid—into the moderator, will shut down the reactor.[78] If the coolant is not available due to a Loss of Coolant Accident (LOCA), the Emergency Core Cooling System (ECCS) will remove the heat by passive means. If the primary coolant tube ruptures, a large flow of water from the accumulators will cool the reactor initially. Later, the core will be cooled by the injection of cold water from a 7,000 cubic metre Gravity Driven Water Pool (GDWP), as a passive water sink located at the top of the reactor building, giving a grace period of three days. After that, the Passive Containment Cooling System (PCCS) provides long-term containment cooling.[79]

The "Status Report 74 – Indian 220 MWe PHWR (IPHWR-220)" enumerates numerous physical-technical modifications undertaken in old atomic power stations.[80] Major modifications introduced in NAPS-1&2 on the basis of standardised Indian PHWR units include: two diverse and fast acting shutdown systems, double containment of reactor building, water filled calandria vault, integral calandria-end shield assembly, zircaloy-2 pressure tube separated from the calandria tube by 4 loose fit garter springs per coolant channel with inter-space between the pressure tube and calandria tube filled and purged with carbon dioxide to monitor pressure tube leak by monitoring the dew point of carbon dioxide. The material of the pressure tubes in KAPS-2 was changed to Zr-2.5 per cent Nb and loose fit garter springs were replaced by garter springs kept tight on pressure tubes.

The major improvements in the designs of units like KGS-1, KGS-2, RAPS-3, RAPS-4, RAPS-5, RAPS-6, KGS-3 and KGS-4, according to the Status Report, include a valve-less primary heat transport system and a unitised control room concept. In addition, the design of these units also includes improvements in the control and instrumentation system and incorporation of computer-based systems to match with the advancement in technology. The older Indian PHWR units have undergone major refurbishment to bring them at par with the latest units. For all old PHWR units, the En Mass Coolant Channel Replacement (EMCCR) campaign has been completed. With this, all Indian PHWR units (except RAPS-1) will have Zr-2.5 per cent Nb pressure tubes with 4 tight fit garter springs. All these efforts intend to strengthen the safety and security of the plants to withstand any anticipated eventuality.

Perimeter Security: Security and safety begin right from the site selection stage and then all through the design stage of Indian nuclear facilities. In the siting of a nuclear power plant, the zoning concept is followed (Fig 3) that helps in enforcing the emergency preparedness as well as periodic exercises for such facilities. Generally, three zones are defined for the control of the population. The innermost zone, called the Exclusion Zone (EZ), surrounds the plant and defines an area directly under the control of the plant. The second zone, an annulus around the exclusion zone, defines the Sterilised Zone (SZ) where the growth of population is limited by administrative control. The outermost zone, the Emergency Planning Zone (EPZ), defines the minimum distance to a high population centre. The Indian siting code[81] defines the exclusion area of at least 1.5 km radius around the plant. This area shall be at the exclusive control of the station and no public habitation shall be allowed in the area. Under design basis accident conditions, a member of the public shall not receive a dose equivalent more than 0.1 Sv for the whole body and 0.5 Sv for the thyroid of children. The sterilised area extends upto 5 km around the plant established by administrative measures. In this area, natural growth is permitted but planned expansion of activities leading to enhanced population growth is not allowed. On the lines of the above, all NPP sites in India have an exclusion boundary radius of 1.6 km, except the Kaiga site, where the radius is 2.3 km. Where more than one twin station is sited, each must have an exclusion radius of 1.6 km.

In the EPZ that expands up to 16 km, though there is no restriction on population settlements, constant monitoring is undertaken for security and emergency planning purposes. Close surveillance is kept over transportation networks, means of communication, etc. Considering the advanced means of communication and transport facilities available now, intruders can stay outside the security circles but traverse the distance easily to enter at the appropriate time. Also, to protect the population from

Fig 3

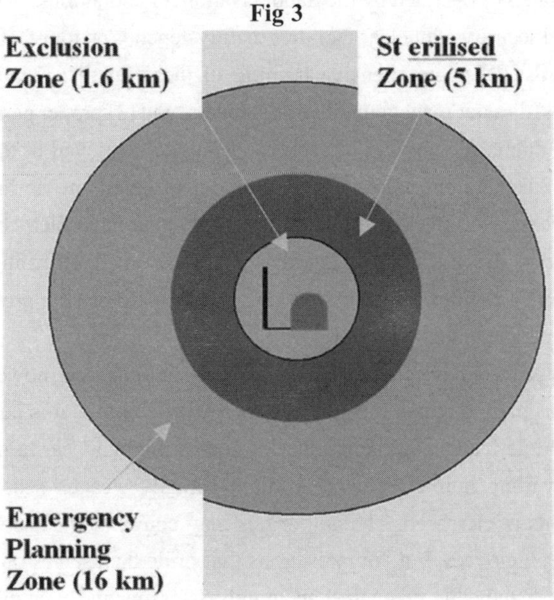

bigger magnitude nuclear disasters, it may be prudent to put in place another security ring covering a larger area, perhaps of 25 km radius.

The CISF is in charge of providing security to the nuclear facilities of the country. It has developed the necessary ability to deploy specially-trained first responders in case of a nuclear attack. Four companies of the CISF have been sanctioned, and specialised training is being imparted to some 400 personnel. This elite force is deployed in four locations across the country: Ghaziabad unit to cater to Delhi and other northern areas, Ranchi unit to cater the eastern areas, Kota unit for the western, and Chennai unit for the southern part. Many officers of these units have already undergone eight weeks of nuclear and biological response training in the United States, and others are being trained to share skills with fellow CISF members in a train-the-trainer approach.[82]

In 2004, India's Border Security Force (BSF) announced that it was forming a battalion with special skills in countering Nuclear, Biological, Chemical (NBC) threats. The special battalion receives training from nuclear experts at BARC. In April 2002, the Chairman of India's Nuclear Power Corporation announced that he was cognisant of the terrorist threat and mentioned that the Department of Atomic Energy (DAE) and CISF have performed security drills at nuclear facilities. The International Atomic Energy Agency (IAEA) has provided security training for the Indian officials. Also, Indian experts have participated in the IAEA-sponsored International Training Course on the Physical Protection of Nuclear Facilities and Materials operated by the Sandia National Laboratories.[83]

The physical security of nuclear facilities mainly depends on four factors: (1) adequate number of guards; (2) comprehensive training of these guards; (3) strict monitoring, warning systems, disaster management arrangements; and (3) proper personnel reliability procedures. No doubt, the number of security personnel deployed in the nuclear power plants must be adequate but increasing the number of guards in the facilities does not necessarily increase the safety of the facilities. More guards, in fact, could increase the threat from insiders. Even if the new guards are well screened, screening procedures are not foolproof, and a rapid increase in new employees increases the probability of some malintentioned people being admitted.

The DAE appears to have attended to all the above four aspects, however, considering India's ambitious plan to expand its nuclear energy programme, it is necessary to avoid complacency. While increasing the number of guards might appear to increase security, certain countervailing human behaviour might actually weaken security, if only the number of guards is increased. The authorities may convince themselves that they are recruiting loyal employees, but "organisations that pride themselves on high degrees of personnel loyalty can be biased against accurately assessing and even discussing the risk of insider threats and unauthorised acts." Therefore, strict implementation and periodical assessment of an advanced personnel reliability programme is most important.

Personnel Reliability, Code of Ethics and Conduct: The effectiveness of any security system is ultimately determined by the training, reliability and integrity of the individuals who operate it. Within the confines of a national nuclear complex, the potentially catastrophic consequences of disloyalty, exploitation or a violent workplace incident are always a cause of concern, therefore, Personnel Reliability Programmes (PRPs) are an essential piece of any nuclear security regime. If the integrity and stability of those with access to nuclear materials is not assured, the most rigorous Material Protection Control and Accounting (MPC&A) system is vulnerable to sabotage or circumvention. However, only limited information on India's programme is available in the public domain and it must be acknowledged that "perfect" PRPs do not exist even in the advanced countries.

Since civilians maintain operational control of nuclear activities, personnel reliability is a serious matter in India. India's nuclear establishment follows a personnel reliability programme designed with several lines of inquiry to develop a comprehensive picture of the individual in question.[84] In the first instance, a background check is conducted to verify the identity, credit history, criminal history, reputation and character of the employee. Psychological and medical screening is used to evaluate the mental health and stability of the individual taking into consideration aspects like depression, schizophrenia, epilepsy, high/low blood pressure and other disorders.

Additionally, a detailed interview to verify background information and elucidate other potential concerns is conducted at the time of employment or when any sensitive task is being assigned. Periodic reviews of job performance and co-worker interaction are standard means of ensuring that an employee's reliability remains high over time, and an individual's after work activities may also be monitored. Issues like alcohol abuse/dependency, drug abuse, conviction of, or involvement, in a serious incident, an adverse medical – physical and mental – condition or serous progressive illness, lack of motivation, suicide attempt or threat if noticed in any employee, may lead to decertification for nuclear duty.

The Atomic Energy Regulatory Board (AERB), realising the importance of personnel ethics in discharging sensitive nuclear duties, has developed a formal code of professional ethical values for the employees to adhere to.[85] In order to ensure all activities in nuclear and radiation facilities in India are conducted in compliance with the Atomic Energy Act, 1962, the officials shall be guided by the principles to (1) to maintain a high level of professional competence; (2) maintain a high level of honesty and integrity and be principled and consistent in application of regulations. The core value the officials need to follow, first, is development, dissemination and unbiased interpretation of safety regulations. Second, the officials need to objectively deal with facts without distortion by personal feelings or biases and ability to evaluate information. Third, a high standard of integrity is highly desired among the officials to maintain the confidentiality of information and live up to the commitments. Lastly, all professionals have to maintain a high standard of honesty, have the courage to choose the right course, be fair in discharging responsibilities and respect the values of others. All the employees of the AERB have to accept the "statement of responsibility" to uphold the highest standards of professional conduct in the performance of their professional duties.[86]

Similarly, the Nuclear Power Corporation of India Ltd. (NPCIL), which runs the nuclear power plants in the country, has mandated a "Code of Ethics and Conduct" asking "commitment for ethical professional conduct from every director and senior employee."[87] The code, consisting of imperatives formulated as statements of personal commitment, bestows responsibilities for the design, construction, operation and maintenance of nuclear power projects. Also the code mandates that employees maintain confidentiality of information, strive to achieve the highest quality, mutual trust and transparency, and avoid a conflict of personal interest with the interest of the company at large.

The NPCIL has also instituted a Vigilance Directorate with the objective to eliminate or minimise factors which provide an opportunity for corruption or malpractices through indepth examination, regular inspection, ensuring prompt observance of proper conduct, and ethics relating to integrity.[88] According to the corporation, it has maintained surveillance on employees who have access to sensitive parts of the plants, and has done regular and surprise inspections to try to detect possible misconduct.[89]

However, occasional reports about incidents of misconduct and carelessness in different departments of the establishment have rendered the public an impression that all is not well in the nuclear industry. Again, putting in place novel regulations does not necessarily enhance reliability, and India has a bad record of implementation of policy measures. It has to ensure that the ambitious nuclear energy expansion programme that India has embarked on is achieved without compromising the safety, security and quality of the industry as a whole.

Material Protection Control and Accounting (MPC&A): Incidents of nuclear material going missing and of smuggling are increasingly reported these days. With the increase in nuclear activities in the decades ahead, such incidents might also increase. It can be speculated whether a nuclear terror plot has already moved beyond the theft of nuclear material as a substantial amount of nuclear material has already gone missing in different parts of the world. The standard procedure is physical protection or material control accompanied by an accounting system to provide precision if physical protection and control fail.[90] Nuclear material control implies the adoption of "control and monitoring measures" to prevent loss. It also involves maintaining a physical inventory of the materials. Regular accounting makes it possible to detect if nuclear materials have been diverted. An effective nuclear MPC&A system tracks the quality and quantity of nuclear materials and their authorised movement, which helps to detect if there has been any unauthorised removal of such materials.[91]

State parties to a safeguards agreement with the IAEA are required to use material control and accounting as a strategy for keeping nuclear materials safe and secure. India, being a responsible party, has devised a comprehensive material protection control and accounting programme comprising three basic elements: (1) the legislative and regulatory framework; (2) an integrated physical protection programme for facilities and materials; and (3) a comprehensive "Nuclear Material Accounting and Control System" (NUMAC).[92]

While all facilities are covered by the multi-layered security system, facility-specific NUMAC arrangements are in place under an Officer in Charge to oversee each facility. The Inventory Information and Control and Data Management Section and a control laboratory compile and preserve the information. The activities of all NUMAC facilities are coordinated through the central NUMAC cell at the DAE. At the top, the Senior Coordination Committee reviews the NUMAC reports to initiate action, if needed. The responsibility of NUMAC is to identify nuclear material by type, nature and amount; to implement the accounting and control mechanism; to ensure measurement capabilities and statistical analysis of reported data as efficient; to oversee auditing practices and implement inspection and verification practices; and to ensure the compliance of constructive measurements, periodic inspection, verification and auditing and documentation of inventory changes and discrepancies thereof.[93]

The radiation leak in April 2010 in New Delhi's Mayapuri scrap market raised serious questions with regard to the nuclear safety and security in India.[94] The IAEA, while demanding an explanation from India, called it "the most serious global instance of radiation exposure since 2006." But, a deeper understanding of the issue would reveal that the incident was not owing to a lack in India's regulatory or technological competence, but because of the inevitable gap between the knowledge and technology it possesses and the magnitude of the challenges on the ground. First of all, Cobalt-60 was used in the Delhi University Chemistry Department irradiator that was received from Canada in 1970, much before the setting up of AERB. It is easy to point fingers at the

AERB as it had no inventory of radioactive materials sourced from abroad prior to its own existence. But, as per the end-user agreement, the onus is on the supplier to ensure return of the defunct radioisotopes. At best, the user could have taken the responsibility of their safekeep or disposal.

However, all these years, BARC has been collecting the materials from the users for disposal. How the gamma cell irradiator of Delhi University was overlooked is undoubtedly a matter of serious concern. First, the facilities that received such materials before the establishment of the AERB have not been accounted for by it subsequently. Second, the personnel in charge of these materials in Delhi University have retired and since the irradiator was not in use for 25 years, it was completely forgotten by the subsequent staff in charge that it contained radioactive material. Third, neither is the scrap market equipped with radiation detection devices nor have the scrap workers any radiation-related awareness. So, there exist serious gaps at each level, starting from the suppliers' responsibility to the users' onus, from waste disposal to public awareness.

This does not mean that India has no capability to safeguard its radioactive sources or to quickly respond to a radioactive disaster. In fact, the Delhi Police was able to promptly trace the source of the supply and BARC was able to effectively contain the situation. Also the medical team responded efficiently in saving many lives. But what is worrisome is the complacency and callousness about possible accidents like this. Before the AERB was set up in 1983, the Directorate of Radiation Protection (DRP) was responsible for the radiation protection programme, including radiation surveillance in hospitals, industries and research institutes. This suggests that the coordination between the DRP and AERB was absent after the former was established. However, BARC has now prepared a comprehensive inventory of all the radioactive materials imported, used and disposed of in the country.

Security During Transportation: Considering the magnitude of use of radioactive material and the expanse of nuclear related facilities in the country, provisions for safe transport of radioactive materials are of the utmost importance to protect against advertent and inadvertent opening, theft, sabotage or unlawful removal. Since India is part of the UN Convention on the Physical Protection of Nuclear Material (INFCIRC/225/Rev.1), the AERB has stipulated a Safety Guide on security of radioactive material during transport (AERB/NRF-TS/SG-10) that prescribes the requirements for ensuring safety in the movement of radioactive material through the public domain.[95] This guide specifies rules, regulations and standard procedures to be followed in the packaging, shipment and protective measures to be arranged during the process of transportation. Different security levels are specified for different materials (Category I to 5) depending upon their degree of fissile characteristics and the danger involved. This includes, amongst others, prior approval for the shipment, a special vehicle, security locks, appropriate training of the personnel involved, additional security and escort by armed guards, secure communication support and on line tracking system, etc.[96]

Beside the physical arrangements of transport systems, India is a member of the Container Security Initiative (CSI) and the automated container screening and information exchange provisions of the CSI arrangement help in intercepting the movement of such materials. At present, only the Jawaharlal Nehru Port Trust (JNPT), Mumbai, is part of the initiative. India may consider making its other major ports CSI-compliant in the future. Also, at the major transit points like border crossings, airports and other sea ports, radiation monitoring devices have been installed to track the unauthorised movement of radioactive material. The police and border security forces have been given the necessary training to identify and take necessary action if such an event is noticed.

Air Defence Provisions: There have been reports in the media that claimed that the Atomic Energy Commission was seeking "no-fly zones' over nuclear installations to prevent terrorist attacks from the air.[97] Within a month after 9/11, New Delhi promulgated no-fly zone restrictions around nuclear power plants. However, no information is available regarding whether these facilities are adequately protected by anti-aircraft defences. Nevertheless, security at India's nuclear installations has been improved in many other ways. (The Indian Coast Guard deploys additional boats off the coast of Bombay to guard BARC.) Also, additional anti-aircraft guns have been requisitioned for deployment to the Narora atomic power plant in Rajasthan and for two atomic power plants in southern India.[98]

Taking no chances with its security following the Mumbai terror attacks (26/11), India has decided to tighten security around its key nuclear installations. As a step in this direction, the Directorate General of Civil Aviation (DGCA) has declared a no-fly zone around the Kalpakkam nuclear plant in the southern state of Tamil Nadu.[99] The civil aviation agency has issued notices, prohibiting any air activities up to 10,000 ft above Kalpakkam. However, the status of other nuclear facilities is unknown. Though BARC is a sensitive nuclear research facility at Trombay, it may be impossible to make it a no-fly zone as it comes in the flight path of the main runway at the airport in the country's financial capital.[100] Therefore, it is expected that the facility must be secured through alternative means of air defence.

The other two concentric squires of security arrangements are more in the nature of regulatory and emergency preparations and the outermost blanket is the military protection against any external aggression. While various legal provisions – both national and international treaty obligations – provide the basis for controlling the use or misuse of radioactive materials, the 18 Emergency Response Centres with quick response teams are located in various parts of the country to contain any nuclear disaster promptly. All these protective layers are arranged primarily to mitigate both the design basis threats and threats that may emanate beyond the design so that the benefits of nuclear technology are exploited fully while protecting the workers, the environment and the public at large from the adverse impact of national nuclear activities. However, the apprehension and fear of a nuclear disaster will continue to emerge in India, firstly, as a corollary of the global concern for nuclear terrorism and, secondly, due to the volatile regional politico-security environment that India situated in.

Notes

1. Unstarred Question No. 3097, by Yogi Adityanath and M.K. Raghavan, "Threat to Atomic Power Plant," Parliament Debate (Lok Sabha), answered on March 15, 2011, by Minister of State in the Ministry of Home Affairs Shri Mullappally Ramachandran, [Online: web] accessed on May 10, 2011, URL: http://164.100.47.132/LssNew/psearch/QResult15.aspx?qref=103590.
2. Ibid.
3. "Critical Infrastructure Protection," Department of Homeland Security, USA, [Online: web] accessed on May 14, 2011, URL: http://www.dhs.gov/files/programs/critical.shtm.
4. Robert A. Miller, Irving Lachow, "Strategic Fragility: Infrastructure Protection and National Security in the Information Age," *Defence Horizons*, November 01, 2007. http://www.carlisle.army.mil/DIME/documents/Miller%20and%20Lachow%20Strategic%20Fragility.pdf.
5. Tadjibayev A. Furkhat and Sattarova Y. Feruza, "Categorization of Critical Infrastructures and Critical Information Infrastructures," *International Journal of Advanced Science and Technology*, Vol. 8, July 2009, p. 19, URL: http://www.sersc.org/journals/IJAST/vol8/3.pdf.
6. Charles D. Ferguson and Philip D. Reed, "Seven Principles of Highly Effective Nuclear Energy Programs," Council on Foreign Relations, May 26-29, 2009, [Online: web] accessed on May 14, 2011, URL: http://www.cfr.org/content/thinktank/Ferguson_SevenPrinciples_NuclearEnergy.pdf, p. 7.
7. Trevor Findlay, "The Future of Nuclear Energy to 2030 and its Implications for Safety, Security and Nonproliferation," URL: http://www2.carleton.ca/cctc/ccms/wp-content/ccms-files/nef_part3.pdf, p. 15.
8. UNSC Resolution 1540 (2004) establishes binding obligations on all UN member states under Chapter VII of the UN Charter to take, and enforce, effective measures against the proliferation of WMD, their means of delivery and related materials. If fully implemented, it can help ensure that no state or non-state actor is a source or beneficiary of WMD proliferation. "Resolution 1540 (2004)," URL: http://daccess-dds-ny.un.org/doc/UNDOC/GEN/N04/328/43/PDF/N0432843.pdf?OpenElement.
9. The summit convened by President Obama in 2010 reaffirmed the fundamental responsibility of states, consistent with their respective international obligations, to maintain effective security of all nuclear materials, which include nuclear materials used in nuclear weapons, and nuclear facilities under their control; and emphasised the importance of robust national legislative and regulatory frameworks for nuclear security. "Communiqué from Washington Nuclear Security Summit," URL: http://www.america.gov/st/texttrans-english/2010/April/20100413171855eaifas0.6155773.html.

10. Findlay, n. 7, p. 14.
11. DBT includes such characteristics as the number of attackers, their training, and the weapons and tactics they could use that can be defended against by the inbuilt design of the reactors that can withstand such attempts without releasing radioactivity.
12. Igor Khripunov, Carlton Stoiber, "Nuclear Security and Nuclear Counterterrorism: Streamlining and Updating the Legal Framework," Centre for International Trade & Security, University of Georgia, 2010, p. 12.
13. "Application of Radiation in Medicine, Industry and Research," http://www.aerb.gov.in/T/sj/book/chapter9.pdf, p. 146.
14. Charles D. Ferguson, "Assessing the Vulnerability of the Indian Civilian Nuclear Program to Military and Terrorist Attack," http://npolicy.org/userfiles/image/Assessing%20Vulnerability%20of%20Indian%20Nuclear%20Program%20to%20Attack_pdf.pdf, accessed on June 20, 2011.
15. Martin Matishak, "International Partners to Discuss Removing Radiological Materials From Lighthouses," http://www.globalsecuritynewswire.org/gsn/nw_20110525_4387.php, May 25, 2011.
16. "DAE, CISF Review Security of Nuclear Power Plants," *The Times of India*, April 30, 2011.
17. "Terror Threat to N-Sites," The *Times of India*, November 23, 2006.
18. "Security Beefed up at BARC," *The Times of India* (New Delhi), August 13, 2006.
19. Andrew Prosser, "Nuclear Trafficking Routes: Dangerous Trends in South Asia," Centre for Defence Information, November 24, 2004, http://www.cdi.org/PDFs/TraffickingSmuggling.pdf, p. 9.
20. "Five Arrested for Alleged 'Uranium' Smuggling, say Police," http://www.spacewar.com/reports/Five_arrested_for_alleged_uranium_smuggling_say_police_999.html, September 11, 2008.
21. "Water Cooler at Indian Nuclear Plant Contaminated," *Voice of America*, November 29, 2009, http://www.voanews.com/english/news/Water-Cooler-at-Indian-Nuclear-Plant-Contaminated-78087742.html.
22. Ankica Cizmek, "Nuclear Security and Nuclear Security Culture", Proceedings of the 8th International Conference on Nuclear Option in Countries with Small and Medium Electricity Grids, Dubrovnik, Croatia, March 16-20 2010, S5-171.
23. Military Police, Army Regulation 190–54, "Security of Nuclear Reactors and Special Nuclear Materials," Headquarters, Department of the Army Washington, DC, April 30, 1993, URL: http://www.fas.org/irp/doddir/army/ar190-54.pdf.
24. Daniel Hirsch, "The Truck Bomb and Insider Threats to Nuclear Facilities," Nuclear Control Institute, 1987 URL: http://www.nci.org/g-h/hirschtb.htm.
25. Black and VEATCH, "Cyber Security for the Nuclear Power Industry," http://www.bv.com/Downloads/Resources/Brochures/rsrc_ENR_NuclearCyberSecurity.pdf.
26. "Mahalingam's Body Identified; Handed Over to Family," June 14, 2009, http://www.indianexpress.com/news/mahalingams-body-identified;-handed-over-to/476238/.
27. Times News Network, "Kaiga Nuke Plant Leak was Inside Job: Kakodkar," *The Times of India*, November 30, 2009.
28. Preety Acharya, "Senior Barc Scientist Found Murdered," http://www.dnaindia.com/mumbai/report_senior-barc-scientist-found-murdered_1351839, February 24, 2010.
29. "Another Scientist Found Dead," URL: http://www.deccanherald.com/content/56283/another-scientist-found-dead.html.

30. Charles D. Ferguson, "Assessing the Vulnerability of the Indian Civilian Nuclear Program to Military and Terrorist Attack" [Online: web] accessed on May 17, 2011, URL: http://npolicy.org/userfiles/image/Assessing%20Vulnerability%20of%20Indian%20Nuclear%20Program%20to%20Attack_pdf.pdf, p. 156.
31. Ibid.
32. Vishal Thapar, "Ammo Fires: Not Quite Accidental," *Hindustan Times*, August 5, 2001.
33. Raj Chengappa, *Weapons of Peace* (New Delhi: HarperCollins, 2000), p. 422.
34. Kishore Kuchibhotla and Matthew McKinzie, "Nuclear Terrorism and Nuclear Accidents in South Asia," http://www.stimson.org/southasia/pdf/reducingnukes-section5.pdf.
35. *Ibid.*
36. Michael Krepon and Zaid Haider, "Reducing Nuclear Dangers in South Asia," Report No. 50, Henry L. Stimson Centre, January 2004, p. 24.
37. Ferguson, n. 30.
38. B. Raman, "Al Qaeda's Shadow over India?," *International Terrorism Monitor*, Paper No. 242, South Asia Analysis Group, http://www.saag.org/papers23/paper2267.html.
39. David Albright, *Al Qaida's Nuclear Programme: Through the Window of Seized Documents*, Nautilus Institute Special Forum 47, November 6, 2002, URL: www.nautilus.org/fora/special-Policy-Forum/47_Albright.html#sect2.
40. *The 9/11 Commission Report: Final Report of the National Commission on Terrorist Attacks Upon the United States*, Official Government Edition (Washington, DC: US Government Printing Office, 2004), URL: http://www.gpoasccess.gov/911/pdf/full-report.pdf, p. 172.
41. "India - Maoist Insurgency (1980 – First Combat Deaths)," *Armed Conflicts Report*, February 2010 http://www.ploughshares.ca/libraries/ACRText/ACR-IndiaAP.html.
42. "India is 'Losing Maoist Battle," http://news.bbc.co.uk/2/hi/south_asia/8256692.stm.
43. Ibid.
44. Ashok Handoo, "Naxal Problem Needs a Holistic Approach," *Press Information Bureau*, http://www.pib.nic.in/newsite/erelease.aspx?relid=50833.
45. "Rising Maoists Insurgency in India", *Global Politician*, January 15, 2007.
46. Ibid.
47. "No Threat to Kaiga Nuclear Plant," http://naxalwatch.blogspot.com/2007/07/no-threat-to-kaiga-nuclear-plant.html, July 31, 2007.
48. Seema Mustafa, "Naxals Quietly Expand Base," *The Asian Age*, October 14, 2007.
49. Manasi Kakatkar-Kulkarni, "A Naxal Threat to India's Nuclear Arsenal?," http://india.foreignpolicyblogs.com/2010/06/29/a-naxal-threat-to-indias-nuclear-arsenal/.
50. Mark Thompson, "An Unstable Nation with WMD – and Extremists Who Would Die for Them. How Afraid Should we be?," *Time*, January 14, 2008.
51. Statement by Tapan Choudhury, Adviser (Minister), Ministry of Science & Technology of Bangladesh at the 51st Session of General Conference of IAEA Vienna, September 17, 2007, http://www.iaea.org/About/Policy/GC/GC51/Statements/bangladesh.pdf.
52. "Testimony of Kamal Mitra Chenoy, U.S. Commission on International Religious Freedom, Hearing on Communal Violence in Gujarat, India and the U.S. Response," June 10, 2002, http://coalitionagainstgenocide.org/reports/2002/uscirf.10jun2002.kamal.pdf.
53. "Design Basis Threat (DBT)," http://www-ns.iaea.org/security/dbt.asp?s=4.
54. "Design Basis Threat," http://www.dtic.mil/doctrine/jel/doddict/data/d/18945.html.
55. Ibid.
56. Mark Holt and Anthony Andrews, "Nuclear Power Plant Security and Vulnerabilities," *Con-*

gressional Research Service, August 23, 2010, p. 3.

57. Ferguson, n. 30.
58. Rajesh M. Basrur and Friedrich Steinhäusler, "Nuclear and Radiological Terrorism Threats for India: Risk Potential and Countermeasures," http://jps.anl.gov/vol1_iss1/3-Threats_for_India.pdf, p.7.
59. "Research N-reactor CIRUS to Shutdown Permanently on December 31," *Daily News & Analysis*, December 18, 2010.
60. Declan Butler, "Reactors, Residents and Risk," http://www.nature.com/news/2011/110421/full/472400a.html.
61. Ibid.
62. "Massachusetts Congressman Says Nuclear Plants Are Vulnerable," *New York Times*, March 25, 2002.
63. Nuclear Energy Institute, *Evaluation of Aircraft Impact on Nuclear Power Plant Structures*, Report NEI-02-04, 2002.
64. Department of Atomic Energy, *Nuclear India*, July-August 2000, available at: http://www.dae.gov.in/ni/niju100/niju100.htm.
65. Helmut Hirsch, "Vulnerability of VVER-1000 Nuclear Power Plants to Passenger Aircraft Crash," WISE, November 2001, http://www.antenna.nl/wise/terrorism/112001vver.html.
66. Hui Zhang, "Radiological Terrorism: Sabotage of Spent Fuel Pools," *INESAP: International Network of Engineers and Scientists Against Proliferation*, issue 22, December 2003, pp 75-78.
67. Rajesh M. Basrur and Friedrich Steinhäusler, "Nuclear and Radiological Terrorism Threats for India: Risk Potential and Countermeasures," http://jps.anl.gov/vol1_iss1/3-Threats_for_India.pdf, p. 4.
68. Ha-Vinh Phuong, "Physically Protecting Nuclear Materials in Transport," *IAEA Bulletin*, Spring 1985, http://www.iaea.org/Publications/Magazines/Bulletin/Bull271/27104582224.pdf, p. 22.
69. Ritu Sarin, "Hunt for Yellow Cake," *The Indian Express*, June 4, 1998.
70. "Uranium: Resources, Production and Demand," Nuclear Energy Agency, Organisation for Economic Cooperation and Development, 1995, p. 195.
71. An Integrated Approach to Nuclear Safety and Nuclear Security, World Institute for Nuclear Security, 2010, p. 5, 10.
72. "Indian Nuclear Reactors Prepared for any Internal, External Threat," http://www.dnaindia.com/mumbai/report_indian-nuclear-reactors-prepared-for-any-internal-external-threat_1475513, December 2, 2010.
73. Mukesh Kukreja, et al., "Damage Evaluation of 500 MWe Indian Pressurized Heavy Water Reactor Nuclear Containment for Aircraft Impact," Paper # J03-2, Transactions of the 17th International Conference on Structural Mechanics in Reactor Technology (SMiRT 17) Prague, Czech Republic, August 17 –22, 2003, p. 1.
74. N.F. Zorn and G.I. Schueller, "On the Failure Probability of the Containment under Accidental Aircraft Impact," *NED*, Vol.91, 1986, pp. 277-286.
75. A.D. Roshan, P. Shylamoni, and Sourav Acharya, *Monograph on Siting of Nuclear Power Plants*, AERB, Civil & Structural Engineering Division, http://www.aerb.gov.in/t/sj/Siting.pdf, p. 13.
76. Kukreja, et al. n. 73.
77. "Abstract," Ibid.

78. K.S. Parthasarathy, "India's Innovative Nuclear Power Reactor," http://www.thehindu.com/sci-tech/technology/article450927.ece, June 10, 2010.
79. Ibid.
80. "Status Report 74 - Indian 220 MWe PHWR (IPHWR-220)," http://aris.iaea.org/ARIS/download.cgi?requested_doc=report&doc_id=74&type_of_output=pdf, April 4, 2011.
81. "Site Considerations of Nuclear Power Plants for Off-site Emergency Preparedness," AERB Safety Guide No. AERB/NPP/SG/S-8, Atomic Energy Regulatory Board, Mumbai, October 2005, http://www.aerb.gov.in/T/PUBLICATIONS/CODESGUIDES/S-8.PDF.
82. "Biological Overview," http://www.nti.org/e_research/profiles/India/Biological/print/index_2287.prt.
83. Arian L. Pregenzer, "Securing Nuclear Capabilities in India and Pakistan: Reducing the Terrorists and Proliferation Risks," http://cns.miis.edu/pubs/npr/vol10/101/101prege.pdf.
84. Rajesh M. Basrur and Hasan-Askari Rizvi, "Nuclear Terrorism and South Asia," *Cooperative Monitoring Centre Occasional Paper/25*, Sandia National Laboratories, February 2003, http://www.cmc.sandia.gov/cmc-papers/sand98-050525.pdf, pp. 37-38.
85. Code of Ethics, Atomic Energy Regulatory Board, Mumbai, Government of India, http://www.aerb.gov.in/t/publications/ethics.pdf.
86. Ibid, p. 5.
87. "Code of Ethics and Conduct," http://www.npcil.nic.in/main/CodeofEthics.aspx.
88. "Vigilance," http://www.npcil.nic.in/main/Vigilance.aspx.
89. "Director's Report," *Annual Report 2004-2005*, Nuclear Power Corporation of India Ltd, p. 17.
90. Michael Levi, *On Nuclear Terrorism*, (Cambridge, London: Harvard University Press, 2007), p. 100.
91. Basrur and Rizvi, n. 84, p. 38.
92. Based on K. Raghuraman, from DAE, presentation in an international workshop on "Protection, Control, and Accounting of Nuclear Materials: International Challenges and National Programs" at the National Academy of Sciences, Washington, DC. Christopher Eldridge, "Domestic MPC&A Program," in *Protection Control and Accounting of Nuclear Materials*, National Academy of Sciences, Washington, DC, http://books.nap.edu/openbook.php?record_id=11343&page=39, pp. 39-40.
93. Ibid., p. 40.
94. "Biggest Radiation Crisis in 4 Years May Shut DU Labs," *Hindustan Times*, April 30, 2010.
95. "Security of Radioactive Material During Transport," *AERB Safety Guide No. AERB/NRF-TS/SG-10*, AERB, January 2008, http://www.aerb.gov.in/T/PUBLICATIONS/CODESGUIDES/sg-10.pdf.
96. Ibid., pp. 13-16.
97. "Indian Atomic Energy Body Wants 'No Fly Zones' Over Nuke Facilities," *Deutsche Presse-Agentur*, February 5, 2002, in Lexis-Nexis Academic Universe, February 13, 2005, http://www.lexis-nexis.com.
98. Ibid.
99. "India Declares Kalpakkam Nuclear Plant no-fly Zone," December 17, 2008, http://www.brahmand.com/news/India-declares-Kalpakkam-nuclear-plant-no-fly-zone/821/1/12.html; Vinay Kumar, "Kalpakkam Nuclear Plant no-fly Zone," *The Hindu*, December 17, 2008.
100. "Nuclear Power Plants set to get no-fly Zone Status," www.news.chennaionline.com, April 25, 2008.

6

Artificial Intelligence in Military Applications

Arun K. Singh

> *Our machines will become much more like us and we will become much more like our machines.*
>
> — Rodney Brooks

Introduction

Since the dawn of civilisation, humans have endeavoured to be in control of the environments and surroundings. This quest resulted in many discoveries and inventions, most notable among them being machines. Humans used machines as an aid to make life comfortable, effective and efficient, and aimed to develop machines capable of working like human beings, if possible. The computer is one of the most important machines which has not only raised hopes in this regard but has also contributed significantly in every sphere of human endeavour. The human approach to problem solving is one such. It is based on abstract thought, logic, reasoning and recognising of patterns. But computers and human beings are different. A computer is yet to understand all situations and simultaneously adapt to an evolving one.

The military systems, including weapons, will become smart; too fast, too small, too many, and will create a complex environment for humans to monitor, control and direct them. Information-based systems will lead to data overload that will make it a challenge for humans to directly intervene in decision-making. Weapons and other military systems already under development will function at increasingly higher levels of complexity and responsibility, without meaningful human intervention and control.

In future military conflicts, the norm of engagement will be to act rapidly. The military architectures of tomorrow will consist of a new array of sea, ground and space-based sensors, Unmanned Combat Aerial Vehicles (UCAVs), and missile defence technologies. These will take advantage of directed energy weapons. Military forces will be both faster and more agile. Opponents will take advantage by operating faster than a defender can observe, orient, decide how to respond and act on that decision. The attacker will, thus, place himself inside the defenders Observe, Orient, Decide and Act (OODA) loop, destroying an adversary's ability to conduct an active defence.[1] To execute the OODA process faster than the enemy is the core concept of future digital and information warfare. Automated systems, assisted by artificial intelligence in some form or the other, may be a way out for this problem. The advances gained in the field of artificial intelligence technology can be utilised by unmanned systems to assess operational and tactical situations and decide on an appropriate action. Information will drive the success of command and control. These systems will collect data, have the ability to analyse it, and provide recommendations to the commander. The difference between providing a recommendation and acting on a recommendation may be only a software twist.

Artificial Intelligence (AI) is the branch of computer science focussing on creating machines that can engage in behaviour that humans consider intelligent. AI aims to improve machine behaviour in tackling complex tasks. Smart machines have now become a reality and researchers are creating systems which can mimic human thought, understand speech, beat the best human chess player, and achieve many other advantages. With the introduction of web-enabled infrastructure, rapid developments have been made in the application of AI techniques in the recent past. AI is the key technology in many of today's applications in all fields, including the military.

AI methodologies are being applied to support decision-making at all levels of military operations such as assessment of force readiness, reliability and capability, complex missions planning and integration of data from multiple sources[2]. Research in the field of AI is also addressing the challenges presented by supporting such decision-making in rapidly changing environments. The use of such technology opens up endless possibilities in the military. This paper aims to trace the contours of AI, examine current efforts to utilise AI and explore its potential applications in the military.

Genesis and Recent Past

The first electronics computer was developed in 1941; however, the field of AI research was formally founded later, at a conference at Dartmouth College, in 1956. Early work in AI focussed on using cognitive and biological models to simulate and explain human information processing skills. In the 1990s and early 21st century, AI achieved its greatest successes. AI has advanced rapidly in the past decade, due to greater use of the scientific method in experimenting with, and comparing, approaches that systematise and automate intellectual tasks. Thus, it is relevant to any sphere of human intellectual activities.

The success can be attributed to the incredible power of modern computers, a greater emphasis on solving specific sub-problems, the creation of new ties between AI and other fields working on similar problems. AI is seen and perceived by different people or groups of people differently. The definitions of artificial intelligence can be broadly put into two approaches: one centred around humans and the other centred on rationality.[3] The human centred approach must be an empirical science involving hypothesis and experimental confirmation, while the rationalist approach involves a combination of mathematics and engineering.

There have been efforts to introduce new creative approaches and refine the best one. Recent progress in understanding the theoretical basis for intelligence has gone hand in hand with improvements in the capabilities of real systems. Various sub-fields of AI have become more integrated. AI has found some common ground with other disciplines. A better understanding of the problems and their complex properties, combined with increased mathematical sophistication has led to workable research agendas.

Fields of AI

In AI, the problem of intelligence simulation is generally divided into a number of specific sub-problems. These consist of particular capabilities that researchers like an intelligent system to display. For difficult problems, most of the algorithms require large computational resources and the amount of memory or computer time required becomes very high. With rapid strides in computer technology, research and utilisation, the field of AI witnessed new frontiers. Russell and Norvig explain, "AI encompasses a large variety of sub-fields ranging from general purpose areas such as learning and perception to such specific tasks as playing chess, proving mathematical theorems, writing poetry, and diagnosing diseases. AI systematises and automates intellectual tasks and is, therefore, potentially relevant to any sphere of human intellectual activity. In a sense, it is a truly universal field."[4] The various fields and sub-fields that received more attention in order to solve larger problems are:

- **Learning:** The centrality of learning was discussed by Turing in 1950. From the very beginning, machine learning has been central to AI research. The ability to find a pattern in a stream of input is called unsupervised learning whereas supervised learning includes both classification and numerical regression. Classification is used to determine which category something belongs in. This is done after seeing a number of examples of things from several categories. Regression takes a set of numerical input and output examples and attempts to discover a continuous function that would generate the outputs from the inputs. In the case of reinforcement learning, the agent is rewarded or punished based on good or bad responses.

- **Natural Language Processing:** This gives machines the ability to read and understand the languages spoken by human beings. Text mining and machine translation are examples of some basic applications of natural language processing.
- **Perception:** Perception provides agents with information about the world in which they exist. Perception is initiated by sensors. Machine perception is the ability to use inputs from various sensors such as cameras, microphones, sonar, etc to deduce aspects of the world. Computer vision is the ability to analyse visual input. Facial recognition, object recognition and speech recognition are some of the selected sub-problems
- **Social Intelligence:** In order to obtain social intelligence capability, artificial intelligence has to establish able human interaction and also possess the emotions that people have during their everyday lives. Social skills and emotions play two important roles for an intelligent agent. First, it should be able to foresee the actions of others, by knowing their motives and state of emotions. This involves elements of game theory, decision theory, as well as the ability to model human emotions and also the perceptual skills to detect emotions. Also, it is expected that for good human-computer interaction, emotions need to be displayed by an intelligent machine also. It must appear polite and sensitive to the humans it interacts with. At best, it should have normal emotions and at least, it should appear polite.
- **Creativity:** Artificial intelligence deals with the development and exploration of systems that exhibit creativity. It includes systems capable of such things as scientific invention, visual artistry, music composition and story generation, etc. A section of AI addresses creativity both theoretically from a psychological perspective and practically via specific implementations of systems that generate outputs that can be considered creative. Artificial intuition and artificial imagination are the areas related with computational research.
- **General Intelligence:** Many researchers hope that their work will finally be included into a machine with general intelligence, combining all the other skills and exceeding human abilities at most of them.
- **Knowledge Representation:** Knowledge representation is one of the important and most familiar concepts in AI. Most of the problems that machines are expected to

solve will require extensive knowledge about the world. Among the things that AI needs to represent are objects, properties, categories and relations between objects, situations, events, states and time, causes and effects, and many other less well researched domains. Knowledge representation and knowledge engineering are central to AI research.

- **Planning:** Planning is the sub-field of AI devoted to finding action sequences that achieve the agent's goals. Intelligent agents should be able to lay down goals and accomplish them. They need a way to imagine the future and be able to select choices that maximise the value of the available choices. They should have a representation of the state of the world and be able to make predictions about how their actions will change it. Multi-agent planning uses the cooperation and competition of many agents to achieve a given goal.

Tools Used to Solve Problems of AI

In the course of years of research, AI has developed a large number of tools to solve some difficult problems in computer science. A few of the most common of these methods are mentioned below:

- **Search and Optimisation:** Search is the sub-field of AI devoted to finding action sequences that achieve the agent's goal. Several problems in AI can be solved in theory by intelligently searching through many possible solutions. Reasoning can be reduced to simply performing a search operation. Planning algorithms search through trees of goals and sub-goals, attempting to find a path to a target goal. This process is called means-ends analysis. Robotics algorithms for moving limbs and grasping objects use local searches in configuration space. Several learning algorithms use search algorithms based on optimisation. In the case of most of the real world problems, simple exhaustive searches are rarely sufficient. Therefore, heuristics supplies the programme with a best guess for the path on which the solution lies. Also, in the case of many problems, it is possible to begin the search with some form of a guess and then incrementally refine the guess until no more refinements can be made.
- **Logic:** Logic is the primary vehicle for representing knowledge. It is used for knowledge representation and problem solving. However, it can be applied to other problems also. AI uses several different forms of logic research. Propositional or sentential logic is the logic of statements which can be true or false. There is well developed technology for reasoning in proportional logic First-order logic also permits the use of quantifiers and predicates. It can express details about objects, their properties, and their relations with each other. Fuzzy logic is a version of first-order logic. It allows the truth of a statement

to be represented as a value between 0 and 1, rather than simply True or False. Fuzzy systems have been widely used in modern industrial and consumer product control systems and can be used for uncertain reasoning. Several extensions of logic have been intended to handle many domains of knowledge. Other forms of logic designed to help with default reasoning and the qualification problem include default logics, non-monotonic logics and circumscription

- **Probabilistic Methods For Uncertain Reasoning:** A large number of problems in AI such as learning, reasoning, planning, perception and robotics call for the agent to operate either with uncertain or incomplete information. A number of powerful tools using methods from probability theory and economics have been devised by AI researchers to solve these problems. Bayesian networks are a very common tool that can be used for a large number of problems like learning, reasoning, planning and perception, etc. Probabilistic algorithms can also be used for filtering, prediction and finding explanations for streams of data, helping perception systems to analyse processes that occur over time. Mathematical tools have been developed that analyse how an agent can make choices and plan, using decision theory, decision analysis, information value theory.
- **Classifiers and Statistical Learning Methods:** Classifiers and controllers are two types of AI applications. Classification forms a central part of many AI systems, however, controllers also classify conditions before inferring actions. Classifiers are functions that make use of pattern matching to determine a closest match. They can be tuned as per examples, making them very attractive for use in AI. These examples are known as patterns or observations. Each pattern belongs to a certain predefined class in the case of supervised learning. All the observations combined with their class labels are known as a data set. When a new observation is received, that observation is classified based on earlier experience. A classifier can be trained in many ways.
- **Neural Networks:** A neuron is a cell in the brain whose principal function is the collection, processing, and dissemination of electrical signals. The brain's image processing capacity is considered to emerge mainly from a network of neurons. A neural network is an interconnected group of nodes, similar to the large network of neurons in the human brain. Neural networks are designed to distinguish patterns in data and forecast an output from a given set of data. Neural networks need to be trained on the data before they can predict or learn. In this way, they learn from examples, similar to the way a child learns. Computer learning skills that are developed for neural networks are used in a class of computer programmes called 'expert systems'. Expert systems also learn from experience and get better at their job, the longer they

do.

- **Control Theory:** Control theory is the foundation of AI and deals with designing devices that act optimally on the basis of feedback from the environment. Initially, the mathematical tools of control theory were quite different from AI, but the fields are coming closer together. Control theory has many important applications, especially in robotics.
- **Languages:** AI researchers have developed several specialised languages for AI research, including Lisp and Prolog. In AI, the automation or programming of all aspects of human cognition is considered from its foundations in cognitive science through approaches to symbolic and sub-symbolic AI, natural language processing, computer vision, and evolutionary or adaptive systems. It is inherent to this very complex problem domain that in the initial phase of programming a specific AI problem, it can only be specified poorly. Only through interactive and incremental refinement does more precise specification become possible. This is also due to the fact that typical AI problems tend to be very domain specific, therefore, heuristic strategies have to be developed..

Applications of AI

General

The probable applications of artificial intelligence are plenty. Application of AI is possible in all fields requiring intelligent analysis, precision and automation. They stretch from the military to the entertainment industry, to big establishments dealing with large amount, of information such as banks, hospital and insurance: AI can also be used to predict customer behaviour and detect trends. There are many general fields where AI can be very usefully utilised for autonomous planning and scheduling, autonomous control, medical diagnosis, logistics planning, and language understanding, problem solving, game playing.[5] Some of the important applications are appended below:

- **Pattern Recognition:** Pattern recognition is the area of research that studies the operation and design of systems that identify patterns in data. When a programme makes observations of some kind, it is often programmed to compare what it sees with a pattern e.g face, fingerprint or handwriting recognition. Important application areas are image analysis, character recognition, speech analysis, man and machine diagnostics and person identification.
- **Bio-Informatics:** Bio-informatics is the application of computer technology for the management of biological information. AI provides several powerful algorithms and

techniques for solving important problems in bio-informatics. Approaches like neural networks, hidden Markov models, Bayesian networks and Kernel methods are ideal for areas with more data but less theory. The goal in applying AI to bio-informatics is to extract useful information from the wealth of available data by building good probabilistic models.

- **Data Mining:** An AI powered tool that can discover useful information within a database that can then be used to improve actions, data mining is the process of extracting patterns from data. Data mining is seen as an increasingly important tool by modern business to transform data into business intelligence, giving an informational advantage. It is currently used in a wide range of profiling practices such as marketing, surveillance, fraud detection, and scientific discovery.
- **Expert Systems:** An expert system is a computer programme that represents the reasoning process with knowledge of some specialist subject with a view to solve problems or give advice.[6] It is the knowledge-based applications of artificial intelligence that have enhanced productivity in almost all fields such as business, science, engineering, and the military. With advances in the last decade, today's expert systems clients can choose from dozens of commercial software packages with easy-to-use interfaces. Diagnosis and trouble-shooting explain the development and testing of a condition-monitoring sub-module of an integrated plant maintenance management application based on AI techniques. There are mainly knowledge-based systems, having several modules, sub-modules and sections.
- **Computer Vision:** It is essential for a computer to perceive objects. Vision includes both the acquisition and processing of visual information. AI enabled technologies have made possible many amazing achievements: vehicles that are able to steer themselves safely along highways, and computers that can recognise and interpret speech or facial expressions. AI supported vision technology has made many applications possible. Some of them are like 3D modelling, image stabilisation, image synthesis, surgical navigation, handwritten document recognition, and vision-based computer interfaces. While explaining the success of an autonomous system trial supported by computer vision, Russel and Norvi state:

> The ALVIN computer vision system was trained to steer a car to keep it following a lane. It was tried in the Carnegie Melon University (CMU) NAVLAB computer controlled minivan and used to navigate across the United States for 2,850 miles and it was in control of steering the vehicle 98 percent of the time. A human took over the other 2 percent mostly at the exit ramps. NAVLAB has video cameras that

transmit road images to ALVIN, which then computes the best direction to steer, based on experience from previous training runs.[7]

- **Image Processing:** Perception appears to be an effortless activity for humans, however, it requires a significant amount of sophisticated computation. The team associated with image formation and processing is concerned with research issues related to the acquisition, manipulation, and synthesis and distribution of images. In AI, applications include video phone, video conferencing, teleconferencing, and multimedia databases. Progressively, this research has combined image or vision with audio or speech. For example, in the video indexing project, the group is using both visual and audio cues to derive semantic labels for video shots.
- **Robotics:** Robots are physical agents that perform tasks by manipulating the physical world. Robots comprise several systems working together as a whole. Robots are widely used in assembly plants, space stations, and hospitals and now also in homes. Other types of mobile robots include the unmanned land vehicle, unmanned aerial vehicle and autonomous underwater vehicle.
- **Knowledge Representation and Reasoning:** The representation of knowledge and the reasoning processes that bring knowledge to life are the two concepts central to the field of AI. Knowledge representation means encoding real world, common sense, etc in a format that is both readable and understandable by the computer. Logical agents comprise the representation of knowledge and the reasoning processes that bring knowledge to life. Logic is the primary vehicle for representing the knowledge throughout, and semantic webs describe things in a way that computer applications understand.
- **Gaming:** Game playing was one of the first tasks taken up by AI. Games, unlike other problems, are interesting because they are difficult to solve. Games, like the real world, require the ability to make some decisions even when calculating that the optimal decision is not feasible. Games also penalise inefficiency severely. Game playing research has contributed in many ideas on how to make best possible use of time. AI techniques are used in computer and video games to produce the illusion of intelligence in the behaviour of non-player characters. The techniques used typically draw upon existing methods from fields that include control theory, robotics, etc. IBM's Deep Blue became the first computer programme to defeat the world champion in a chess match when it performed better than Gary Kasparov in an exhibition match.

Military Applications

The military applications of artificial intelligence are spread over large areas of military functions. Some of the military functions where AI techniques are being used or have potential use are given below.

Operations

- **Command and Control:** Command and control is considered one of the most important functions of military operations. In a networked-centred battlefield scenario, with a host of sensors deployed at different stages and vast amounts of data flowing among various centres, the time available for decision-making is at a premium. The information overload can sometimes impair the decision-making, hence, intelligent filtering of information is required to take timely and appropriate decisions. AI is used in playing a decisive role in reducing the load on the human beings in the loop and, at times, taking autonomous decisions, as and when warranted.
- **Navigation:** The availability of the Global Positioning System (GPS), Inertial Navigation Systems (INS) and autopilot along with host of sensors and on-board computers has helped in overcoming certain human limitations and resulted in safe and efficient management of operating aircraft.
- **ISR:** Intelligence, Surveillance and Reconnaissance (ISR) are the key elements of battlefield management. Over time, the battlefield scenario has undergone dramatic change and so have the means of identification, surveillance and reconnaissance. Advancement in technology in many spheres has offered sensors with high sensitivity, small sizes and better visibility. AI has contributed significantly in this regard in terms of ground, aerial, space and underwater ISR capabilities. Unmanned Aerial Vehicles (UAVs) using AI offer tremendous potential as intelligence, surveillance and reconnaissance platforms for early detection of security threats and for acquisition and maintenance of situational awareness in a crisis condition. Using their capabilities effectively requires addressing a range of practical and theoretical problems. Developments in the field of hardware and software technologies, as well as economies of scale, make UAVs feasible for increasingly diverse airborne observation missions. Expert systems are promising technologies that manage information demands and provide required expertise. Thus, they are well suited to many of the tasks associated with environmental impact assessment. While highlighting the contribution of artificial intelligence in battlefield surveillance using the Geographical Information System (GIS), Maj Jagmohan Singh of the project management organisation, battlefield surveillance system , Army HQ concludes:

Transparency of the battlefield is a critical factor influencing the outcome of future battles. Battlefield transparency would provide a framework for `scientific' and deliberate decision-making. The dependence of commanders on paper maps and sand models for operational planning will have to be replaced by the latest GIS tools. These tools permit dynamic visualisation of a 3D terrain model for seamless access, query and analysis across multiple types of military geographical data. Mapping and analysis is done using various GIS technologies incorporating satellites and aerial imagery, and photography of the target area. The future technologies would further enhance the visualisation techniques and enable the commanders to take timely decisions to defeat the adversaries. However, emphasis needs to be focussed on refinement of some critical technologies such as Multi-Sensor Data Fusion (MSDF), AI and interoperability issues.[8]

- **Weapon Systems:** The weapon technology has seen constant change and has gained more lethality and effectiveness in its evolution. A host of modern weapons is in use or in the process of development, which can change the landscape of the battlefield. Missiles, directed energy weapons, standoff weapons, autonomous weapons, etc are a few examples of intelligent weapons and have even greater potential in the future.
- **Communications and Computers:** Communication is the core of all activities. In the age of modern communication, the geographical boundaries have come closer and visibility has improved to a great extent. The advent of satellites and availability of the internet has revolutionised communication. In the future, success on the battlefield will depend on the maintenance of network connectivity and management of information from a large variety of sources. This will also make real-time communication more important. The non-availability of real-time information can hamper the decision-making ability of soldiers fighting the war. It may result in failure of the mission and even danger to personal survival. Wren, Ichalkaranje and Jain have commented on the contribution and maturity of AI:

> Intelligent Decision Support Systems have the potential to transform human decision-making by combining research in artificial intelligence, information technology, and systems engineering. The field of intelligent decision-making is expanding rapidly partly due to advances in artificial intelligence and network-centric environments that can deliver the technology. Communication and coordination between dispersed systems can deliver just-in-time information, real-time processing, collaborative environments, and globally up-to-date information

to a human decision-maker. At the same time, artificial intelligence techniques have demonstrated that they have matured sufficiently to provide computational assistance to humans in practical applications.[9]

A network-centric environment facilitates leveraging artificial intelligence to allow soldiers to access and share information throughout the entire network. A network-centric environment provides coordination, where each node in the network helps provide a flawless, decentralised organisation of intelligent resources.

Maintenance

- **Repair and Overhaul:** The fighting capability of the forces depends upon the serviceability and availability of the range of equipment held in its inventory. Most of the modern-day equipment used for military applications has a certain defined life-span. Also, the demand of the battlefield has ensured that highly sophisticated equipment should be made available for combat. This demands a system with quick fault diagnostic capability, easy maintainability and highly trained human resources along with modern ground facilities. Presently, expert systems are in use to analyse the faulty Printed Circuit Boards (PCB) of radars or aircraft avionics, using Automatic Test Equipment (ATE). Built-in test systems are encouragingly being used with modern development of weapons. Techniques such as expert system and robotics are in use in military applications, however, they have the potential to be exploited at a much greater scale to expedite automation.
- **Logistics:** Logistics is the life-line of military operations. The various models of operations research have been employed in effective management of the logistics operation. The system of simulation has helped in optimising operations and AI has great potential in assisting in planning and keeping the supply chain effective and efficient. Russell and Norvig have highlighted:

> During the Persian Gulf crisis of 1991, US forces deployed a Dynamic Analysis and Replanning Tool (DART) to do automated logistics planning and scheduling for transportation. This involved up to 50,000 vehicles, cargo and people at a time and had to account for starting point, destinations, routes, and conflict resolution among all parameters. The AI planning techniques allowed a plan to be generated in hours that would have taken weeks with older methods. The Defence Advanced Research Project Agency (DARPA) stated that this single application more than paid back its 30-year investment in AI.[10]

Administration

- **Security:** Security is one of the most vulnerable aspects of military establishments. Proper scrutiny and flow of men, material and equipment in its different role demands fool-proof security of all resources and establishments. This has gained more importance in today's hostile and unpredictable internal and external environments. AI techniques like face recognition and biometrics become relevant in the use of identity access management and access control. They are also used to identify individuals in groups that are under surveillance. The US Department of Defence (DoD) Common Access Card, is an identity (ID) card issued to all US Service personnel and contractors on US military sites. This card contains biometric data and digitised photographs. It also has laser-etched photographs and holograms to add security and reduce the risk of falsification. However, this has now become a common feature for many establishments and is in use widely.
- **Medical:** AI has helped in a big way in the advancement of medical sciences, resulting in a large array of intelligent machines capable of doing many functions with great sensitivity and accuracy. Also, medical diagnosis programmes based on probabilistic analysis have been able to perform at the level of expert physicians in several areas of medicine. Under operational conditions, this could define the fine line between life and death for a casualty.
- **Education and Training:** In the military domain, models have been primarily developed and applied in the areas of training and exercises, defence planning, operational planning, etc. Training is one of the important areas of the military sphere where AI has been successfully employed in terms of war-gaming and simulation. It encompasses the areas of operational and ground training, consisting of simulation of flying machines, missiles, radar system and fault diagnosis in maintenance practices. AI has been used effectively in teaching the Arabic language to the US forces and training them to be conversant with the local language before deploying them in the GulfWar. DARWARS is a research programme intended to accelerate the development and deployment of military training systems. It was envisioned as a low-cost, mobile, web-centric, simulation-based, "lightweight" system designed to take advantage of the presence of the Personal Computer (PC) and of new technology, including multi-player games, virtual worlds, off-the-shelf PC simulations, intelligent agents, and on-line communities. DARWARS is DARPA's core training superiority initiative[11].
- **Planning:** Planning has been an important function in all military activities. Humans have been central to decision-making, and wish to continue to be so. However, modern tools have been able to overcome the limitation of human beings to a great

extent in many areas and have proved their edge in spheres like data processing, pattern recognition, etc. AI has the potential to strengthen the planning process in different areas of the military. Autonomous planning and scheduling comprises one of the powerful applications of AI. Russell and Norvig explain this as:

> NASA's Remote Agent Program became the first on-board autonomous planning to control the scheduling of operations for a spacecraft. Remote agent generated plans from high level goals specified from the ground, and it monitored the operations of the spacecraft as the plans were executed – directing, diagnosing, and recovering from the problems as they occurred.[12]

The Future of AI

AI has moved through its birth to the phase of early enthusiasm and great expectations to realism. It began as an attempt to answer some of the most basic questions about human existence by understanding the nature of intelligence. However, it has grown into a scientific and technological field affecting many aspects: business, commerce and society. Commercial success of applications like expert systems gave a boost to the AI industry and as Russell and Norvig said, "Overall, the industry boomed from a few million dollars in 1980 to billions of dollar in 1988."[13] The development of the knowledge-based system added value to AI and helped in the development of various tools to handle practical sub-problems. A gentle revolution in the field of robotics, computer vision and knowledge representation, apart from others, is visible. On the future of AI, Russell and Norvig observed, "Encouraged by the progress in solving the sub-problems of AI, researchers have started looking at the 'whole agent' problem again."[14] One of the most important environments for intelligent agents is the internet. Also, AI technologies bring about many internet tools such as search engines, recommender systems, and website construction systems.

The prospective power of technology will continue to rouse both hopes and fears. Some researchers believe that artificial intelligence will eventually exceed the limits of progress. Ray Kurzweil has used Moore's Law that describes the exponential improvement in digital technology to calculate that desktop computers will have the same processing power as human brains by the year 2029. He also predicts that by 2045, artificial intelligence will reach a point where it is able to improve itself at a rate that far exceeds anything conceivable in the past, a scenario that science fiction writer Vernor Vinge termed the "technological singularity."[15] As per predictions made by robot designer Hans Moravec, cyberneticist Kevin Warwick and inventor Ray Kurzweil, humans and machines will merge in the future into cyborgs and that will be more capable and powerful than either.[16] Kurzweil further argues:

> Artificial intelligence will necessarily exceed human intelligence for several reasons. First, machines can share knowledge and communicate with one another far more efficiently than can humans. As humans, we do not have the means to exchange the vast patterns of inter-neuronal connections and neurotransmitter-concentration levels that comprise our learning, knowledge, and skills, other than through slow, language-based communication. Second, humanity's intellectual skills have developed in ways that have evolutionarily been encouraged in natural environments. Those skills, which are primarily based on our capabilities to recognize and extract meaning from patterns, enable us to be highly proficient in certain tasks, such as distinguishing faces, identifying flying objects and recognizing language sounds. Unfortunately, our brains are less well suited for dealing with more complex patterns, such as those that exist in financial, scientific or product data. The application of computer-based techniques will allow us to fully master pattern recognition paradigms. Finally, as human knowledge migrates to the web, machines will demonstrate increased proficiency in reading, understanding, and synthesizing all human–machine information.[17]

Any technological progress has taken some gestation period before it is in use up to its full potential. It is likely to be so with the future of AI. It is only a question of time when the field of AI will get matured and develop to its full potential. Till that time, the development work is likely to continue and its benefits in current capability will continue to be harnessed by military planners in the days to come.

As the world becomes more and more network-centric, the complementary roles of man and machine will continue to enhance the capabilities of both. The outcome of the collaboration of man and machine will certainly bring many opportunities and also throw up many challenges for the management of future battlefields. The trend so far has shown an increasing level of capability enhancement of war-making inventories in almost all spheres of military activities such as weapon systems, weapon delivery platforms, battle support systems, etc. The contribution of technological advancements, especially in the field of AI, has substantially impacted the capability enhancement process and also added complexities in the field of military planning and operations. It is evident that as the systems are getting more complex, they are progressively reducing the human role in many areas of human activities. As processing speed becomes faster and data overload becomes unavoidable, decision-making is progressively likely to become difficult for human beings.

The effective use of such technologies will require rapid, effective, and close interaction among many different systems. It will involve sophisticated command and control links as well as a variety of technical means, including reconnaissance sensors, communication links, computers, display systems, and weapon platforms. This kind of interaction will require radical changes in the architecture and integration of these interconnected and widespread intelligence absorbing, processing, and application systems. Right now, the architectures for this kind of system of systems are in the developmental stages and yet to be matured. The actual achievement of solutions for the integration of such large, complex systems will be a long process involving extensive experimentation. At least another decade, probably two, will be required. Humans may retain symbolic authority, but automated systems move too fast and the factors involved are too complex for real human comprehension. When computers are designed and programmed by other computers, humans will find it difficult to understand and even more difficult to intervene successfully. In a sense, this will be true that the new systems with dominant AI will enable people to accomplish far more in war and peace than was even conceivable before their development. But the simple fact remains. The farther we extend our reach outside human space, the more we require the assistance of machines.

Conclusion

Humans and computers have their own strengths and limitations. AI has been focussing to make machines intelligent so that both come at par. Since the early days, humans have strived to create intelligent machines. AI methodologies are commonly being applied to support decision-making processes at different levels of military operations. Today, AI can perform many activities in many fields. Some of these are autonomous planning and scheduling, game playing, autonomous control, diagnosis, logistics planning, robotics, and language understanding, problem solving, etc.

There are now millions of robots working in factories around the world, assembling everything from cars to electric appliances to defence equipment and performing hazardous and precision jobs. Unmanned space probes have been exploring deep space for decades, and sophisticated robot vehicles are now searching for signs of life on the surface of Mars. But the power of the computer is rapidly increasing, and with new technologies on the horizon, thinking computers are probably only decades away from becoming a reality. And unlike human brains, computers are precise in their calculations, and their memory does not fade over time. Computers are already being programmed to understand speech and computerise telephones.

AI began as an attempt to answer some of the most fundamental questions about human existence by understanding the nature of intelligence, but it has grown into a scientific and technological field affecting many aspects of the military, commerce and society. Even as AI technology becomes integrated into the fabric of everyday life, AI researchers remain focussed on the grand challenges of automating intelligence. Work is progressing on developing systems that converse in natural language, that perceive and respond to their surroundings, and that encode and provide useful access to all of human knowledge and expertise. Future generations may treat tactical warfare as appropriate for the business of machines and not for people at all. Humans may maintain control at the highest levels, possibly making strategic decisions about the overall objectives of a conflict. But even these will increasingly be intimated by automated information systems. In the future, direct human participation in warfare is likely to be less. Instead, the human role will take other forms such as strategic directions. It may perhaps be limited to no more than the policy decisions like whether to go for conflict or not.

AI in the military is used in numerous ways. Due to the increased robustness, reliability, and durability of most military programmes and hardware, AI has become an integral part of the battlefield.

Notes

1. Thomas K. Adams, "Future Warfare and the Decline of Human Decision-Making", *Parameters*, Winter 2001-02, pp. 57-71.
2. L. F. Arrowood, M. R. Hilliard, H. L. Hwang and M. L. Emrich *Challenges in Applying Artificial Intelligence Methodologies to Military Operations* (New York: ACM, 1986), pp. 408-414 available at http://portal.acm.org/citation.cfm?id=12853.
3. Stuart J. Russell and Peter Norvig, *Artificial Intelligence: A Modern Approach* (New Delhi: Pearson Prentice Hall, 2007, 2nd edition), pp. 29-30.
4. Ibid., pp. 29.
5. Ibid., pp. 55-56.
6. Peter Jackson, *Introduction to Expert Systems* (New York: Addison- Wesle Publishing Company,1994), p. 3.
7. Russell and Norvig, n. 3, p. 55.
8. Maj Jagmohan Singh, "The Importance of GIS in Battlefield Surveillance," available at http://www.gisdevelopment.net/application/military/defence/mi04de02pf.htm.
9. Gloria Phillips-Wren, Nikhil Ichalkaranje and Lakhmi C. Jain, *Intelligent Decision-Making: An AI-Based Approach* (Springer Publishing Company, Inc, 2008) Available at http://portal.acm.org/citation.cfm?id=SERIES11878.1628784.
10. Russell and Norvig, n. 3, p. 56.
11. http://en.wikipedia.org/wiki/DARWARS.
12. Russell and Norvig, n. 3, p. 55.
13. Ibid., p. 52.

14. Ibid., p. 55.
15. Ray Kurzweil, *The Singularity Is Near* (New York: Viking, 2005).
16. Ibid.
17. Ray Kurzweil, "Reinventing Humanity: The Future of Machine – Human Intelligence," The *Futurist*, March-April 2006, p. 44. Available at http://www.wfs.org/futuristorder.htm.

7

Rise of Islamist Insurgency

A. V. Chandrasekaran

Introduction

At the conclusion of World War1, Britain, France, Italy and a few other European nations had established their direct or indirect rule throughout the erstwhile Ottoman lands. In 1920, only four Muslim countries—Turkey, Saudi Arabia, Iran, and Afghanistan— remained independent of some form of non-Muslim rule.[1] The retreat of Western colonialism began slowly in the aftermath of World War II. The collapse of the Soviet Union in 1990 brought independence to additional Muslim nations. Muslims in large numbers were turning towards Islam as a source of identity, meaning, stability, legitimacy, development, power and hope that "Islam is the solution." Beginning in the 1970s, Islamic symbols, beliefs, practices, institutions and organisations won increasing commitment and support throughout the world of one billion Muslims stretching from Morocco to Indonesia and from Nigeria to Kazakhstan. In most Muslim countries, an element of radical Islamisation occurred, paving the way for both establishing Islamic schools and expanding Islamic influence in state schools. The year 1973 was an epochal one for the Muslims in their war against the non-Muslims. It was in 1973, during the Arab-Israel War that the Organisation of Petroleum Exporting Countries (OPEC), by hiking the price of oil, made the West pay dearly for its continued support to Israel. Japan, a non-Christian country, was one of the worst affected and this move of targeting all non-Islamic countries saw a new rise of pan-Islamism not seen hitherto. The last three decades of the 20th century witnessed the rise of Islamic movements in different parts of the world and their transformation into epicentres of terror, opposing the existing social and political order.

In 1979, the year Osama Bin Laden left university, several epoch-making events shook the Muslim world: the Islamic revolution in Iran, the peace deal between Israel and Egypt, the Soviet invasion of Afghanistan and the occupation of the Grand Mosque at Mecca by a radical Wahhabi group. Sadat's peace deal with Israel was considered a sellout of Islam by most Islamic countries, and the deposition of the Shah of Iran, Mohammed Reza Pahlavi, was an apt example of what could be done about such regimes; the Soviet invasion emphasised the imminent threat from the West, and for the Saudis' in particular, the occupation of Islam's holiest shrine by Juhaiman ibn Said-Ul-Utaiba, a hardline preacher, and 400 radicals, in November 1979, cast the royal family in Riyadh in poor light.

The success of the Iranian Islamic revolution became a source of inspiration for the revolutionary movements, particularly the Shiite movements, which sprang up in the 1980s. They were led by religious militants drawing their inspiration from Ayatollah Khomeini, who promoted the vision of an Islamic Caliphate. The Hezbollah and Hamas movements in Lebanon and Palestine are the torch-bearers of this goal. There is the 1,400-year legacy of Shi'ism, a legacy of martyrdom and suffering, resting on an ancient grievance: the belief that Islamic history was derailed when political power passed out of the hands of the family of the Prophet Muhammad in the 7th century. The Palestinian Islamic Jihad movement was the group most profoundly affected by the Iranian revolution. From its inception, the Islamic Jihad endorsed the Iranian revolution as an ideal movement to be implemented in other parts of the Muslim world. According to them, the Iranian revolution brought home the old truth that "Islam was the solution and *jihad* was the proper means for the solution."

The sudden spurt in Islamic insurgency after the 1980s—though the assertion of Islam was witnessed as early as 1973—was intriguing, considering the fact that modern militant Islamism emerged in the late 19th century and Islamist groups had used violence throughout the 20th century.[2] The plausible explanation could be that a new sub-current of pan Islamism emerged in the 1970s, and exhibited itself during the oil crisis of 1973.

The Saudi Royals were always wary of secular ideologies creeping into their kingdom which could result in the royals losing their grip over the nation. To counter this eventuality, as early as 1962, the *Rabitat al-alam Islami*, or Muslim World League, had been set up by Riyadh to fund an international effort to counter, through *da'wa*, the spread of secular ideologies in the Islamic world.[3] They further established a global network of charities for the provision of inter-Muslim aid. It was these norms and networks established by the Hijazi pan-Islamists that enabled the Arab activists in Afghanistan to recruit foreign fighters in the name of inter-Muslim solidarity. The "Arab-Afghan" mobilisation, in turn, produced a foreign fighter movement that still exists today. When the erstwhile Soviet Union began its military incursion into Afghanistan, the desolate, remote land of Afghanistan became the birthplace for thousands of young revolutionary fighters from all over the Arab world. These men learned guerrilla tactics and forgetting their individual nationalities, shared a common bond of having gone to war together thinking they were fighting the threat to Islam, and those who survived came to believe that Afghanistan was only a small battle in a much larger war. Thus, Afghanistan became the global *jihadi* movement's launching pad. These zealots were convinced that if they could defeat a superpower, the day for launching an Islamic Caliphate all over was not far away. [4]

These *jihadists* also firmly believed that their victory against the Soviet Union also was the cause of the disintegration of the Soviet Union into fragmented republics. Since the defeat of Fascism, and the collapse of Communism, *Jihadism* has arguably become the world's next ideological opponent of Western-style liberalism. Islamist insurgency which was also one of the patterns has today emerged as one of the biggest threats confronting the civilised world. The teachings of this broad array of global *jihadist* thinkers, most of whom are unknown names in the West, have convinced, and continuing to convince, countless young, angry Muslim men to commit, or at least support, violent acts of terrorism by intertwining the call for action, with a puritanical interpretation of Islam. By exploiting the religious concepts, histories and beliefs, the most influential contemporary *jihadi* ideologues namely Abu Qatada al-Filistini, Abd al-Qadir ibn abd al-Aziz, Abu Muhammad al-Maqdisi and Nasr Bin al-Fahd have all been spiritual guides and have enjoyed enormous success in building their version of God's army on earth. The first premise of *Jihadism* is that there is a global conspiracy working to destroy Islam. The central conspirators, the *jihadists* argue, are the Christian Crusader countries of the West and their Jewish Zionist allies in Israel. The *jihadist* intelligentsia, which consists of a core group of radical thinkers writing in various places around the world, has exhaustively detailed the nature and implications of this conspiracy. Ayatollah Khomeini's Iran, the Taliban's Afghanistan, and Osama Bin Laden and Al Qaeda as well as terrorists from Morocco to Indonesia have espoused a revolutionary Islam that relies on violence and terror.

Islamist Resurgence

The Muslims, who were a divided group, came together for the first time in 1973 and started exerting their power through the vast oil resources they had under their control during the Arab-Israel War of 1973. The 1973 oil crisis started in October 1973, when the members of Organisation of Arab Petroleum Exporting Countries or the OAPEC (consisting of the Arab members of OPEC, plus Egypt, Syria and Tunisia) proclaimed an oil embargo. This was "in response to the US decision to resupply the Israeli military" during the Yom Kippur War. The effects of the embargo were immediate. OPEC forced the oil companies to increase payments drastically. On October 16, 1973, OPEC announced a decision to raise the posted price of oil by 70 percent, to $5.11 a barrel. This increase in the price of oil had a dramatic effect on the oil exporting nations, for the countries of the Middle East who had long been dominated by the industrial powers were seen to have acquired control of a vital commodity. The traditional flow of capital reversed as the oil exporting nations accumulated vast wealth. Some of the income was dispensed in the form of aid to other underdeveloped nations, thus, paving the way for the establishment of *madrasas* in almost all countries having a sizeable Islamic population to spread Islamic education worldwide, which subsequently branched out to radical Islamic teachings, and this paved the way for the growth of a militant form of Islam largely intolerant of other religions, with a firm belief that the Muslims' task would be to reclaim all Muslim lands occupied, and subsequently to establish an Islamic Caliphate. This control of a vital commodity became known as the "oil weapon," which came in the form of an embargo and cutbacks in oil production from the Arab states to select industrial governments of the world to pressure Israel during the fourth Arab-Israeli War in October 1973. The 1973 incident emboldened the Muslims and the use of foreign Muslim militants was witnessed during the Israeli-Lebanon skirmish of 1975. The 1973 incident became the hallmark for the rise of Islamic fundamentalism and also led to the rise of Islamic insurgency. In 1979, Juhaiman had seized control of the Grand Mosque along with 400 of his followers who were not just Saudis but also included Egyptians, Kuwaitis, Bangladeshis, Yemenis and Iraqis, which stands testimony to the fact that transnational religious violence was starting to appear on the horizon. Radical Islam had already crossed frontiers but it was the Afghan conflict that for the first time saw a huge number of Muslim *jihadists* from all over the Arab world and from other Muslim countries descend on Afghanistan to wage a holy war. Afghanistan reminded Muslims of all colours and races that the unity of Islam is much more important than the superficial differences wrought by colonialism, secular nationalism, and other material ideologies. They were made to feel that they were on the verge of reenacting and relieving the golden age of their blessed ancestors.[5] This probably paved the way for a transnational Islamist insurgency. Muslim insurgents from Algeria, Egypt, Saudi Arabia, and Southeast Asia fought side by side, forging relationships and creating a cadre of veterans who shared a powerful life experience, a more global view, and a heady sense of confidence underscored by the Soviet Union's ultimate withdrawal and subsequent collapse, for which they assumed credit. It is interesting to study how these insurgents are frequently driven by a set of ideas derived from specific writers or schools of thought. They have been inculcated in specific ways of conceiving the state of Islam's relation with the rest. These thinkers have argued for a purer form of Islam, for the establishment of genuine Islamic governments in primarily Islamic countries, for the severing of cultural and economic ties with the West (even to the extent of ceasing to export oil), for the elimination of an American and European presence and influence in these countries, and for the establishment of a homeland for the Palestinian people. And, unfortunately, many—though by no means all—of these thinkers conceive it as legitimate to employ terrorist acts of violence to achieve these goals.

When the Soviets withdrew from Afghanistan in the spring of 1992, the *jihadists* were looking for new arenas where they could fight in defence of the *ummah*. A number of armed conflicts evolved more or less in parallel, notably in Algeria, Somalia, Kashmir, Chechnya and Bosnia. The Islamic militants would invariably get involved in all of these conflicts at one point or another, in varying degrees.

Ironically tracing their intellectual pedigree to the modern fundamentalist *Salafi* movement, the *jihadists* argue that the meaning of the scripture is obvious and eternal and, hence, does not need any additions and innovations from scholars, and argue that this could subvert the truth. These responses coincide with a massive mistrust of Islamic institutions, including educational institutions and their alumni which are all seen as a blasphemy of the official authority. Distrust of the state has a long history in Islam and the *jihadists* feel these regimes are degraded versions of the original rightly guided Caliphate. *Jihadi* tracts regularly refer to leaders of these states as tyrants, traitors and heretics. The Muslim Brotherhood of Egypt and Syria, and Islamic Salvation Front in Algeria all fell under this category of religious zealots.

Islamic Ideologues

Abu al-A'la Maududi (1903-79), the Indian and later Pakistani thinker, was the first Islamist writer to approach *jihad* systematically. In his words, "*Jihad* was most commonly interpreted to mean armed struggle for the defence or advancement of Muslim power. In Muslim tradition, the world is divided into two houses: the House of Islam…in which Muslim governments rule and Muslim law prevails, and the House of War, the rest of the world, still inhabited and, more importantly, ruled by infidels…the presumption is that the duty of *jihad* will continue, interrupted only by truces, until all the world either adopts the Muslim faith or submits to Muslim rule." Shia revolutionaries have a similar perspective. Ayatollah Khomeini (1903-89) contends that jurists, "by means of *jihad* and enjoining the good and forbidding the evil, must expose and overthrow tyrannical rulers and rouse the people so the universal movement of all alert Muslims can establish Islamic governments in the place of tyrannical regimes." The proper teaching of Islam will cause "the entire population to become *mujahids*."

Sunni Ideologues

Sunni Islamist movements all base their ideology on that of the Muslim Brotherhood and/or the Wahhabi movement in the Arabian Peninsula and beyond. This ideology interprets Muslim history as a process of deterioration, particularly since the beginning of the 20th century and after the abolition of the Caliphate and feel that the infiltration of Western morals and culture is largely to blame for this situation.

The literary sources of Islamist strategic thinking are readily available on the internet and in bookstores across the Muslim world. The discussion of strategic issues is most evident in the writings of "mainstream" Islamist movements, which have "research centres" that perform strategic research (such as those affiliated with the Muslim Brotherhood in Egypt). The Muslim Brotherhood is an ideological movement that encompasses a number of organisations in different Arab countries (mainly Egypt, Jordan, Syria, Sudan and Palestine). The principal authors of these strategic writings are such prominent clerics as Sheikh Yusuf al-Qaradawi (Egypt/Qatar), Hasan al-Turabi (Sudan), Sheikh Rashid Ghannushi (Tunisia/London) and Tariq Ramadan.

Some of the prominent strategists in this arena are Ayman al-Zawahiri, Abu Musab al-Suri, Abu Musab al-Najdi, Abu Basir al-Tartusi, Abu Muhammad al-Maqdisi, Fares Ahmad al-Shuwayl al-Zahrani (Abu Jandal al-Azdi), Nasser bin Hamad al-Fahd, Ali al-Hamid, and the late Yusuf al-Ayiri. Their writings focus on methods for re-Islamising the Muslim world (the *jihad* against "apostate" regimes), the milestones toward victory over the "infidel" West, and the strategic goals of the Islamist movement—including the model for the future order of the Islamic world after this victory (e.g., the Caliphate model). Other authors affiliated with Al Qaeda in Iraq (such as Abu Abdallah Ahmad al-Imran al-Najdi and Abu Muhammad al-Hilali) deal directly with the strategy in Iraq. Arguably the most authoritative, if not the best-formulated, strategy can be found in the writings of Al Qaeda's supreme commander, Ayman al-Zawahiri.[6]

In the *jihadist* worldview, Islam's war against these internal and external enemies is an ancient one and central to Islamic military history. This confrontation was at the root of the Prophet's wars against the original apostates and the tribes that abandoned Islam (the "*ridda*" wars). The "enemy" in the eyes of all Sunni Islamist movements is composed of four main groups: (1) the West, led by the United States, which embodies and spreads an anti-Muslim Judeo-Christian political culture; (2) the Jews, Zionists and Israel, which promote Western concepts, anti-Muslim/anti-Arab attitudes, and conflicts initiated by the

"Crusaders"; (3) "apostate" Muslim regimes and rulers; and (4) heterodox and secular or "atheistic" Muslims in general. This last group includes Shiites (*al-Murji'a* and *al-Rafida*), Alawites and Kurds, and has become more central in *salafi-jihadi* strategy discussions since the war in Iraq. The strategic writings of the different Sunni movements deal with the different goals toward each of these "enemy" groups.

The goal as regards the West is an integrated military-economic defeat. Numerous *jihadi* texts attribute the power of the West, and particularly of the United States, to its economic domination. The way to end this domination is to execute attacks designed to severely damage the Western economy.

Some of the well known and leading Islamic ideologues who are extensively quoted and followed today and who propagated *jihad* were:

Taqi al-Deen Ahmad Ibn Taymiyya (1268-1328 AD)

The medieval Hanbali professor Ibn Taymiyya has been the most important inspiration for Sunni radicals of the modern era. Many of today's Islamic radicals attempt to present their own creeds as continuations of the practices of previous scholars such as Ibn Taymiyya. However, just as Ibn Taymiyya took Hanbal's teachings and remade them, present day *Wahhabis* and *Salafis* have reinterpreted Ibn Taymiyya's teachings to suit their requirements. Ibn Taymiyya's own rebellious life and his particular place in Islamic history make him a particularly popular scholar for modern radical 'reformers' of Islam.

Maulana Abu'l a'la Maududi (1903-1979)

Pakistani Abu'l a'la Maududi was an extremely important figure in the development of radical *Salafi* Islam in the 20th century. Maududi founded the *Jama'at-i-Islami* (Society of Islam) in 1941 as a centralised, strictly hierarchical organisation, similar to the Muslim Brotherhood. Maududi's *Jama'at-i-Islami* gave rise to the two most important *Mujahideen* factions in the Afghan civil war, that of Ahmad Shah Masud (who leavened his *Salafism* with traditionalism), and Gulbuddin Hekmatyar.

Talaat Fouad Qassem

He was born in 1958 in Egypt. He was one of the founders of the Egyptian Jamaa Islamiya in Egypt in the early 1970s and the spokesman for the organisation. Talaat Fouad Qassem fled Egypt after Anwar Saadat was assassinated in 1981 and was granted political asylum in Denmark. From Denmark, Qassem, along with two Algerian associates, Kamer Eddine Kherbane and Abdullah Anas, who operated from Milan, Italy, coordinated and recruited Muslim European volunteers to fight in Bosnia in the years

1990-95. They sent, eventually, about 2,000 volunteers to camps in Bosnia later known as the 7 Mujahideen Brigade.

Dr Abdullah Azzam

Palestinian-born Islamist Dr. Abdullah Azzam (1941-89) played a leading role in promoting and developing the modern Islamist concept of *jihad.* Little known in the West despite lengthy stays in the United States, Azzam was responsible for internationalising the Islamist struggle against secularism, socialism, and materialism. As forms of *jihad* erupt from Algeria to the Philippines, it is important to understand the man whom so many Mujahideen cite as their inspiration. By tracing Azzam's thought through his most important influences, mediaeval scholar Ibn Taymiyya, Muslim Brotherhood founder Sayyid Qutb, and Egyptian radical Muhammad Faraj, it is possible to see how Azzam transformed radical Islam from a group of disparate movements defined by national borders into a potent (if scattered) force in the international arena.

"Jihad and the rifle alone; no negotiations, no conferences, and no dialogues." This was the uncompromising answer of 'Abdullah Azzam to the encroachments of the Western and Communist worlds into Islamic lands in the 1980s. Azzam's militant interpretation of the Islamic doctrine of *jihad* contributed to the success of the Afghan Mujahideen, and has been an inspiration since his assassination in 1989 to a new generation of radical Islamists, including Osama bin Laden's Al Qaeda organisation and 'Ayman al-Zawahiri's Islamic Jihad group in Egypt.[7]

Dr. Azzam's contribution to Islamic radicalism was to popularise the idea of a universal and international Islamic *jihad,* rather than the existing condition of each national Muslim group concentrating on a narrow area of concern related to its own circumstances. In 'Azzam's words: "*Jihad* must not be abandoned until Allah alone is worshipped. *Jihad* continues until Allah's Word is raised high, until all the oppressed people are freed, to protect our dignity and restore our occupied lands and *jihad* is the way of everlasting glory." Unlike many earlier *jihad* theorists who had never fired a shot in anger, Azzam also provided an example to young Muslims by actively taking up *jihad* in Afghanistan, providing not only his considerable leadership and organisational skills, but by also serving on the frontline of combat. Azzam's long-term goal was the reestablishment of the Islamic Caliphate. In 1987, Azzam presented a list of reasons why young Muslims should join the Afghan *jihad*:

- In order that the disbelievers do not dominate;
- The scarcity of men;

- Fulfilling the duty of *jihad*, and responding to the call of the Lord;
- Following in the footsteps of the Pious Predecessors;
- Establishing a solid foundation as a base for Islam;
- Protecting those who are oppressed in the land; and
- Hoping for martyrdom.

'Azzam moved to Peshawar with a plan to internationalise the *jihad*. In order to facilitate the movement of Islamist volunteers to the Mujahideen struggle, Azzam created the Mukhtab al-Khidmat (Services Centre) in 1984. This office also served as a means of channeling donations from Islamic charities and wealthy individuals in the Gulf states to support the Mujahideen—sources of funding included the Saudi Red Crescent, Saudi intelligence services, the World Muslim League, and many individuals in the Saudi royal family. Azzam sought to establish that the pursuit of armed *jihad* was obligatory on all Muslims in such a way that could potentially draw the entire *ummah* (Islamic community) into the conflict on behalf of Islam: "*Jihad* means the obligation to fight."

Political Islam's great communicator and travelling salesman, Azzam trotted the globe during the 1980s to promote the Afghan *jihad* against the Soviets. By the time of his death in 1989, he had recruited between 16,000 and 20,000 Mujahideen from 20 countries to Afghanistan, visited 50 American cities to advance his cause, and dispatched acolytes to spread the gospel in 26 US states, not to mention across the Middle East and Europe. His Mujahedeen Services Bureau in Peshawar, Pakistan, served as a way station and training ground for fresh recruits as they arrived to participate in the *jihad*. In his seminal work on the necessity of armed *jihad*, *Join the Caravan* (*ilhaq bil-qafilah*), 'Azzam described both the legal obligations and practical considerations surrounding the concept of *jihad*. The conditions upon which *jihad* becomes *fard 'ayn* (individually obligatory) are outlined in an unambiguous fashion. *Jihad* becomes *fard 'ayn* when disbelievers enter the land of the Muslims. This condition, thus, makes *jihad* currently obligatory for every Muslim until the disbelievers are driven from Muslim lands. "It remains *fard 'ayn* continuously until every piece of land that was once Islamic is regained."

As he wrote in *Defense of Muslim Lands*, his best-known booklet, "With specific reference to the Russians, it is not permitted to negotiate with them until they retreat from every hand span of Muslim territory, and in reference to the Jews in Palestine, likewise." This doctrine roused Bin Laden to issue his 1998 *fatwa* declaring that Muslims must kill Americans in order to expel the United States from Saudi Arabia's holy sites.

Shiite Ideologues

Shiite strategy—the Iranian doctrine of "export of the revolution"—stems primarily from the writings and statements of Ayatollah Khomeini. Many years before the establishment of the Islamic Republic in Tehran, Khomeini expounded his main views in his book *Huk -umat-I Islami va Velayat-i Faqih* (*Islamic Governance*). This book called on the clergy to take upon themselves, not only spiritual authority, but also political power—the basis of the principle of *velayat-e faqih* (guardianship of the Islamic jurists). The "Mahdist" doctrine can be found in much-less-definitive texts: sermons of certain clerics, and some writings of a scattering of Ayatollahs. Some apocalyptic writings that focus on hastening the reappearance of the Hidden Imam are associated with the Iranian Revolutionary Guard.

Afghanistan: The Cradle of the *Jihadist* Movement

The Islamic *jihad* against the West actually started in 1973 during the Arab-Israel War when the Muslims used oil as a weapon to counter the West. The 1979 Soviet invasion of Afghanistan provided a timely outlet, as devout young Sunni Muslims—encouraged by the success of the recent (Shiite) Islamic revolution in Iran, yet simultaneously keen to keep Shiism itself in check—responded to calls from religious leaders to join the holy war against the Soviets. The invasion of Afghanistan by Soviet forces at the end of the 1970s further militarised and augmented the Islamic militants who went to Afghanistan to wage an Islamic insurgency.. The Soviet forces were met with fierce resistance by the Afghan Mujahideen, or Islamic warriors. One faction of these fighters would eventually become the Taliban. The Mujahideen called upon Muslims from all over the world to come and join them in their fight against the Soviets, and thousands answered the call. From all over the Muslim world, young men flocked to Afghanistan to fight off the Soviet invasion. What's more, they won! A ragtag army of Islamic warriors drove back the army of a superpower. This victory made a powerful impression on the consciousness of the Muslim world; it was seen as an expression of God's will.

Guidance and Misguidance

One of the leading proponents of this war, Abdullah Azzam, rightly proclaimed as the Lenin of international *jihad*, developed the notion of international participation in *jihad*. He became an increasingly active propagandist for a pan-Islamic *jihad*, writing books on the subject, and in May 1982, published his first article about the Afghan *jihad* in the Muslim Brotherhood journal of *Al-mujtama.* All his journal articles were published as a book, *Signs of the Merciful in the Afghan Jihad*, which presented stories on the so-called *karamat*—the miracles which occur when the *mujahid* falls a martyr. The book was so popular that ten editions of it were published over the next decade and it continues to inspire *jihadis the* world over. The Mujahideen were made to believe that they are both recreating and revitalising Islam's past glories. Further Divine Favour is also bestowed on the Mujahideen, who heal quickly from, or are unhurt by, wounds that would kill others, and emerge from battle looking like shining moons. Angels or mysterious strangers help the Mujahideen to prevail against overwhelming odds, fire from heaven will knock down enemy aeroplanes and helicopters, dogs refuse to bark when the Mujahideen pass by. In 1984, Azzam wrote *The Defence of Muslim Lands* in which he famously argued that the *jihad* in Afghanistan is an individual duty (*fard'ayn*) for all Muslims. These two books had an enormous influence on the mobilisation of Arabs for Afghanistan.[8] Azzam also kept travelling around the Arab world to enlist support for the Mujahideen (holy warriors). Azzam's efforts—funded and supported by the US, UK, Saudi Arabia, China and others—were largely responsible for the influx of foreign (predominantly Muslim Arab) Mujahideen into Afghanistan. Saudi Arabia became a major transit point for those heading to Afghanistan, simultaneously providing an introduction to the country's fundamentalist Wahhabi culture and religious teachers. But it was the experience in Afghanistan that most profoundly affected the Mujahideen, and it is there that they received ideological grounding in a fundamentalist, violent and militaristic worldview.

A decade of fighting was enough to create a substantial, well organised and well trained army, a strong network of contacts, and a new way of life. One of the clearest aspects of the post-Cold War era was the rise of religion as a social and political movement around the globe, and, by extension, the growing number of religiously-driven conflicts. Militant Islam today is competing for the minds of the Muslim masses. It would not be an exaggeration to state that various hardline Islamic militant scholars who were hitherto forgotten or sidelined, suddenly assumed prominence. Their words were carefully dissected and their radical messages were applied with renewed zeal and fervour.

History has witnessed Muslim fighters fighting in countries not of their origin as early as 1967 when fighters from Sudan and Yemen fought alongside the Arab coalition. This was followed in the Lebanon War in 1975 when Israel fought the miscellaneous Palestinian factions and fighters from Egypt, Syria and Jordan took part in the confrontation. However, a tectonic shift in Islamist insurgency started with the Soviet occupation of Afghanistan. The war in Afghanistan gave rise to the *salafi-jihadist* faction of Salafism, of which Al Qaeda became the most prominent exponent. The invasion was seen by the Muslim nations as a subjugation of Islam and Saudi Arabia cleverly exploited this sentiment, pumped in billions of dollars and paved the way for a trans-border insurgency which today has assumed the proportions of an Islamist insurgency stretching from the Balkans to the Philippines. This call for *jihad* attracted fighters from many Muslim countries. The United States, the United Kingdom, and Saudi Arabia became major financial contributors, with the United States donating "$600 million in aid per year, with a matching amount coming from the Persian Gulf states."[1] The People's Republic of China (PRC) also sold Type 59 tanks, Type 68 assault rifles, Type 56 assault rifles, Type 69 RPGs, and much more to the Mujahideen in cooperation with the Central Intelligence Agency (CIA), as did Egypt with assault rifles. Fighters from most Arab countries, Turkey, Pakistan, Bangladesh, Indonesia, and Philippines also poured in to take part in the *jihad.*

Operation Cyclone was the code-name for the CIA's programme to arm, train, and finance the Afghan Mujahideen during the Soviet war in Afghanistan, 1979 to 1989. The programme leaned heavily towards supporting militant Islamic groups that were favoured by neighbouring Pakistan. The main objective of the CIA during the initial stages of the Soviet invasion of Afghanistan was primarily to ensure that the Soviet exercise would be a costly one. The CIA forged a relationship with Pakistan's ISI (Inter-Services Intelligence) and Saudi Arabia's General Intelligence Directorate to funnel funds and weapons to Afghan fighters (Mujahideen). The CIA's Afghan programme, which started during President Carter's tenure, was primarily conducted by the ISI for the most part. Both the US and Pakistan recognised the potential threat posed by the Soviet occupation of Afghanistan. As the US did not want to be directly involved in thwarting the Soviet invasion, it handed over the operational aspect of the programme to the ISI. The ISI was in charge of providing the funds and weapons to the Mujahideen and setting up training camps. Saudi Arabia's intelligence agency also played a very important role in providing funds which were vital for the success of this exercise. During President Reagan's tenure, however, the focus of the CIA began to change. William Casey took over as Director of the CIA and remained personally involved in the Afghan programme. He took steps to ensure that the CIA played a more aggressive role in ruining the Soviet attempt to occupy Afghanistan. The funds and weapons channeled to the Mujahideen soon stood at staggering levels. The CIA's involvement proved to be successful as the Soviets were never able to gain a strong foothold in Afghanistan. The war proved to be far too costly for them. However, their decision to pull out of Afghanistan caught the US off guard. The US did not have a strategy in hand with regard to their involvement in Afghanistan after the Soviet withdrawal. It was widely perceived that the Soviet backed Communist government put in place in

Kabul would soon be toppled by the Mujahideen. The US remained indecisive over the next course of action in Afghanistan and the ISI grabbed the opportunity to carry out its own agenda in Afghanistan.

The CIA made a historic mistake in encouraging Islamic groups from all over the world to come to Afghanistan." The US provided close to $3 billion for building up these Islamic groups, and it accepted Pakistan's demand that it should decide how this money should be spent. The creation of the Taliban had been "actively encouraged by the ISI and the CIA," and "Pakistan has been building up Afghan collaborators who would sustain Pakistan." The CIA was firmly of the opinion that the more fanatical and fiercer the Islamists were, the more fiercely they would fight the Soviets. It was a decision which came to haunt them a decade later.

Afghanistan today is the product of a war fought by others on its soil. The US and its allies plied this country with Stinger missiles and cash to fuel the Mujahideen's opposition against Soviet occupation. They encouraged the growth of Islamic fundamentalism to frighten Moscow, and of drugs to get the Soviet soldiers hooked. The CIA even helped "Arab Afghans" like Osama bin Laden, "America's nemesis", to fight here. When the Soviets fled Kabul, US money and interest also evaporated, leaving a terrible mess behind. It has to be accepted that the Islamic insurgency haunting the globe is part of the West's legacy of intrusion followed by neglect, and Afghanistan is the last orphan of the Cold War. [9]

Al Qaeda was formed in Afghanistan after the Soviet defeat in 1989 by the various Mujahideen groups who were emboldened by their victory over a superpower and, hence, sought to carry their war to other arenas. Given its geographic location, however, the early Al Qaeda was more involved in militant Islamic struggles in Chechnya, Kashmir, and against the Taliban's Afghan rivals in the Northern Alliance.

Transnational Battlefronts

By 1987, the Soviets had withdrawn from Afghanistan, giving the ISI tremendous experience in guerrilla warfare and sabotage while working with the Central Intelligence Agency; and it also inherited a lot of sophisticated equipment.

Now, flushed with victory, the Mujahideen had three choices: return to their countries of origin and get on with their lives; go back to their countries and start radical movements to bring the "true Islam" to their homelands; or go on to fight for Islamist causes in other lands. Many did indeed return home after the war, only to find that the only profession they had—that of holy warriors—was not at all welcome to their totalitarian governments. And so, the Afghan Veterans, as they came to be called, became involved in terrorist groups in Muslim countries from Egypt to Malaysia.

Others attempted to return to their homelands but were refused entry. Their governments knew better than to allow these young firebrands into their territory to make trouble. Refused admission to their countries of origin, many of the Afghan Veterans sought political asylum in the Western countries, especially in the United States. We should not be surprised to find that the United States granted these requests; after all, the United States had supported the Mujahideen. These mercenaries had fought the USSR, and now the US had to pay the price—a green card and political asylum. Islamic radical mercenaries were granted political asylum not only in the United States, but in Germany, Britain, Switzerland and a host of other Western countries.

Yet a third group of mercenaries stayed on in Afghanistan. Many were recruited by Osama bin Laden into his newborn Al Qaeda organisation. Thus, the end of the Afghan War saw the emergence of a totally new kind of international insurgency; an insurgency that could draw upon hundreds of thousands of Islamic activists, sharing a common extremist ideology, and common goals. What's more, these people were veterans with a decade of fighting experience behind them; they knew warfare in all its aspects. And, perhaps more important than anything else, they knew each other: they had fought together in the trenches of Afghanistan; they knew one another's minds and they shared a common bond of experience. It is these battle-hardened fanatics, now spread all over the world who have formed the nucleus of modern global Islamic insurgency. It is this network of Islamist radicals that now threatens the modern world, as well as the moderate Muslim regimes of the Arab world.

The global insurgents, Bin Laden and Ayman al Zawahiri, adopted a three-stage strategy toward the ultimate goal of spreading Islamic radicalism all over the world. The first stage is to spread their version of Islam to Muslim countries in Central Asia and the Middle East, since these were already home to Islamic radical organisations, some of which had large numbers of supporters. The countries with Islamic movements which could serve as the nucleus of radicalism were Afghanistan, Pakistan, Egypt, Palestine and Jordan. Once this first stage was achieved, these "Islamised" countries could serve as the staging ground for the second stage—the spread of radical Islam to countries with large Muslim minorities: Kosovo, Bosnia, Germany, and the former Islamic republics of the USSR. Later, more countries were to be added to the circle of radical Islam: China—especially Xinjiang province—the Philippines, Indonesia, Malaysia and finally north of Africa. Only upon the completion of this stage, would Islamic radicalism be ready for the final stage—the ultimate battle to spread their rule to the rest of Western society. Some of the regions that witnessed this onslaught of global Islamic insurgency are appended below.

Islamic Insurgency in the Indian Subcontinent

Kashmir

When the Soviets withdrew, the Islamic insurgents trained in Pakistan were all rendered jobless The Pakistani ISI saw the *jihadis* available with them in surplus and immediately hit upon the plan to use them in Kashmir. Jammu and Kashmir (J&K) which has always been a bone of contention between secular India and Islamic Pakistan, has witnessed three battles, including Kargil, over its sovereignty. All the battles had ended badly for Pakistan and the 1971 Indo-Pak War that was fought not on Kashmir, led to the dismemberment of Pakistan's eastern region, paving the way for the establishment of Bangladesh. The Pakistanis knew that they would not be able to match India militarily, and, hence, resorted to this sub-conventional war in line with Zia's philosophy of making India bleed through a thousand cuts. They, therefore, trained people from Pakistan, Afghanistan and other places to fight in Kashmir. Most of these new fighters were mercenaries and were paid to fight in Kashmir. These mercenaries were also told that the Muslim faith was in danger and that they were fighting a *jihad* or Holy War. According to figures released in October 1998 by Indian Home Minister L. K. Advani, 32 percent of the 677 militants killed were foreigners. These *jihadis* included Afghans, Sudanese, Egyptians, Lebanese, and Chechnyans. In fact, these figures point to something far more menacing than Pakistan's geographically narrow fixation on Kashmir—merely one staging ground for a massive pan-Islamic geo-strategic enterprise. [10]

The time of the induction of these battle hardened insurgents coincided with the loss of momentum in the insurgency in Jammu and Kashmir and these insurgents were used to give a fresh impetus to the upheaval in the state. Pakistan created *tanzeems* of foreign militants with a majority of Afghans and other equally motivated cadres from other countries. These groups that were both battle hardened and highly motivated, were controlled and led by Pakistani commanders, and were fighting for what they perceived to the just and righteous principles of *jihad*. One of the first groups to surface and begin a reign of terror was the Harkat-ul-Ansar.

India responded with a combination of military and political initiatives, and, thus, has been able to successfully control the insurgency. Though the insurgency lingers on mainly due to cross-border support, it is a far cry from what it was in the 1990s. However, the foreign insurgents, now mainly from Pakistan, continue to hold sway over the momentum of militancy in Jammu and Kashmir till date.[11] The Lashkar-e-Tayyeba, Al Faran, and Harkat-ul Mujahideen were some of the prominent transnational outfits which were operational in Jammu and Kashmir.

Islamic Insurgency in the Balkans

Bosnia

The battle hardened Mujahideen, on the withdrawal of the Soviet forces, found themselves unwelcome in their own countries. However, some sought, and were granted, asylum in Europe, giving rise to an influx of war-hardened radicals into the continent. Some settled down into life in the West and left their *jihadist* past behind them in the battlefields of Afghanistan. Others were still hungry for action and they were soon given the opportunity to continue their struggle through the *jihadist* front that opened up in Bosnia in 1992.

In March of that year, as the former Yugoslavia was breaking up, Bosnia-Herzegovina, in which the majority of Muslims in the country lived, declared its independence, prompting heavy retaliation by Serbian militias and an ensuing ethnic cleansing campaign by the Slobodan Milosevic regime against the Muslim population. Bosnia would not seem the most obvious place in which to wage a holy war given that the Balkans rang few bells in the minds of the majority of Arabs and that the ultimate aim was still to create an Islamic Caliphate in the Middle East, but the outbreak of the crisis proved a kind of godsend for some of the Afghan Veterans who had nowhere else to go. One of the most important Afghan Veterans who made his way to Bosnia was the charismatic Saudi preacher and fighter Abu Abdel Aziz, sometimes referred to as Barbaros. Abu Abdel Aziz became the *emir* of the Arab Afghan fighters in Bosnia and led one of the two Mujahideen factions that were operating in the war under the command of the Bosnian Army. The other group was led by Al-Zubair Al-Haili, who was also a Saudi and who had also been in Afghanistan. Al Haili's group consisted mainly of fighters from Saudi Arabia and the Gulf region, while Abu Abdel Aziz's faction, called Kattibat Al-Mujahideen, consisted mainly of North African fighters.

Like Abdullah Azzam in the Afghanistan War, Abu Abdel Aziz sought religious sanction for the new project. He went to the heart of the Islamic establishment, Saudi Arabia, and met with prominent scholars, including Sheikh Nasir Ad-Din Al-Albani, Sheikh Abdulaziz Bin Baez and Sheikh Muhammad Bin Otheimin, who all gave their backing to the war. While he was in the kingdom, Abu Abdel Aziz also travelled around giving lectures and encouraging people to join his new *jihad*.

However, the real brains behind Abu Abdel Aziz's faction lay in the Egyptian Afghan Veterans who were the real theoreticians and political strategists of the Bosnian *jihad*. After being forced out of Afghanistan, these Egyptians, who were mainly members of the militant Egyptian group Al Jama'a Al-Islamiya, sought, and were granted, political asylum in Europe. From Western Europe, these Egyptians, along with their cohorts inside

Bosnia, such as Egyptian Afghan Veteran Wahiuddin Misri, succeeded in setting up a network to support the *jihad* there.

One of the most influential figures among these Egyptians was Sheikh Anwar Shaban, and on the outbreak of the Bosnian War, he took it upon himself to make his Islamic Centre a recruitment hub for the *jihad.* Shaban is alleged to have developed a large network to send willing young recruits to do their bit for the holy struggle. The Saudis established special aid organisations for Bosnia such as the Saudi High Committee for Aid to Bosnia-Herzegovina, which was set up by Prince Salman Ben Abdulaziz. Funds were channeled through this and other charities and organisations that were operating in Bosnia. Scores of Islamic charitable organisations opened offices in Bosnia, many of them run from the Gulf. The networks built up by these agencies, however, also proved useful in supplying weapons to the fighters.

The Brotherhood in Egypt also launched initiatives in support of the Bosnian refugees and a number of its members went to work in refugee camps in Croatia. The Egyptian Ikhwan also tried to use the Bosnian conflict as a means of putting pressure on the Egyptian regime to support the Bosnian *jihad.*

Not to be outdone by the Saudis and their allies, Iran was also willing to spend money in Bosnia in order to spread its influence in what it viewed as a bridgehead into Europe. In May 1994, Tehran tried to display its commitment to the Bosnians by opening a new embassy in Sarajevo. It also openly flouted the arms embargo that had been imposed by the United Nations in 1991. In May 1994, for example, an Iranian Air Force transport plane, loaded with explosives and material for weapons production, landed in Zagreb, its cargo bound for the Bosnian Army. The *jihadis* were successful in ensuring Bosnia became an independent state, though the efforts were doubled by the North Atlantic Treaty Organisation's (NATO's) aerial blitz which hastened the Serbs' defeat.

However, as far as Western Europe was concerned, the Bosnian crisis did have an impact, albeit limited, beyond those immediately engaged in the various networks: it served to heighten feelings among Muslim communities that while the West had been prepared to go thousands of miles to strike against Saddam Hussein in 1990, it was slow to assist Muslims who were being massacred on its doorstep. Some Muslims who were living in Europe complained that the Bosnian War had made them feel vulnerable because it had proved that Western governments had shown no compassion even for white Muslims who were part of the same continent. The Bosnian conflict was adopted as part of the discourse of Islamists in Europe and came to represent another example of the Western world's perceived disregard for Islam and Muslims.

These feelings generated a stronger sense of unity among the Muslims in general and *jihadis* in particular that it is their moral obligation to rush to the aid of oppressed Muslims wherever they may be.

Islamic Insurgency in the Caucasus

Chechnya

With Afghanistan over, some of the veterans tried to find another Islamic battlefield where they could continue the *jihad*. Some headed to Chechnya, some to Tajikistan and others to Kashmir. None of these locations was as glamorous as Afghanistan, and only Chechnya really struck a chord with the Arabs. This was largely because of the presence of Chechen communities in a number of Arab countries, including Jordan and Syria, and a general awareness among Islamists that the Soviet Union was Communist and, therefore, infidel. However, these hotspots provided a place to go and a cause to fight for. What started as an insurgency in Chechnya, in a couple of years lost its sheen and what is seen and being witnessed today are nothing but acts of terrorism.

Since 1989, radical Islam has gradually permeated the fabric of Chechnya's socio-political environment. In this regard, during his initiation as Chechen President on November 9, 1991, retired Lieutenant-General of the Soviet Air Forces, Djohar Dudayev was sworn in, holding a Quran, in front of numerous representatives of Islamic religious institutions. During his inauguration ceremony, Dudayev promised to abide by, and to protect, the Islamic faith. The Russian federal government's efforts to establish martial law in Chechnya and to disarm the military branches of the National Chechen People's Congress resulted in an upsurge of Islamic sentiments among the local population and increasing usage of Islamic rhetoric by radical-nationalist elements in Chechnya. Chechen Islamisation was further accelerated by Grozny's frustration that resulted from the failure to achieve international recognition of Chechnya as an independent entity. International refusal to support Chechen separatist aspirations made adherence to internationally accepted norms of governance redundant in the eyes of the Chechen leadership.

Chechnya was under both internal and external pressure to increase the Islamic character of the state and of the struggle. It was at that point in time, before the beginning of the First Chechen War in December 1994, that the Chechen separatists established their first significant ties with Middle Eastern radical Islamists. Forces emerged from a number of Muslim countries that actively supported Dudayev's line of separatism and of strengthening Islam's integration into the Chechen society as an additional factor of political contention against Moscow. Groups of missionaries, who called themselves "preachers of Islam", arrived in the North Caucasus from Syria, Jordan, Saudi Arabia, United Arab Emirates (UAE), Turkey, and Libya. Many of these Arab fighters were Afghan Veterans, whose incursion in Chechnya was sanctioned by the leadership of Al Qaeda and other global *jihadi* organisations The Islamic missionaries who infiltrated Chechnya were representatives of fundamentalist political Islam in its Salafi-Jihadi interpretation who encouraged the Chechens to reject Sufism and follow a radical interpretation of Islam. In addition to "Wahhabi" propagators, Chechnya became a popular destination for Middle Eastern militants and mercenaries, including the Afghani Mujahideen, who were supplied with weapons and transferred to the Caucasus. The most prominent figure among the foreign fighters in Chechnya was Ibn al-Khattab, who arrived in Chechnya along with eight other fighters in spring 1995. Khattab and his companions established a "foreign holy warrior" battalion, which played a critical role in Chechen military operations from1996-99 and offered military training to Chechen separatists.

It is apparent that this influx of support from abroad played a decisive role in Dudayev's shift towards Islamic values, and his consequent disengagement from the secular model of government. Islam settled in as the main form of Chechen self-identification in the post-Soviet period and quickly became a symbol of opposition to the modern Russian state and to the Christian civilisation altogether.

Islamist ideology was put to active use during the First Chechen War in 1994-96. The fight for independence (as it was perceived by most Chechens at the time) received its political and spiritual grounding in the militant interpretation of the Quranic verses that call for armed struggle against "infidel" occupiers of Muslim territories. The idea of militant *jihad* – armed resistance aimed at completely eradicating the *kafirs* (non-Muslims) from Chechen territory – became a ubiquitous notion. The spirit of *jihad* penetrated practically all Chechen regions; it inspired and unified different layers of society, especially the younger generations. Green headbands inscribed with statements taken from the Quran were worn by many young Chechens, who vowed to fight without regard to their own lives, as warriors of Islam. In this light, the perpetrators of numerous terrorist and guerrilla attacks throughout the war, including the ones masterminded by Shamil Basayev in Budyonnovsk (1995) and Pervomayskoye (1996), wore green Islamic headbands, thereby clearly exhibiting Islamist characteristics. Both attacks are generally referred to as watersheds of the First Chechen War that influenced the strategic and political relations between Yeltsin's administration and the separatist Chechen government. The Russians suffered heavy losses during the First Chechen War.

During the Second Chechen War, Russian military commanders perceived the war as a chance to atone for the losses suffered in the war in Afghanistan (1979-89), and during the First Chechen War (1994-96). The Russian military also wished to demonstrate to Russia's neighbours including NATO, that Moscow would maintain a no-tolerance policy towards Islamist insurgents, regardless of foreign governmental and non-governmental criticism.

The military success in Chechnya simultaneously entailed a number of political rewards for Moscow, including reestablishing territorial integrity, strengthening national unity, restoring motivation among the armed forces and defending Russia's authority in the international arena.

The price of military success, however, proved to be daunting: thousands of civilians, Russian soldiers and Chechen fighters perished in the war, with displaced persons numbering in the hundreds of thousands. Russian Generals managed to complete their main mission towards the beginning of 2001, when the main Chechen formations were defeated. At the end of January 2001, Putin transferred the control of the military operation from the Defence Ministry to the special forces, noting that the military campaign would continue.

Although the separatists were defeated from a military perspective, as long as the notorious leaders such as K. Hattab, Gelayev, Yandarbiyev, Raduyev, Saydulayev, and Basayev remained active, complete victory over the Chechen insurgents remained a distant notion. Russian analysts correctly assessed that without the liquidation of these Islamist warlords, low-intensity warfare in Chechnya could have lasted for a very long time. This assessment was substantiated by the tragic terrorist attacks that followed in Chechnya and in Russia itself – airliner bombings, assassinations of pro-Moscow Chechen leaders, and unprecedentedly brutal attacks in the Moscow Theatre siege (2002), Moscow Metro (2004), and in Beslan (2004).The Moscow Theatre (Nord Ost) siege was a devastating terrorist event, conducted by a few dozen Chechen terrorists belonging to the Special Purpose Islamic Regiment (SPIR). Armed with automatic weapons and explosives, the assailants took 850 hostages and demanded the complete withdrawal of Russian forces from Chechnya. The siege was led by Movsar Barayev, who was killed, along with most of the terrorists and 129 hostages, in the controversial counter-terrorist operation conducted by the Russian Special Forces.

Russia's policy of intensified targeted killings, simultaneously targeting both Maskhadov's and Basayev's factions, proved decisive in curtailing Chechen resistance as a whole. This policy resulted in virtually absolute annihilation not only of the most notorious "Wahhabi" terrorists, but also of many "moderate" separatist leaders. Thus, by treating both Chechen factions as a single "separatist" threat, Moscow managed to achieve two crucial objectives: severely hampering foreign Islamic presence in Chechnya and undermining the overall structure of Chechen separatism as a whole.[12]

The current President of Chechnya is Ramzan Kadyrov and is apparently in control of a brutal militia force called "Kadyrovtsky" which he has assigned to operate against the rebel forces. Kadyrov and his forces have been the targets of numerous allegations of violent human rights abuses. There have been appeals to the authorities regarding the abduction or disappearance of relatives. The control over security in Chechnya has been transferred from the Federal Russian forces to the local security forces. Chechnya's oil wealth also continues to be an important issue, with legitimate Russian and Chechen interests competing for the benefits of the oil reserves.

Insurgency in the Middle East

Iraq

Since the end of the major phase of the war in Iraq and the collapse of the former Baathist regime of Saddam Hussein in May 2003, Iraq—like Afghanistan in the 1980s, and Bosnia and Chechnya in the 1990s—has turned into a magnet for *jihadi* volunteers. Unlike the case of Afghanistan, Bosnia, and Chechnya, the vast majority of the volunteers that streamed into Iraq are Arabs, while only a few fighters are from non-Arab Muslim countries or emigrant communities in the West. The one possible reason for the predominantly Arab composition of *jihadists* in Iraq may be the fact that Iraq is an Arab country, occupied by the "Crusaders," thus, stimulating the *jihadi-salafi* individuals and groups. An additional reason may be the ease with which Saudis, Kuwaitis, Jordanians, or Syrians can cross the borders to Iraq. Furthermore, the Sunni *jihadi* groups, and many other Islamists, even from within the Saudi and other Arab Islamic establishments, view the insurgency in Iraq as a legitimate *jihad* not only against the Americans, but against the Shias as well.

The insurgency that has grown in Iraq since the downfall of the regime of Saddam Hussein and Allied occupation in April 2003, has gripped the country in a spiral of lawlessness and anarchy. Despite the presence of over 150,000 Allied forces and the training of thousands of local Iraqi police and security forces, Iraq is still dominated by armed insurgents who are weakening and sabotaging post-war reconstruction in the areas of law and order, oil production, and road infrastructure. The radically inspired factions that had emerged from the Afghan War in the early 1990s formed a new, radical, armed, and ideologically fanatical Diaspora. Saudi fundamentalist clerics, such as Sheikh Ali Bin Khudayr and Sheikh Nasir bin Hamad al-Fahd, both of whom were disciples of Sheikh Hamoud al-Shuaybi were leading personalities in this trend. Such figures are believed, along with others, such as Yusuf al-Ayyri, to have sanctioned the new *jihadi* factions that began to emerge to wage insurgent attacks in Iraq in the late spring of 2003. In November 2004, a group of Saudi clerics issued a call for Iraqis to undertake a *jihad* against "occupation" targets in the country. This element was not indigenous to Iraq but its near neighbours in Saudi Arabia and Jordan were also host to such groups. They found it easy to infiltrate the border into Iraq in the chaos that ensued following the fall of Saddam Hussein.

The *jihadi* elements quickly gained ground in Iraq. Their ideology of puritanical theology and militancy through violent action—packaged as *jihad*—appealed to those in Iraq who were left powerless in the ensuing breakdown in law and order and chaos in their own society. It became quite clear that common cause could be made in turning the global message of the *jihad* groups into a local insurgent struggle against the Western occupation of Iraq. Thousands of Arab Mujahideen elements had entered Iraq before, during, and after the war as part of the rallying cry to wage *jihad*.

Even before the outbreak of the war, Arab volunteers were reported to be crossing into Iraq to begin training led by militant *jihadi* groupings. As the country slid under Allied occupation and the first suicide bombings against prominent targets in Baghdad took place, sources pointed to the Arab Mujahideen as the operatives.

The presence of such elements has added a new dimension to the Sunni face of insurgency in Iraq. The involvement of Arab Mujahideen in this context reflects the global nature of the conflict as it unfolds in Iraq. This trend is symbolised by the Arab *jihad* fighters with their extreme violent tactics and assaults on Allied Coalition targets and local Iraqis deemed "collaborators," such as police and National Guard personnel. Their motivation is centred on the ideology of a global *jihad* to end Western domination in Muslim lands.

Though a semblance of normalcy has returned to Iraq, it still represents a pressure cooker ready to burst as the warring *jihadi* factions of Shias and Sunnis are yet to be brought together.

Insurgency in Asia

Afghanistan

The Taliban insurgency took root shortly after the group's fall from power following the 2001 War in Afghanistan. There is a huge presence of forces from NATO countries under the banner of the ISAF (International Security Assistance Force) to counter the Taliban and restore normalcy in Afghanistan. The Taliban continue to attack Afghan, US, and other ISAF troops with impunity and many terrorist incidents attributable to them have been registered. The war has also spread over the southern and eastern borders of the country to Pakistan, in particular the Waziristan areas. The Taliban conduct low-intensity warfare against the Afghan National Army and Coalition forces. There are many players now in Afghanistan that are operating against the NATO Coalition forces: the Haqqani network and the Hezb-e-Islami Gulbuddin Hekmatayar and there is also a Taliban group in Pakistan. The US military commanders call the Afghan Taliban Big T and they call the Pakistani Taliban Little T. The Afghan Taliban's main goal is to remove the foreign forces and their backed government from Afghanistan. Their leadership councils are intact and they operate in almost all parts of Afghanistan in one form or the other. The Taliban control most of the countryside from Herat (northwestern Afghanistan) to Kandahar (southern Afghanistan) to Kunar (northeastern Afghanistan). Taliban fighters are also said to have started operations in the northern city of Mazar-i-Sharif.

The Pakistani Taliban's main goals are very unclear and they do cross the border to Afghanistan to fight NATO forces but their main concern seem to be in the Pakistani tribal areas. There is also the Hezb-e-Islami militia which operates in northeastern Afghanistan. The insurgency continues strongly in 2011. The Taliban continue attacking and ambushing NATO and Afghan troops as well as targeted assassinations of government officials.

In addition, Islamic insurgencies are currently raging in Yemen, Philippines, Pakistan and Indonesia. The Central Asian Republics have all been infested with transnational Islamic insurgency.

What Drives the Insurgents?

The following motivations are particularly salient among the *jihadis*:

- **Justifying the Act:** The ideology describes—and statements by insurgents reflect—the need to defend Islam from attack as an individual duty for each and every Muslim; participation in *jihad* as the ultimate proof of one's worthiness as a Muslim; and failure to participate in *jihad* as an act of heresy.
- **Shaping the Mental Framework of the Attacker:** Ideology shapes the mental framework of the insurgent by constantly repeating the West's real or perceived infractions against Islam. This tends to employ conspiracy theories to further incite fear and hatred of the West. These conspiracy theories may involve a gross exaggeration of real infractions (e.g., accusing the United States of killing many more civilians in a military operation than have actually been killed), or a fabrication of lies (e.g., accusing the White House or Mossad of being behind 9/11). These conspiracy theories are often designed to deflect blame from Muslims (e.g., blaming the West, as opposed to Osama

bin Laden, for 9/11), thus, portraying Muslims as victims. This ongoing victimisation of Muslims, has created a siege mentality among some Muslims, who have accepted the notion that they are under consistent attack and humiliation.

- **Revenge:** The statements and wills of the insurgents reflect an intense desire to exact revenge upon the enemy by inflicting upon him the same pain that he has allegedly inflicted on the insurgent's brethren. Revenge is perhaps the single most important motive and motivation for a person.
- **Restoring Honour and Manhood:** As statements across the board suggest, the insurgents feel that they need to perpetrate a suicide attack in order to restore their honour and, by extension, the honour of an Islam that has been subjected to repeated humiliation by the West over centuries and up to the present time. Related to this, many insurgents, including the suicide bombers, seem to believe that perpetrating a suicide bombing is a manly deed—a belief that is exploited by the leadership of the various groups, which often appeal to Muslims to be "real men" and defend the honour of Islam.
- **Commitment:** A strong commitment to the cell or larger group appears as a frequent motive for insurgents. Commitment to one's kin, a small social group, or larger community—which in some cases may be explained by primordial bonds—is intensified, in the case of globalised suicide attacks, by a shared sense of victimisation. The internet plays a crucial role in providing a sense of brotherhood, a sense of solidarity, belonging, pride, and empowerment to these insurgents.
- **Martyr's Benefits:** The statements and wills that we have examined strongly suggest that suicide bombers believe that by becoming martyrs, they will reap a number of benefits. They firmly believe that the act of martyrdom is a service to God, and pleasing to Him. Because of their willingness to sacrifice their lives in the service of God, they believe that God rewards the martyr by washing away all of the martyr's sins. Furthermore, the martyr enjoys the benefits of paradise, a reservation for scores of his or her family members in heaven, and a wedding to the *houris* (black-eyed virgins) of paradise. Although the possibility of sexual motivations driving male suicide attackers is sometimes dismissed by researchers, statements made by the bombers, as evidenced here, are replete with references to the women of paradise. While this fact, in itself, does not prove that suicide bombers die and kill for sexual pleasure, it is nevertheless clear that sponsoring groups continuously promise these rewards to would-be-bombers. And yet, it is fair to assume that these groups would not consistently preach the rewards of paradise if they did not believe that these promises would not resonate at some level with would-be-bombers. That said, there

is no evidence suggesting that the benefits of sexual pleasures are either a necessary or a sufficient factor for a person to become a suicide bomber.

- Martyrdom operations furthermore are portrayed as the weapon of the weak in an asymmetric battle against a materially more superior enemy. In this battle, the Mujahideen, who do not possess the weaponry and technological sophistication of the West, nevertheless defeat the West with their will power, selflessness, as well as ingenuity, illustrated in the Mujahideen's ability to beat the West at its own game by utilising the West's technologies against itself.
- **Indoctrination and Incitement:** Ideology, again, enables individuals to perpetrate the act of killing and dying by helping to articulate the justification for the act; by shaping the mental framework of the attacker; and by helping the insurgent to morally disengage from his act and from the victim.

Insurgents' Battles Against Americans

The Islamic insurgents have been so motivated by the likes of Osama Bin Laden who would coax his Islamic insurgents to hit wherever American interests rest, thereby hurting American interests all over the world. The targets can be varied, ranging from military, economic or even civilians. The Khobar Towers bombing in 1996 in Saudi Arabia, the bombing of the USS *Cole* in the port of Aden in Yemen, the bombings of the US Embassies in Nairobi and Dar-es-salam in 1998, the 1983 bombing of the United States Embassy in Beirut, the bombing of the United States Marine Barracks also in 1983, and the bombing of the World Trade Centre in 1993, all fall under this category of hurting Americans over the globe.

This plan is primarily to spread in the territory and open new and several battlefronts with the Americans to disperse their forces and deny them the chance to focus on one region. There were plans to attack US economic interests, including gas and oil pipelines and infrastructure, power generating dams, and strike oil tankers through explosive laden speed boats in international waters. These were revealed during the recent arrest of an Al Qaeda operative in Pakistan. The recent shooting of two United States Air Force personnel at Frankfurt airport in Germany, by an Albanian Islamic terrorist, Arid Uka, on March 02, 2011, also falls under this category.

Global Vs National Battles

The implication of this kind of conflict is that Islamic insurgents from all over the world would come to a particular country to fight for the Islamic cause. This was the trend which caused the spread of global Islamist insurgency and was widely seen in Afghanistan, Kashmir in India, Chechnya, Bosnia, Iraq, Yemen, and the Philippines.

One factor that worked in Al Qaeda's favour was that the aftermath of 9/11 did not alter the fact that individuals who had trained in camps in Afghanistan were present in a multitude of countries in the world. In many cases, these fighters, who were affiliated with Al Qaeda, had been present in these regions before 9/11, including in Africa (Somalia, Kenya), Southeast Asia, Chechnya, Kashmir, Central Asia, Western Europe, the Middle East, and North America. Training camps would soon reemerge, first, in Central Asia, then spread to Asia, Southeast Asia, the Far East, and Africa. As the centre of gravity of Al Qaeda shifted increasingly to its affiliates, Al Qaeda suddenly appeared not only as a highly robust, but also as a truly global network of terrorists and insurgents, whose members were able to strike in such distant places as Aceh, Chechnya, Indonesia, Iraq, Kashmir, Kenya, Morocco, Saudi Arabia, and Yemen. In sum, Al Qaeda's forced reliance on local groups, brought about by the pressures exerted on the group after September 11, helped render the group more resilient. As Bruce Hoffman put it a year after the most deadly terrorist attacks on the US homeland, "Al Qaeda has, in fact, proved to be remarkably nimble and adaptive—and the group's strength derives precisely from this flexibility." The movement consists of "smaller international Sunni extremist groups who have benefited from Al Qaida links," such as the Zarqawi network, Ansar al-Islam, the Libyan Islamic Fighting Group, and the Islamic Movement of Uzbekistan." A second level of threats was posed by "small local groups, with limited domestic agendas, that work with international terrorist groups in their own countries. These small local groups have an autonomous leadership, pick their own targets, and plan their own attacks. The foreign *jihadists* draw on broad support networks, have wide appeal, and enjoy a growing sense of support from Muslims who are not necessarily supporters of terrorism. The Sipah-e-Sahaba and its more militant offshoot, Lashkar-e-Jhangvi, two radically anti-Shia *salafi-jihadis*t terrorist outfits previously focussed on Kashmir as well, have increasingly adopted the goals of global *jihad*. Perhaps the most well-known of groups to have turned from a local to a global outfit is Jemaah Islamiyya (JI), an Indonesia-based group that is bent on establishing an Islamic Caliphate throughout all of Southeast Asia.

Strategies and Plans for Enhancing the Scope of Islamist Insurgency

The transnational insurgent movements, especially Al Qaeda, have an overarching narrative, and continue to attract followers from a multitude of countries. All the while, the interplay of the Al Qaeda Core (AQC) with its affiliated groups, associated groups, and inspired adherents provides an increasing number of pathways to violence. A number of successful and unsuccessful plots in the past decade, and especially the last two years, serve as a stark reminder that the global *jihad* remains devoted to striking its enemies, often with ingenuity.

In 2004, Al-Suri, a radical Islamic scholar, posted a massive, 1,600-page book on the internet titled, *The Call of the International Islamic Resistance*—a treatise that outlines future strategies for the global *jihad* movement, placing terrorist attacks and decentralised urban warfare at the forefront of methods that will guarantee success to the global *jihad* movement.[13] (Al-Suri, who was captured in Quetta in October 2005, saw his role as that of educating the "third generation" of Muslim fighters, i.e., more dispersed Mujahideen who did not receive systematic training in the Afghan camps. Among his recommendations to the new generation of Mujahideen was his call on Muslims to wage a decentralised global *jihad* against the United States and other infidel countries. Links to the organisation's leadership cadre should be kept at a minimum in order to evade enemy security advances. In August 2005, after the London bombings, he encouraged sleeper cells around the globe to launch a general front as part of a "global conflict" against the entire West and its allies. In this decentralised war, Al-Suri believed that propaganda and *jihadist* indoctrination was of key importance. He recalled the failure of the *jihadist* experience in Syria, blaming the defeat of the Muslim Brotherhood on a lack of strategy and planning, a lack of ideological grounding, a dearth of *jihadist* theory and weaknesses in the foundations of propaganda. Al-Suri, whose writings are prominently featured on websites close to Al Qaeda such as the Global Islamic Media Front (GIMF), has become one of, and possibly the prime, theoretician of Al Qaeda after 9/11 who acts in a systematic and organised manner, and exhibits the patience of the first generation of Al Qaeda that is often lacking in younger *jihadists* such as Zarqawi. Al Suri's 1,600-page treatise is a "masterpiece of strategic thought."[14] Almost all Sunni terrorist Islamist insurgent groups operating around the globe have an affiliation to Al Qaeda, making Al Qaeda the single largest global insurgent group. Henceforth, for all practical purposes, Al Qaeda would be cited as an example of a global insurgent organisation.

Adaption by Transnational Insurgent groups

Al Qaeda has emerged as the sole global terrorist group though there are various regional groups operating in the peripheries of their neighbouring countries.

First, Al Qaeda increased its media production in the years following 9/11 to compensate for the loss of its training camp infrastructure and its corresponding centrality among *jihadist* groups. This increase also reflected its maturation as a terrorist organisation seeking to capitalise on its newly-found brand recognition.[15] Spurred on by the thoughts and actions of fellow insurgents such as Abu Musab al-Suri and Younis

Tsouli (aka Irhabi007), AQC embraced the agenda-setting power of the internet, hence, Al Qaeda's supremo Ayman al-Zawahiri's assertion that at least half of the overall battle against the Crusader-Zionist foe takes place in the media. A look at the number of official Al Qaeda releases demonstrates the steadily growing output of media productions on the part of the group, from six in 2002 to 11 in 2003, 13 in 2004, 16 in 2005, 58 in 2006, and peaking in 2007 with 97 releases. The number of media releases dropped to 49 releases in 2008 and picked up slightly to reach 79 releases in 2009, but seemed to drop again in 2010. After 2003, Al Qaeda proved particularly skillful at exploiting the widespread negative sentiment about the American invasion and occupation of Iraq. It would seize upon the Ethiopian occupation of Mogadishu in a similar way, urging the erstwhile Islamist militia turned *jihadist* group Al Shabaab to "fight on" as "champions of Somalia."

The second element of Al Qaeda's strategic evolution after 9/11 was its determination to exploit the perceived weaknesses of the West. Al Qaeda and its scions have increasingly monitored, identified, and exploited gaps in Western defences by reading Western literature and downloading material from Western websites. This new *jihadi* tactic was exemplified by a new genre of *jihadi* publications termed "*jihadi* strategic studies"—writings that draw on Western secular-rationalist sources, identify and analyse the weaknesses of both parties, consider political, economic, and cultural factors in the conflict, and recommend realistic strategies. The *Inspire* magazine, an English language *jihadist* magazine produced by Al Qaeda in the Arabian Peninsula (AQAP), illustrates this trend. The first edition of *Inspire* featured a "Message to the American People and Muslims in the West" by Anwar al-Awlaki, a dual US and Yemeni citizen—an article that points to a future of religious intolerance for Muslims in the United States. Al-Awlaki contextualises this prediction with examples of racism from American history.[16] In follow-on editions, *Inspire* amplified examples of Islamophobia in the West, such as the proposed Quran burnings and protests over the establishment of mosques, to underline his arguments and rein force Al Qaeda's narrative of a war against Islam.

Third, since 9/11, Al Qaeda has become more political in terms of its communiqués as well as the timing and targeting of its attacks. The group has attempted to create a rift between the United States and its allies, conducting attacks against Spanish, British, German, and other forces to undermine popular support for the war efforts in Afghanistan, Iraq, and other theatres. Osama bin Laden's offer of a truce to the European countries in April 2004 served a similar goal, as he withheld that offer from the United States. Further, the group began exploiting the Western political calendar, as was most clearly evident in the timing of the March 11, 2004, attacks in Madrid, which were carried out just prior to the Spanish presidential elections. A plot that disrupted Oslo, Norway, in July 2010, is another indicator of Al-Qaeda's interest in attacking "peripheral" Western nations allied with the United States and Israel.

A fourth strategic adaptation in the post-9/11 period is Al Qaeda's emphasis on economic *jihad*, foremost by targeting oil facilities in the Middle Eastern and Gulf states. Prior to the 9/11 attacks, Bin Laden acknowledged the strategic importance of the energy sector, as is evident in his 1996 declaration of war, where he called upon the Mujahideen to "protect this (oil) wealth and [do] not include it in the battle as it is a great Islamic wealth and a large economic power essential for the soon to be established Islamic state. The insurgents have declared the "bleed-until-bankruptcy" strategy as far as American economic interests are concerned.

Fifth, Al Qaeda's mergers with militant groups, including Jama'at Tawhid wal Jihad in Iraq, the Salafist Group for Preaching and Combat (GSPC) in Algeria, al-Shabaab in Somalia, and the reconstitution of AQAP, have all resulted in a fundamental structural shift. Rather than an organisation with cells spread in scores of countries, Al Qaeda in 2011 is better understood as a multipolar organisation with a central hub in North Waziristan and a small number of autonomous regional nodes. By offering their organisational acumen to Al Qaeda, these organisations extend Al Qaeda's ideological and operational influence in their respective regions, while also allowing Al Qaeda to engage in networking, propagandising, and resource mobilisation in active conflict zones. These nodes create resilience and dynamism in the movement, amplify the world's perception of Al Qaeda, and even provide a degree of redundancy should Al Qaeda suffer a devastating blow in Pakistan.

The most consequential implication of Al Qaeda's structural transition into a multi-polar entity lies in the resulting locations, targets, and tactics of terrorist violence. Thus, the most likely theatres for current and future attacks against local and Western targets are those in proximity to the main territorial hubs of the Al Qaeda Core and its affiliates, such as Afghanistan, Algeria, Iraq, Pakistan, Somalia, Yemen, and their neighbours.[17] It is not a coincidence that Al Qaeda's tactics such as suicide bombings have been introduced precisely in these regions, where *jihadist* cells, including Al Qaeda affiliates, have sprung up. Algeria, Somalia, and Yemen, for example, have seen prolonged periods of localised, brutal violence, but radical Islamist groups in these countries traditionally shunned the use of suicide bombings against Western targets until Al Qaeda solidified its affiliations in these areas. Besides the adoption of suicide attacks, the use of Vehicle-Borne Improvised Explosive Devices (VBIEDs) offers additional evidence of knowledge transfer to these regional nodes.

Transnational Insurgents' Score Card

The first, and most obvious, strength is that after regrouping along the Afghan-Pakistan border, Al Qaeda has been able to reestablish a limited safe haven in an active conflict zone. This allows Al Qaeda to link up to other like-minded groups either directly involved in the conflict or living parasitically off the war economies of that conflict. These associated organisations can then share training resources, fund raising and mobilisation networks, and opportunities for propaganda. Al Qaeda can facilitate violence locally, enable *jihadist* attacks abroad, and shape propaganda as consultants to a violent *jihad*.[18]

The second of these strengths is that Al Qaeda's foundational ideological assumption remains convincing to politicised demographics; the United States is, in their perception, waging a war on Islam as evidenced by its occupation of Muslim countries. As long as US military is present in Arab and Muslim countries—a political reality beyond Iraq and Afghanistan, given current events in Yemen, Libya, and Somalia—Al Qaeda's propaganda will resonate.

Major Global Attacks

August 07, 1998	—Bombing of the United States Embassy at Kenya and Tanzania. (To mark the 8th anniversary of the arrival of American forces in Saudi Arabia).
October 12, 2000	—USS *Cole* attacked by suicide terrorists in Aden.
September 11, 2001	—World Trade Centre and Pentagon attacks.
March 11, 2004	—Madrid train bombings.
July 07, 2005	—London underground train bombings.
November 26, 2008	—Terrorist attack in Mumbai.

Conclusion

Islamist insurgency continues to enable the violence of others, orient that violence especially towards the United States and its allies in a distributed game of attrition warfare, and foster a dichotomous "us versus them" narrative between the Muslim world and the rest of the international community. The insurgent groups have adapted to changing environmental pressures at the strategic, ideological, and structural levels, and the aggregation of these adaptations has fundamentally changed the nature of the *jihadist* threat to the West. This evolved threat is not inherently more dangerous, as counter-terrorism efforts today focus on, and disrupt, capability earlier and more consistently than prior to September 2001. This multifaceted global *jihad* will, however, continue, despite this overarching consistency.

Notes

1. Samuel P. Huntington, The *Clash of Civilizations and the Remaking of World Order* (Penguin Publishers, 1996), pp. 210-211.
2. Thomas Hegghammer, "The Rise of Muslim Foreign Fighters," *International Security*, Vol.35 No.3, Winter 2010/11, pp. 54 & 56. .
3. Jason Burke, *Al Qaeda: The True story of Radical Islam* (IB Tauris Publishers, 2006), pp. 56-57.
4. Jarret M. Brachman, *Global Jihadism Theory and Practice* (Routledge, 2009), pp. 8-9.
5. Charles Lindhol and Jose Pedro Zuqete, *The Struggle for the World, Liberation Movements for the 21st Century* (Stanford University Press, 2010), p.127.
6. Quintan Wiktorowicz, ed., *Islamic Activism* (Indiana University Press, 2004), pp.186-187.
7. Andrew McGregor, "Jihad and the Rifle Alone—Abdullah Azzam and the Islamist Revolution," *The Journal of Conflict* Studies, Fall 2003.
8. Thomas Hegghammer, *Jihad in Saudi Arabia: Violence and Pan-Islamism Since 1979* (Cambridge University Press 2010), pp.41-42.
9. Sanjay Suri, India Abroad News Service, March 6, 2001.
10. Robert G. Wirsing, *Kashmir in the Shadow of War: Regional Rivalaries in a Nuclear Age* (ME Sharpe Publishers, 2003), pp.115-116.
11. Lt Col Vivek Chadha, *Low Intensity Conflicts in India: An Analysis* (Sage Publications, 2005), pp.130-131.
12. Artem Kroupnev, "Radical Islam in Chechnya," International Insitute of Counter-Terrorism, September 23, 2009.
13. Stephen Ulph, "Setmariam Nasar: Background on Al-Qaeda's Arrested Strategist," *Terrorism Focus 3*, No. 12, March 28, 2006.
14. Reuven Paz, "Al Qaeda's Search for New Fronts: Instructions for Jihadi Activity in Egypt and Sinai,"PRISM Occasional Papers 3, No. 7, October 2005.
15. Vahid Brown, *Cracks in the Foundation: Leadership Schisms in Al-Qa'ida 1989-2006* (West Point, NY: Combating Terrorism Centre, September 2007).
16. Anwar al-Awlaki, "Shaykh Anwar's Message to the American People and Muslims in the West," *Inspire*, Issue 1, Summer 2010. This is a reprint of the speech published as an audio file. It was released originally on March 10, 2010, and again in July 2010.
17. Assaf Moghadam, "Shifting Trends in Suicide Attacks," *CTC Sentinel 2.1*, January 2009.
18. Alex Gallo, "Understanding Al Qa'ida's Business Model," *CTC* Sentinel 4.1, January 2011.

8

Role of the IAF in National Defence

Nishant Gupta

Human aspirations for acquiring the ability to manoeuvre in the medium of air are probably as old as humanity itself. From time immemorial, man has had a fantasy and a deep-rooted desire to get airborne. Almost all the epics mention some kind of employment of air power by the divine forces. Air power has drawn the imagination of philosophers, literary scholars, futurists, scientists and military leaders alike. Due to the human imagination, the innovations and tireless efforts of several enthusiasts, the exploitation of the 'third dimension' became a reality and, thus, air power was born.

Flying activity started with the invention of the kite and progressed with the creation of lighter-than-air balloons and airships. What revolutionised the concept and capabilities of air power was the invention of heavier-than-air aircraft. Thereafter, the launch of the Sputnik started the era of exploitation of space.

The roles of air power expanded with the development of technology and doctrines. Due to primitive and nascent technology, use of air power was initially restricted to auxiliary roles such as reconnaissance, observation and communication. Subsequently, as a counter-measure to reconnaissance and bomber aircraft, the concept of air superiority was born and a need for the fighter aircraft was generated. During World War II, new fighter aircraft were invented and since then, the requirement of air superiority has become integral to any force deployment. With the enhancement of airlift capability and reach of aircraft, air transport operations and strategic bombing gained ascendency and became the game changers. In the due course of time, air power evolved from being a peripheral to an influential force and, finally, attained the status of a dominant force.

Prior to turning the focus on the Indian Air Force (IAF), it is important to discuss air power and its evolution. The scope of this paper is restricited to the pre-independence era and the contribution of the IAF would be analysed in the background of its limited means and the overarching influence of colonial rule. Contrary to common belief, the IAF was created as an independent force and not as an arm of the Army. Nevertheless, the initial role was limited to support of the Army as the strategic role was retained by the Royal Air Force (RAF), a colonial force. Despite being a small Air Force, the IAF contributed immensely in the North-West Frontier Province (NWFP) and the Burma Campaigns during World War II.

Understanding Air Power

The term 'air power' was first used in 1908 by H.G. Wells in his novel *The War in the Air* which was much ahead of its time.[1] Even after a century, it is difficult to define air power in absolute terms. Winston Churchill had also expressed that "*air power is the most difficult of all forms of military force to measure, or even to express in precise terms*". Nevertheless, several attempts have been made to explain the concept. "The ability to do something in the air," the definition of air power given by Billy Mitchell, an early advocate of air power, is rather general and calls for further explanation. The definition as per the Joint Doctrine of the Royal Air Force (RAF), "the ability to project power from the air and space to influence the behaviour of people or the course of events"[2] and the American *Heritage Dictionary* meaning, "the organised, integrated use of aircraft and missiles for purposes of foreign policy, strategy, operations, and tactics"[3]are also not adequate to understand the meaning of air power. The following definition published in America's *Air & Space Power Journal* is a good attempt:

> Air power is the integrated employment of all air and space forces to control and exploit the air and space environments to achieve national security objectives. Air power exploits the properties of its operating medium to realise unique operational characteristics and, thus, employ unique capabilities to provide the nation a broad range of military options. [4]

However, no definition can cover the numerous dimensions of air power. Air power extends warfare to the 'third dimension' and should not be confused with aircraft or missiles only. Rather, air power includes all the systems which can be used to exploit the air-space continuum like space vehicles, aircraft (fixed-wing, rotary-wing, manned, unmanned), guided missiles, balloons, radars, etc. Like national power, air power too has several intangible components, including men, training, morale, policies and strategies. Synergy among all the elements of air power is necessary for the best exploitation of the third dimension towards achieving national goals and objectives during war, conflict and peace. At the same time, air power is not just confined to the air force but includes all the national aviation resources and related capabilities, military as well as civil.

Evolution of Air Power

Kites

The first written account of employment of a kite, the first man-made object that could fly with some degree of control from the ground, in a war, dates back to 200 BC. A kite was flown by the Chinese Gen Han Hsin of the Han Dynasty to calculate the distance up to which opponent forces were deployed. With knowledge of this distance, his troops made a tunnel to get past the defences, surprised the enemy, and won the battle.[5] Since then, kites have been used in different innovative ways for various purposes, including war. For example, during World War I, man-lifting box kites were used to increase the viewing range in signal and observation duties. During World War II, kites were used to create barrages which prevented airplanes from flying too low over targets. Kites were also used for target practice and pilots lost at sea raised the Gibson-Girl box kite so that they could be found.

Balloons

The first air display of a balloon flight (unmanned) by two brothers, Joseph and Jacques Montgolfier on June 04, 1783, at Annonay, in France, had created phenomenal anxiety amongst the thinkers. When Benjamin Franklin was asked, "Of what use is it?" he had made the famous reply "What is the use of a newborn baby?"[6] He had also envisaged the concept of "vertical employment" and estimated that 5,000 balloons, with two men each, would make the defence of any sovereign country difficult, as such a force might appear at any place and at any time. Although at that time he was promising too much with too little capability, he could definitely visualise the future.

First Air Unit

Le're Compagnie d'Ae'rostiers, the French balloon unit, was the very first organised **air unit** in the history of air power, and the one which paved the path for the formation of air forces of the world. The unit was authorised by the Committee of Public Safety by passing an Act on April 2, 1794. In just about a month's time, *Entreprenant* (Enterprise), the only balloon of the unit, was deployed for observation duties against the Austrians and Dutch in the **Battle of Fleurus**. The application of air power influenced the battle and enabled the French occupation of much of Belgium.[7]

Dirigibles and Commercial Airline

Although experiments were conducted on dirigibles for quite some time, the LZ4 was the first significant dirigible to get airborne on July 01, 1908.[8] It was named after its German inventor Count Ferdinand von Zeppelin. The 446-foot-long Zeppelin with 5,30,000 cubic feet of gas drew national attention when it made a 12-hour flight over Switzerland. Within less than a year, the Zeppelin was used by the world's first commercial airline Deutsche Luftschiffahrts-Aktiengesellschaft (German acronym for "German Airship Travel Corporation"), commonly known as Delag. However, in May 1937, the Germans permanently discontinued airship transport in favour of airplanes.[9]

Aircraft

December 17, 1903, is one of the most significant dates in the evolution of air power as on this day, the first flight of a heavier-than-air aircraft was exhibited by the Wright Brothers at Kitty Hawk. It was the Signal Corps of the USA which took the lead in envisaging the first military use of an aircraft and advertised for an aircraft "capable of carrying two men and sufficient fuel supplies for a flight of 125 miles, with a speed at least 40 miles per hour. It must remain aloft for at least one hour and land without damage."

Preliminary Experiments with Aircraft

During 1910-12, various possible exploits of aircraft in war were demonstrated. Daring and enthusiastic aircraft pilots experimented with the various usages, including photo-reconnaissance, dropping of dummy bombs, firing a rifle from a biplane at a target on the ground, take-offs and landings on naval ships, communication from the ground using the radio as well as carrier pigeons, firing a machine gun from the air (as the aircraft performance had permitted carriage of some more weight in addition to that of the pilot and his observer). These experiments, which were displayed by courageous and passionate aircraft pilots in peace-time, enhanced the importance of air power among military as well as political leaders.

First Air Campaign: Italian Air Campaign in Tripoli

The very first deployment of an aircraft for military use, along with observation balloons and airships which had already been in service for quite some time, was in the **Italian air**

campaign in Tripoli in October 1911. As a part of Special Army Corps fielded against the Turkish forces, the Aviation Unit of the Italian Specialist Battalion Headquarters had sent the 'air fleet' with five pilots under the command of Captain Carlo Piazza of the Eighth Field Artillery to Libya, then part of the Ottoman Empire. Under this campaign, the world's first combat flight took place on October 23, 1911, when Commander of the Air Fleet, Captain Piazza, took off to reconnoitre Turkish positions. During this flight, which lasted for 61 minute, he discovered several enemy encampments.

The first combat bombing, which was widely reported and had a great impact on the thinking of airmen, was the dropping of four grenade-like bombs of four pound each on the Turkish positions by Second Lieutenant Giulio Gavotti.

This campaign had many firsts for an aircraft, including the first dropping of propaganda leaflets, spotting of artillery, night bombing, reconnaissance missions and use of radio communication. The vulnerabilities of the aircraft and the pilots were also exposed during the campaign.

The first ever air campaign was historically successful and received wide reportage as the courageous pilots had proved the valuable use of aircraft in war-time. The campaign also led to a great philosophical impact. **Giulio Douhet**, then a provisional battalion commander, and a great proponent of air power, got the first chance to substantiate his advocacy of air power theory with facts and figures. His extensive report not only analysed various air power considerations but also drew interesting inferences regarding several pertinent dimensions of air power, including recruitment and training of airmen, types of aircraft to be procured, requirement of organisational set-ups, framework of aviation and aircraft industry. Later on, Douhet authored *Command of the Air*, a landmark work on air power.

Air Power in World War I

As per the Schlieffen Plan, Germany had planned to avoid a two-front war by swiftly defeating the Allies on the western front in the first six weeks and then deploying the forces to the eastern front against Russia, presuming that Russia would take six weeks or more to mobilise. However, in the battle of Marne, at the western front, Allied airmen had observed the movement of German forces through aerial reconnaissance. This gave the Allied commanders enough time to plan and act, and deprived the Germans of the benefit of surprise and initiative. On the other hand, at the eastern front, the Germans gained the advantage of air reconnaissance against Russia in the battle of Tannenburg. Gen Paul von Hindenburg acknowledged the importance of air power by conveying, "Without airmen, no Tannenburg!"[10]

When the Great War started, aircraft were wooden biplanes with open cockpits. Their speed was below 100 miles per hour and range, endurance and weight carrying capacity was very limited. The aircraft and technology available at that time were too primitive to be decisive, but they were of importance in the conduct of warfare. Nevertheless, if these early influences of air power had occurred on only one of the fronts, their effect would not have been neutralised and the final outcome of the war might have been different.

Roles and Functions

Various roles and functions of air power evolved during the war. Artillery-spotting and directing fire became one of the most important aspects of air activity during World War I. The observer used to see the target, monitor the shell fall and guide the pilot. The role of the pilot was, by and large, restricted to flying the aircraft, while the observer, who was different from the pilot, was like the captain of a ship. Short and long range reconnaissance and patrolling services were other important roles. Furthermore, landing and picking up agents behind enemy lines at night was undertaken. Long range reconnaissance became possible due to appropriate modification in cameras. Photographs of the entire battle front upto a depth of 100 km behind enemy lines became feasible. Long range reconnaissance photography even led to deployment of dedicated teams for early processing and analysis of photographs and communication of the information to all concerned. Thus, the camera played a significant role in enhancing the use of aircraft in reconnaissance.

Air Superiority and Fighter Aircraft

The need to counter the reconnaissance and bomber aircraft led to the origin of the concept of fighter aircraft. Initially, the utility of fighter aircraft was questioned as some analysts felt that it would not be of any gain for the ground forces as it would neither collect any information nor drop bombs on enemy forces. Nevertheless, it was observed that without air superiority, the operations of other aircraft were highly vulnerable. Thus, the concept of air superiority was firmly established.

The Fokker EI was the first effective, efficient and successful fighter aircraft. It used a machine-gun mounted on the centre-line of the aircraft to fire forward. The machine-gun firing through the propeller was of great advantage to the pilot as he could align the flight of his machine with that of the enemy and fire.

The advent of fighter aircraft led to a seesaw battle for air supremacy which resulted in greater focus and investments in technology improvement and strengthening of the aircraft industry.

The degree of prominence and influence gained by aircraft during the progress of the war can be judged from the fact that France, Britain and Germany alone collectively produced about 50,000 aircraft in the first ten months of 1918, whereas in August 1914, at the beginning of World War I, the total number of aircraft available collectively with these nations was less than 1,000.[11]

Physical Damage Vis-à-vis Psychological Impact

Air power created a profound psychological impact, far greater than the actual physical destruction. The loss of life during the war was so high that 2,500 killed and wounded every day was considered as 'ordinary wastage'. However, the psychological impact of air power was so phenomenal that in January 1916, ten British casualties in the air drew unprecedented public and political attention and even caused a panic like situation.[12]

Although the fighters were primarily to protect friendly aircraft, aerial fighting gave the fighter pilot's profession phenomenal fame and heroism. *Fighter aces*, the fighter pilots who got at least five kills in aerial fighting, acquired the status of demigods. While bomber and reconnaissance crew also played vital roles, including destruction of some enemy aircraft in self-defence, *ace* status was generally won by fighter pilots only.

Even though military aviation did not determine the outcome of the Great War, the aircraft had established its real significance in the conduct of warfare, though in support of the army. In World War I, control of the air space over the battlefield gained importance and the basic techniques developed during the Great War were used for the rest of the 20th century.

Inter-war Years

Air Control and Air Policing

The vast expenditure during the Great War had led to virtual bankruptcy of most of the participating nations. Economic considerations led to downsizing and demobilisation of forces. The impact of budgetary constraints on the RAF was severe and can be judged from the fact that in just six months, its aircraft inventory was drastically decreased from a noteworthy figure of 22,271(in October 1918) to just about 200 by March 1919.[13] Ironically, demilitarisation efforts enhanced the importance of air power. How?

Maintenance of ground troops to address colonial insurgents operating at distant frontiers of the empire was very costly and time consuming. Air power provided a viable, cost-effective, responsive and prompt alternative under the doctrine of air control. As per the doctrine, in place of the long drawn process of sending troops to a remote and isolated place, an aircraft would fly to the troubled area, conduct reconnaissance, inflict the necessary punishment and return within hours, saving money and time, while reducing the requirement of ground troops.

Although 'air policing' against insurgents was first undertaken by the French in Morocco in 1913-14 prior to the Great War, it gained prominence with the RAF's post World War I campaign in Iraq in 1920. In *air policing,* aircraft were used in the roles of reconnaissance, bombing of rebel towns, close air support and artillery spotting. Air policing was extensively undertaken in the NWFP. In fact, the Indian Air Force's first employment was in this role. Air policing and casualty evacuation not only saved soldiers' lives but also heightened the morale for colonial soldiers and demoralised colonial rebels.

Innovative Roles

During these campaigns, there were major innovations as well.

- Aircraft were used in the transport role to maintain garrisons in remote areas or surrounded by rebels through aerial supplies of food and ammunition.[14]
- Light bombers were modified for the casualty evacuation role. In 1925, in Morocco, the French had created the world's first large scale aerial medical evacuation system and evacuated 987 wounded and sick soldiers to rear hospitals by air.[15]
- Aerial photography was used for cartography and mapping.

During air control, at times, air power fully replaced the ground troops and acted independently, while on other occasions, it supported the army as an effective force multiplier. The coordination between the army and air force led to the conduct of air-ground operations in an effective manner. The basic missions of air power in conflicts with non-state actors have remained almost unchanged since then.

Strategic Bombing

Post World War I, some aviation theorists contemplated that in the future, striking directly at civilian centres with bombs or chemicals would bring nations to their knees because civilians would not be able to withstand such pounding, physically as well as psychologically. The impact of bombing on civilians would be immediate and direct, whereas the navy and army have an indirect and late impact on the masses.

Thus, the doctrine of strategic bombing was born. As per the doctrine, which was conceived by Douhet and promoted by the two Chiefs of the Air Staff of the RAF,

Sykes and Trenchard, bombers would attack the nerve centres, militaries, industries and populations of the opponent nation. This would create shock effect and break the morale of the population, leading to complete breakdown of the adversary's will to fight, and the nation would give up the war even prior to the actual defeat of the armed forces. The technology of precision bombing had not yet arrived and strategic bombing implied area bombing and mass destruction. The doctrine had created a phenomenal public fear of mass bombing even before World War II started.

World War II

Offensive/Defensive Balance

Application of air power continued to gain importance with improvement in technology coupled with evolution of doctrines. The most dramatic technological advances just before and during World War II were the development of the jet engine, the advent of new fighters, radars, ballistic surface-to-surface missiles, surface-to-air missiles, and atomic bomb. Radars, coupled with fighters and ground defence weapons, enhanced the defensive capabilities and challenged the earlier concept that 'bombers would always get through.' Trenchard's idea about keeping fighters to the minimum was no longer valid and the focus increased on defensive assets, including fighter aircraft. [16]

Doctrinal Divergence

As the technology was advancing, militaries of all the powerful nations got busy in developing doctrines for the optimal utilisation of air power in line with their geo-political imperatives. While Britain and America believed in strategic bombing, France, Germany and the Soviet Union were of the opinion that air power was to be used in conjunction with the ground forces to expedite the defeat of the enemy's army. Bombing at the enemy forces, even behind the front, was part of their philosophy but not the strategic bombing of cities, nerve centres, economic infrastructure, etc. However, the German air doctrine had catered for a retaliatory (or out of provocation) long-term bombing independent of ground forces, but not as a preemptive initiative.[17]

Such differences in the strategic points of view of the major forces dictated the way the air war was fought. While Germany and the Soviet Union focussed on operational air warfare in cooperation with frontline armies, Britain and the United States evolved long-range bombing, air-sea coordination, and an effective air supply system.

Political Receptivity

Political receptivity, an important element for the growth of air power, also played a significant role in the success of Allied air power. While Hitler was more inclined to the army view, Winston Churchill and Roosevelt were air power enthusiasts. Churchill and Roosevelt accepted a high level of commitment for air power exploitation and supply whereas, on the other extreme, Hitler got progressively disillusioned with air power, and by 1944, he even threatened to disband it and replace it with anti-aircraft defences and surface-to-air weapons like the V-1 flying bomb and V-2 rocket.[18]

Ascendency of Air Power

During World War II, air power went through a transition from being a peripheral to an influential entity. It played a dominant role in most of the theatres and was decisive in at least two battles—the Battle of Britain and the Battle of Midway. By and large, air power was used for attaining air supremacy and supporting the strategic aim of destruction of the enemy's armed forces. The Battle of Britain and the atomic bombing of Hiroshima and Nagasaki were the exceptions where cities as well as the civilian populations were targeted for mass destruction as per the doctrine of strategic bombing. Having discussed the evolution of air power, let us now focus on the jouney of the IAF.

Birth of the IAF

Background

Within a decade of the first successful heavier-than-air flight (and within just three years of the first military use of an aircraft in Tripoli), the Military Flying School was set up in India at Sitapur in Uttar Pradesh in December 1913. Civil flying clubs also came up in Delhi, Bombay (now Mumbai), Calcutta (now Kolkata) and Lucknow in the late Twenties. Much before the IAF was born, Indian enthusiasts like Lt Indra Lal Roy, Distinguished Flying Cross (DFC), Lt S.G. Welingkar, Military Cross (MC) and Sardar H.S. Malik had made a mark in professional military flying while serving with the Royal Flying Corps (RFC) of Great Britain during the Great War.

Independent Service or An Air Arm?

When the demand for Indianisation of the armed forces was pressed upon by the Legislative Assembly, the Skeen Committee (under the chairmanship of Lt Gen Sir Andrew Skeen, KCB KCIE CMG, Chief of the General Staff) was constituted in June 1925 to look into the matter. As far as formation of the IAF is concerned, the committee had recommended grant of King's Commission to the deserving Indians to form the Air Force as an Air Arm of the Indian Army. It was Air Vice Marshal John M Salmond, Air Officer Commanding (AOC) in India (later Marshal of the RAF) who strongly objected to the proposal and advocated for an independent status for the IAF.[19]

Thus, the Indian Air Force came into being as an independent Service on October 08, 1932, when the Legislative Assembly passed the Indian Air Force Act (XIV of 1932). With four Wapiti aircraft, six Indian officers trained in the UK at Cranwell and 22 *hawai sepoys* (technical airmen), 'A' Flight of the IAF No. 1 (Army Cooperation) Squadron of the IAF was made operational on April 01, 1933, at Drigh, Karachi. Rs 12,77,930 was the initial proposed budget which was to be spent over five years.

Formation of the IAF as a separate Service, from the very beginning, was a significant decision. The foresight of the British in understanding the significance of air power can be judged from the fact that the RAF was the world's first independent air force to come into being, although the first flight of the heavier-than-air aircraft was made across the Atlantic Ocean.[20] The RAF, Royal Canadian Air Force, Royal Australian Air Force and South African Air Force are the only four independent and continuously serving air forces of some significance which are older than the IAF. Although the IAF was conceived and established as an independent Service, due to the colonial rule, it was primarily tasked with the tactical role while the strategic role was preserved by the Royal Air Force as a policy matter. Thus, the deployment and objectives of the IAF were dictated by the colonial rulers.

IAF in National Defence

Deployment at NWFP

After about three years of dedicated training and indoctrination, in April 1936 'A' Flight of the IAF moved to Peshawar for active service. Thereafter, the flight moved to various bases, including Chaklala and Miranshah. Initial operational assignments were of 'air policing' or 'watch and ward' against armed tribal guerrillas in the Waziristan Campaign in the NWFP. The roles included reconnaissance, attacks on the armed tribals while providing support to the army columns, engaging the guerrillas on the ground and VIP movements. The flight moved around to different cantonments as per operational requirements. No.1 Squadron continued operations in the NWFP, along with the RAF squadron, till World War II changed the priorities.

Achievements

During the first deployment, the IAF exhibited a high degree of professionalism, enthusiasm and propensity to innovate. Tremendous technical acumen, coupled with an attitude to face the challenges was demonstrated. The flying standards and serviceability of the aircraft were also admirable. An unrelenting desire to overcome the equipment deficiency was displayed time and again. Some of the significant achievements are given below:

- In September 1937 itself, 'A' Flight, comprising just four pilots, logged 337 flying hours in operational sorties, a feat hitherto not achieved by any RAF flight in India. In May 1939, this record was further improved by logging more than 410 flying-hours with just four pilots and four Wapitis.[21]
- At Miranshah, in spite of logging 1,400 hours of operational flying over a period of three months, a record 100 per cent aircraft serviceability was maintained.[22]
- In the Army Cooperation role, the IAF was amazingly prompt in responding to the emergency calls by getting airborne in Hurricanes in just about three and a half minutes[23]—an exceptionally good performance, comparable with current standards of a modern Operational Readiness Platform (ORP).
- The Hurricanes were effectively used by the IAF by innovatively developing the technique of semi-dive bombing, virtually as successfully as dive bombers.[24]
- A Category 'E' (beyond economical repair) Lysander of 28 RAF Squadron was made serviceable by the IAF technicians and added as the thirteenth aircraft to the No.1 IAF Squadron.
- To address the problem of non-availability of the tail wheel tyres of Lysanders, No. 1 Squadron successfully replaced it with a wooden wheel and continued operational flying. No. 28 RAF Squadron tried to copy the same but failed and got grounded.
- The IAF leadership exhibited foresight and a spirit of experimentation in administrative issues as well. In 1936 itself, the IAF had started an inter-community common Mess for all the airmen, irrespective of the community they belonged to. Whereas, the Indian Army continued with separate Messes for Hindus and Muslims for a long time, and took several years to get over this baggage.

Command of the Squadron to an Indian Officer

For the first seven years, the fledgling IAF was commanded by British officers. On September 03, 1939, Squadron Leader Subroto Mukherjee became the first Indian to command the first squadron of the IAF. There must have been two reasons for this decision. Firstly, Indian officers were ready to take on this responsibility as they had undergone the required training and had also gained adequate operational experience in the NWFP. Secondly, on this very day, Britain had declared war against Germany for invading Poland and, thus, Britain was consolidating all its resources for World War II.

Indian Air Force Volunteer Reserve (IAFVR)

Initially, though it was not envisaged that the war would eventually come to Asia, it was important to concentrate on the coastal security of India and protection of the sea lines of communication. To tide over the lack of resources in terms of trained pilots and equipment, the Indian Air Force Volunteer Reserve (IAFVR) was established on the recommendations of the Chatfield Committee, an Expert Committee on the Defence of India (1938-39). The IAFVR took over the coastal defence role from the RAF Squadrons which were required elsewhere more urgently.[25] Initially, five Coastal Defence Flights (CDFs) were formed at Karachi, Bombay, Cochin (now Kochi), Madras (now Chennai) and Calcutta. Thus, with the help of volunteers, mainly with a pilot's licence and flying club experience, and land-based aircraft, the naval aviation component of the military was born as a part of the IAF. Volunteers were to serve in the General Duties Branch of the IAFVR for the duration of the war. The flights at Bombay had twin-engine Dragon Rapides and Dominies and rest were Wapiti and Audax aircraft.[26]

Inadequate Force Levels

In spite of raising of the IAFVR, the actual force level consisting of three squadrons (two RAF and one IAF) and five IAFVR flights was much less than the approved level of 21 squadrons(11 RAF and 10 IAF), six CDFs and two Conversion and Training Units.[27] Thus, the IAF had to meet the national defence challenges with very limited and inadequate resources. One more CDF was formed at Vishakhapatnam with two Wapitis by the end of March 1942. No. 4 CDF was the first IAF unit to be sent on operational service to Burma, after the commencement of the Japanese offensive. [28] Towards the end of 1942, the CDFs were disbanded and maritime surveillance was taken over by the RAF.

First Burma Campaign

Background

On December 7, 1941, Japan attacked the US forces at Pearl Harbour in Hawaii with a stunning blow and surprised the world. Immediately after that, Malaya and Singapore fell to the Japanese and the eastern border gained importance with the Japanese invasion of Burma on January 15, 1942. The IAF was initiated into World War II during the First Burma Campaign.

Air Assets

The Japanese had superior aircraft like Zero fighters and Oscars, and complete air superiority. By February 1942, the Japanese Air Force had deployed about 200 aircraft, and the number increased to 400 after the fall of Singapore. No. 4 CDF, with Wapiti and Audax aircraft, No. 3 CDF, with Blenheim aircraft, and No. 1 IAF Squadron, with Lysanders, participated in the campaign. As the CDF aircraft were of old vintage and of hardly any consequence, their usage was, by and large, restricted to communication duties only. No. 1 Squadron was of significance because by the time it was deployed, most of the air assets of the Allies had been withdrawn and only two RAF Squadrons, No. 28 RAF Squadron flying Lysanders, and No. 67 RAF Squadron flying Buffaloes, along with a few American Volunteer Group (AVG) pilots, with some assorted aircraft, were left in the theatre.

Air Operations

On February 1, 1942, No. 1 Squadron, a sizeable force at that point in time, with a dozen Lysanders sponsored by the citizens of Bombay, arrived at the Toungoo airfield in Burma. On the very first night, Toungoo airfield was bombed twice by the Japanese but there was no significant loss as the squadron had observed adequate ground defence measures.[29] Squadron Leader Karun Krishna "Jumbo" Majumdar, a young squadron commander, immediately planned a befitting response and innovatively modified a Lysander to carry two 250 lb bombs each. On February 03, he flew the first retaliatory **counter- air sortie** to bomb the airfield of Mae-Haungsuan. To avoid detection and air opposition, he flew at tree-top level, completely surprised the enemy and achieved a direct hit and destroyed an aircraft along with the hangar. The exploratory flight and bombing was a great success and the following day, the squadron went ahead in full force, using all the 12 Lysanders for bombing and scored direct hits on the wireless station, dispersed aircraft and buildings.[30]

It is pertinent to note that the pilots of 28 RAF Squadron, collocated on the same airfield with the same type of aircraft, did not take the initiative of modifying the Lysander into a bomber. Rather, having seen the successful attacks by the IAF, they followed the lead. Moreover, this daring and innovative act was exhibited under severe force asymmetry conditions against the enemy who was on a victory run.

The IAF, with its humble resources, continued to contribute in the war efforts by undertaking bombing, strafing, tactical and photo reconnaissance, support to the Army and VIP duties. As the resources were meagre to meet the requirements, No. 1 Squadron was split up into three flights and these were deployed at Mingladon, Lashio and Toungoo airfields—an apt example of flexibility.

Due to the unique training in the NWFP, the slow moving Lysanders could successfully operate against the Japanese Oscars which were far superior in speed, armour as well as manoeuvrability. In spite of the Japanese air superiority, No. 1 Squadron lost only one aircraft in the campaign.

Allied Retreat

The IAF, along with American Volunteer Group (AVG) and RAF, contributed to the best of their abilities. But the better equipped and more advanced enemy continued to dominate and the Allied forces were forced into the "longest retreat". Nevertheless, the rear guard action was also of great importance. W.W. Russell has mentioned in *Indian Air Force (Ten Years Old*) "The army was the first to admit that all the air forces in the campaign, the American Volunteer Group, the RAF and the IAF, did all in their power to stem the advance of the better equipped and more numerous enemy. The IAF with their Lysanders carried more than their share in this stupendous rearguard action." Thus, No. 1 Squadron paved a strong foundation for the growing IAF.

Awards and Honours

No. 1 Squadron performed well and contributed much beyond its resources. For the outstanding performance and historic feat, Squadron Leader Majumdar became the first IAF pilot to earn a DFC and the technical in-charge Warrant Officer Harjinder Singh (later Air Vice Marshal) was awarded the Member of the British Empire (MBE). Even the Chinese appreciated their invaluable service from the Lashio airfield and as a token of appreciation, presented some of the pilots with gold wings.

Second Burma Campaign

Background

After the withdrawal of the Allies by mid-1942, there was a lull at the Burma front for eighteen months. The Japanese gainfully utilised this time by strengthening and fortifying their defences while the Allies reorganised and augmented their forces to counter the Japanese threat. The battlefield was still a real challenge and was considered an "impossible theatre of operations" owing to the lack of railways and roads, the mountainous terrain, heavy monsoon rainfall, and being the world's worst malarial area.

Southeast Asian Command

For appropriate conduct of operations in the eastern theatre, on November 01, 1943, the Allies established a centralised command called the Southeast Asian Command, with Lord Louis Mountbatten as its Supreme Allied Commander. The responsibility of air operations in Bengal and Assam was given to the Eastern Air Command (EAC) which worked under Air Command Southeast Asia. For effective operations, the EAC was further divided into:

- Tactical Air Force.
- Strategic Air Force.
- Troop Carrier Force.
- Photographic-Reconnaissance Force.

Motif

The Allies wanted to capture upper Burma so that they could connect the existing roadhead at Ledo through the jungles and mountains to China to feed the bomber force established in China. They simultaneously planned a campaign in central Burma to capture Akyab.

On the other hand, to stop the Allies and to make further ingress into Indian territory, the Japanese had also planned two separate attacks: a subsidiary attack at Arakan(Operation HA-GO) to draw and engage the main Allies reserves down south; and the main offensive (Operation U-GO) in central Burma sector to capture Imphal-Kohima and interdict the railway line passing through Dimapur. Thus, the Second Burma Campaign was fought at two fronts—the Arakan Front and the Imphal Front.

Air Assets

The Allies had augmented their air power considerably and had established numerical supremacy over the enemy. As on November 16, 1943, there were 723 aircraft in the sector, collectively belonging to 48 RAF Squadrons (519 aircraft) and 17 USAAF (USA Air Force). Squadrons (204 aircraft). By May 1944, the strength was further augmented to 64 RAF Squadrons and 28 USAAF Squadrons. All the nine squadrons of the IAF participated in the war but Nos. 1, 6, 7 and 8 IAF Squadrons contributed the most during the campaign. Although the numerical strength of the IAF squadrons deployed along with the Allies was comparatively less, their contribution to the war efforts was fairly tangible due to their intensive efforts and indomitable spirit. On the other side, the Japanese had just about 250 aircraft at Heho, Ani-Sakan, Rangoon and Chiangmai airfields, with more aircraft at rear bases in Siamand in the Netherlands East Indies.

The Arakan Front

The Allies seized the initiative and commenced the northern Burma campaign in December 1943 with Gen Stilwell's forces and, subsequently, on January 19, 1944, the British XV Corps started the advance near the Arakan coast. The advancing XV Corps was suddenly halted when the Japanese launched Op HA-GO on February 03, 1944. Initially, the Japanese were successful in splitting and besieging the units and formations. The 5th Indian Division, 7th Indian Division and Administrative Headquarters were forced to organise themselves into defensive 'boxes' as they were surrounded and isolated.[31]

The Japanese plan to neutralise the surrounded forces failed due to air power. Dakotas airlifted 26th and 36th Divisions from Chittagong and augmented the isolated forces. The Japanese could not withstand the significant air support and their attack was neutralised by February 24, 1944. The Japanese went wrong in their calculations as they did not factor in the role of enemy air support.

Air Power Challenges and Contribution

In addition to the enemy interference from the ground as well as the air, air power faced several challenges, including the dense forest and the significant camouflaging skills of the Japanese, which made recognition of targets difficult. Moreover, the Japanese had eighteen long months to fortify their defences and made high quality underground shelters which were difficult to address from the air.

The Allies had achieved air superiority by the time land operations commenced. During the first 13 days of the offensive, the Japanese lost 65 aircraft against the Allies' losses of just three Spitfires.[32] Air superiority was of great advantage as it enabled free movement of own troops and supplies by air while denying the same to the Japanese.

Contribution of the IAF

No. 6 Squadron (with Hurricane reconnaissance aircraft) and No. 8 Squadron (with Vultee Vengeance dive bombers)[33] of the IAF were fully involved in this sector from the very beginning since their deployment in November 1943. Till January, the air effort was primarily towards Japanese positions behind the forward line and in support of the Army's advance. However, after the launch of Operation HA-GO, the focus shifted in support of the besieged forces.

No. 6 Squadron

No. 6 Squadron flew reconnaissance sorties relentlessly and achieved a monthly average of 16,000 photo prints. Maximum photo prints in a day were 1,500. The squadron became to be known as "the eyes of the XIVth Army".[34] The pilots generally flew in pairs—the leader and the weaver—and were affectionately called the "Arakan Twins."[35]In addition to photo reconnaissance, the Hurricanes carried out innumerable duties, including providing air cover to the Allied troops, watching enemy movements in the front line as well as in the rear, penetrating enemy camouflage, assessing the extent of Allied bombing, maintaining contact with isolated troops, dropping mail, medical supplies and special instructions.

No. 8 Squadron

No.8 Squadron was tasked to bomb and destroy enemy installations and lines of communications in the rear. The demand from the forward troops was so high that it used to receive 4 to 5 calls every day. To address the well fortified hill positions of the Japanese, a new tactics was devised along with the ground troops. Enemy positions were attacked by artillery barrage for a few hours. Thereafter, the Vengeance would conduct air raids, flying in the box formation of six aircraft. The last box would be a dummy to give sufficient time to own troops to climb up the hill and surprise the Japanese. The tactic proved to be very effective. During the operations, the squadron flew 1,420 sorties and dropped 13,79,250 lb of bombs.[36] At the later stage, Nos. 2, 4, 9 and 10 IAF Squadrons also operated in the area.

Recognition

The IAF, along with the Allies, vigorously supported the courageously fighting troops of XV Corps and air maintained them till the Japanese were thrown back with heavy losses. The extent of the contribution of the squadrons can be judged from the recognition and congratulatory messages they received. Gen Messervy and 7th Indian Division thanked No. 6 Squadron for the support, particularly in Tara Ga Area on March 30. Maj Gen Lomax, Commander 26 Indian Division, sent an appreciation message for support by the squadron. Similar messages were received by No. 8 Squadron as well. The efforts of the IAF were widely recognised and Squadron Leader Mehar Singh and Flight Lieutenant Rawal Singh were awarded the DSO and MBE respectively.

The battle had a great significance on World War II as this was the first defeat the Japanese faced in the eastern sector and thereafter the Allies maintained their victorious stance while the Japanese kept on losing the battles and withdrawing their troops.

The Imphal Front

Japanese Objective

The greatest Japanese threat to India was from the Imphal and Kohima fronts. On March 8, 1944, the Japanese launched Operation U-GO and attacked Imphal to cut off the road and rail link to Dimapur and sever the supply route maintaining Stilwell's force and the US **'over the hump'** airlift to China. Other objectives were to break into the Brahmaputra Valley and the capture the airfields. The Battle of Kohima also started around the same time.

The Japanese 15th Army had moved into the north and south of the Manipur plains to capture Imphal with a lightning campaign. The Japanese were confident that they would be defeating the besieged IVCorps before the arrival of reserves of Gen William J. Slim's 14th Army drawn from the central sector to the Arakan front to counter Operation HA-GO.

Air Operations

While Imphal was held by No. IV Indian Corps, Kohima was guarded by a mixed garrison of 3,500 troops. For augmenting the defences by the end of March, the USAAF airlifted the 5th Indian Division from the Arakan front (except for one brigade which was deployed at Dimapur). 7th Indian Division was also flown into Dimapur. The last remaining brigade of Gen Wingate also joined.[37] At the same time, 50th Para Brigade was also airlifted from Punjab into Imphal and reinforcements were also ordered from India to the central front. Overall, more than 60 percent of the troops fighting the Japanese in Burma were Indians. Nos. 5, 7, 17, 23 and 26 Indian Divisions were either engaged or were deployed as back-up, and went forward on the offensive as soon as the siege was broken.

The Japanese got the initial successes and managed complete isolation of Imphal and IV Corps by April 9. The only contact available was through the air. **Operation Stamina**, one of the greatest air supply operations in the history of war, was undertaken to air supply the army and the civilian population.

The importance of the air operation is highlighted by Lt Gen Sir Geoffrey Evans as, "The British and Indian soldiers lived and fought in diabolical conditions but, unlike with the Japanese, their rations, monotonous though they were, came regularly and medical arrangements were of the highest order. And *British, Indian and United States Army Air Force pilots never hesitated to fly through the worst weather conditions to deliver supplies and attack enemy positions*"[38] (emphasis added).

IAF Operations

No. 1 Squadron (flying Hurricanes) and No. 7 Squadron (flying Vultee Vengeance) were actively involved at this front. During the four months of active operations, No. 1 Squadron, under the leadership of Squadron Leader Arjan Singh (who later became the Marshal of the Indian Air Force), flew 1,600 sorties with a total of 2,200 operational flying hours although during this period, the squadron itself was besieged as the Imphal airfield was within the artillery range of the enemy. [39] The ground staff, despite being under the constant threat of attack from the land as well as air, produced a high standard of maintenance and serviceability that could not be matched by any other RAF squadron operating in the entire Burma front.

On April 10, during a routine sortie, Squadron Leader Arjan Singh spotted the Japanese on a hill 10 km northeast of Imphal and immediately attacked them, while calling in his complete squadron for this task. This was the nearest the Japanese could ever come to Imphal during the four-month-long battle.

No. 1 Squadron served in the war for the longest period (14 months at a stretch) and carried out 4,813 sorties, with a total of 7,220 flying hours.[40] The contribution of the squadron was appreciated and acknowledged by Lord Mountbatten who himself flew to Imphal and pinned the DFC on Squadron Leader Arjan Singh.

No. 7 Squadron, commanded by Squadron Leader Hem Chaudhry, also proved its mettle despite bad weather and severe monsoon conditions. Because of the monsoon, every morning, before the crack of dawn, the squadron personnel travelled a distance of 20 km, often in ankle-deep mud, to reach the airfield at Uderbund. Despite such irritants, the squadron persistently bombed enemy dumps, troop concentrations and lines of communication over a wide area extending as far as Kalewa and Fort White in the south, and the villages on the river Chindwin in the east. In the month of April, the squadron flew 344 sorties with a total of 630 operational flying hours.[41] One of the important achievements of the squadron was destruction of a bridge on the Manipur river. The bridge was neutralised by Flight Lieutenant P. C. Lal (later Chief of the Air Staff during the 1971 War with Pakistan), diving through clouds and poor visibility.[42]

Japanese Defeat

Finally, the siege of Imphal got over on June 22, 1944, when contact was established between 2nd British Division advancing from the north and 5th Indian Division, 14 km north of Imphal, on the road to Kohima. Air power played a decisive role in the battle. The Japanese strategy of encircling the Allied bases and forcing a retreat failed because of large-scale air supplies and close air support. The battle of Imphal-Kohima has been reported to be one of the decisive battles of the 20th century. But the fight continued as the Japanese were driven out of India and the Allies went on the offensive.

In the Burma theatre, the IAF flew 16,000 sorties involving 24,000 operational flying hours and was employed in all classical roles, except airlift. (Incidentally, the Srinagar airlift was the first, and the most important post-independence air operation). During the war, the IAF grew from one incomplete squadron to nine combat squadrons but, by and large, continued to fly primitive aircraft like the Hurricane, whereas the Allies were flying much superior aircraft like the Spitfire, Thunderbolt and Mosquito. The human resource also expanded exponentially from 16 officers and 144 other ranks to 1,400 officers and 23,000 airmen. In recognition of their services, IAF personnel were awarded 22 DFCs and a host of other decorations. March 25, 1945, was a historical day for the IAF, when, for its war efforts, it was honoured with the prefix "Royal", which continued till India became a republic on January 26, 1950.

Growth of the IAF

The first flight of the IAF took more than six long years to grow to the strength of a squadron. By that time, World War II had already started and as per the Defence of India Plan of 1941, which was approved on March 12, 1941, the IAF was required to be built up to a 10 squadron force at the earliest. Thus, two squadrons were raised immediately on April 01, 1941. Although World War II had reached the doorstep of India, and the Andaman and Nicobar Islands were occupied by the Japanese on March 23, 1942, no expansion materialised during the next year.

This made the IAF leadership feel that the British were deliberately hindering their growth since a robust and independent air force could be detrimental to their own colonial rule.[43] Being worried about the slow growth of the IAF 'Jumbo' Majumdar, the Commanding Officer of No.1 Squadron, met the Chinese head of the state Generalissimo Chiang Kai-shek at Lashio and deliberated upon the option of moving to China rather than reverting back to India. He planned to raise a new volunteer group **(Indian Air Volunteer Group)** and join the Chinese, fighting against the Japanese with support from the US. While envisaging faster growth under the aegis of China, and with aircraft and equipment support from the US, he had assumed that convincing Winston Churchill would not be difficult, once the consent of the US President Roosevelt and the Chinese Premier was obtained. After raising the required number of squadrons, the **Indian Air Volunteer Group** (a trained and well equipped force) was to come back to India and gift the nation a "ready-made air force." All the personnel of the squadron had also agreed to the plan as they were ready to go to any extent to see the embryonic IAF grow. [44]

By the end of February 1942, the defeat of the Allies resulted in commencement of their withdrawal from Burma. The defeat had a significant impact on the British psychology and changed their attitude towards the IAF. Moreover, every single squadron became important for the Allies and the IAF had already proved its mettle in the war. Aware of the frustration among the IAF personnel, the Commander-in-Chief, Gen Sir Archibald Wavell himself reached Lashio and addressed the squadron. While highlighting the benefits of growing in India, he assured the expansion of the IAF to ten squadrons at the earliest.

Most likely, that is why the IAF saw an unparalleled expansion on April 01, 1942, when four squadrons were raised on the same day (refer Table 1 below).[45]

Table 1

No. 1 Squadron	April 1, 1933
No. 2 Squadron	April 1, 1941
No. 3 Squadron	April 1,1941
No. 4 Squadron	April 1, 1942
No. 6 Squadron	April 1, 1942
No. 7 Squadron	April 1, 1942
No. 8 Squadron	April 1, 1942
No. 9 Squadron	April 13, 1943
No. 10 Squadron	April 20, 1944
No. 12 Squadron	December, 1945

Thus, K.K. Majumdar, with his foresight and passion to give the nation a potent Air Force, virtually compelled the British rulers to immediately raise the strength of the IAF. Never again has the IAF experienced the creation of four squadrons in a single day.

Conclusion

The IAF was born as an independent air force during the inter-war years and started its journey of operations from the NWFP. The Burma campaign was the first regular war in which the IAF got engaged during its formative years and contributed immensely toward the Allies victory. During World War II, the IAF grew from a single squadron to a nine-squadron force and got the opportunity to work with the British, Americans as well as the Chinese. Circumstantially, the IAF was exposed to joint operations with leading air forces of the world.

As far as strategy and doctrine are concerned, the RAF was the mentor of the IAF. Nevertheless, IAF leaders proved themselves better than their mentors on several occasions. The first counter-air strike by 'Jumbo' Majumdar, the modification of Lysanders and Hurricanes to carry bombs, employment of Hurricanes (a reconnaissance

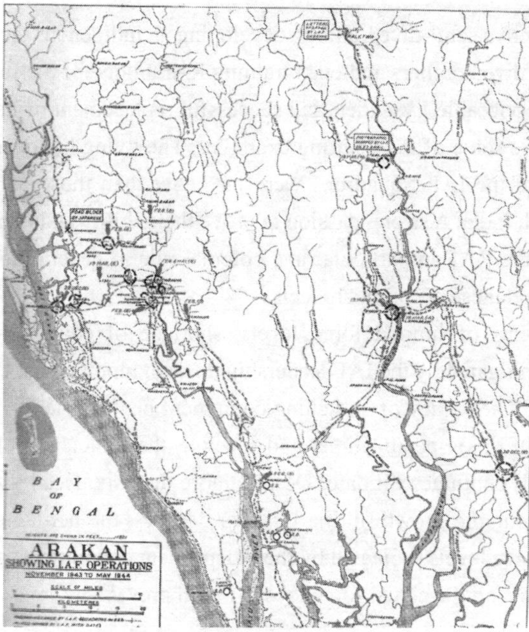

BATTLE FOR IMPHAL AND KOHIMA
SHOWING I.A.F. OPERATIONS
FEBRUARY – AUGUST 1944
SCALE OF MILES

aircraft) as an effective semi-dive bomber, developing an indigenous technique for using Vultee Vengeance dive bombers and even training RAF pilots for the same, rectification of the RAF's unserviceable Lysander, and successful replacement of its tail wheel with a wooden wheel are some of the befitting examples. The flying hours and serviceability records of some of the IAF Squadrons were far better than those of RAF Squadrons operating in British India. A strong passion to prove their ability and thereby to come out of the shadow of the RAF in particular and colonial rule in general had been the main driving force behind these accomplishments.

The impediments of limited force levels, shortage of equipment and primitive technology were mitigated by the IAF leadership through innovations, courage, élan and indomitable spirit. The legacy of stretching equipment beyond the Original Equipment Manufacturer's (OEM's) specifications and meeting the deficiency of spare parts by innovative methods continues till date. Despite more than six decades of independence and substantial economic growth in the last two decades, the heritage of a substantial gap between the force levels projected by the independent committees, authorised by the political leadership, and the actual force levels, is still prevalent.

Notes

1. Tony Mason, *Air Power: A Centennial Appraisal* (London: Brassey's Ltd, 1994).
2. AP 3000 of RAF, Chapter 2 accessed at http://www.raf.mod.uk/rafcms/mediafiles/374B96A2_1143_EC82_2E93053B8A5AF3EF.pdf.
3. http://www.thefreedictionary.com.
4. Lt Col Johnny R. Jones, "Air Power" published in America's *Air & Space Power Journal* and accessed at /http://www.airpower.maxwell.af.mil/airchronicles/cc/jjones.htm.
5. www.gombergkites.com/nkm/hist1.html accessed on May 16, 2011.
6. Hal Marcovitz, *Benjamin Franklin: Scientist, Inventor, Printer, and Statesman* (New York: Infobase Publishing,2006) p.119.
7. http://www.centennialofflight.gov/essay/Lighter_than_air/Napoleon's_wars/LTA3.htm, accessed on September 08,2011.
8. A dirigible is a lighter-than-air rigid flying machine.
9. http://www.centennialofflight.gov/essay/Commercial_Aviation/germany/Tran19.htm,accessed on July 03,2011.
10. Sebastian Cox and Peter Gray, *Air Power History: Turning Points from Kitty Hawk to Kosovo*(London: Frank Cass Publishers , 2002),p.96.
11. Walter J. Boyne, *The Influence of Air Power upon History* (New York: Pelican Publishing Company,2003), pp.48-49.
12. Ibid., p.79.
13. Ibid., p.127.
14. However, proponents of air power overlooked the role of aircraft in transport and no major progress was made in this direction for quite some time.
15. James S. Corum , "Air Power in Small Wars:1913 to the Present" in John Andreas Olsen, ed ,

A History of Air Warfare (New Delhi: Vij Books, 2010), p. 330.

16. Boyne, n.11, pp. 133-135.
17. Richard Overy, "Air Power in Small Wars:1913 to the Present" in Olsen, ed., n.15, p. 27.
18. Ibid., pp. 51-52.
19. Air Chief Marshal P.C. Lal, *My Years with the IAF* (New Delhi: Lancer International, 1986), p.11 and Rana T.S. Chhina, *The Eagle Strikes: The Royal Indian Air Force 1932-1950* (New Delhi: Ambi Knowledge Sources, 2006), pp.8-9.
20. The Royal Air Force was raised in 1918 by merging two existing air Services, the Royal Flying Corps and Royal Naval Aviation Service. The USAF became an independent Service much later, in 1947.
21. A.L. Sehgal, ed., *Birth of an Air Force: Memoirs of Air Vice Marshal Harjinder Singh* (New Delhi: Palit & Palit, 1977), pp.67-75.
22. Ibid., p.67.
23. Arthur Hughes, "The Story of the IAF on the North-West Frontier 'Watch and Ward'" reproduced in Chhina, n.19, p.51.
24. Ibid., p.53.
25. Sehgal, n. 21, p. 153.
26. Lal,n.19, p. 23. Wapities were obsolete even at that time and in the Mess they were informally called "What-a-pities".
27. Jasjit Singh, *Defence from the Skies* (New Delhi: Knowledge World, 2007), p. 11.
28. M.S. Chaturvedi, *History of the Indian Air Force* (New Delhi: Vikas Publishing House, 1978), p.17.
29. However, during the 1965War, the IAF overlooked the ground defence measures and suffered heavy losses, particularly at Pathankot and Kalaikunda airfields.
30. Later on (in 1944), Hurricanes were also modified in the similar manner and were used to bomb the Japanese.
31. The Sinzweya administrative area is famously called the "Admin Box."
32. Bishweshwar Prasad, ed., *History of the Indian Air Force 1933-1945* (Delhi: Combined Inter-Services Historical Section India and Pakistan, 1961), p. 105.
33. In early 1943, IAF No 7 & 8 Squadrons had received a new type of aircraft, the Vultee Vengeance dive bomber. At that time, no one in India knew about the technique of dive bombing and the IAF took the initiative to develop its own techniques and also trained some of the RAF squadrons.
34. Chaturvedi, n.28, p.36.
35. The IAF continued with the tactics of flying in pairs for several decades.
36. Prasad, n.32, pp. 109-110 and Chaturvedi, n.28, p.37.
37. To fight the Japanese, the "long range penetration force" of Gen Wingate's soldiers, commonly known as the Chindits, were flown in by gliders and landed in northern Burma, behind the enemy lines.
38. Geoffrey Evans, "Imphal-Kohima" in Noble Frankland and Christopher Dowling, ed., *Decisive Battles of the Twentieth Century Land-Sea-Air* (London: Sidgewick & Jackson,1976), p. 261. Geoffrey Evans commanded the 5th Indian Division in the closing stages of Imphal Battle.
39. Chaturvedi, n.28, p.41
40. Ibid., p.43, and Lal, n.19, p. 45.
41. Chaturvedi, n. 28, p. 41.
42. Lal, n.19, p. 36.

43. After the armed mutiny of 1857, the British were very cautious in equipping and arming Indian military. In order to maintain the superiority of the British forces, they never supplied the latest technology to the Indian forces.
44. Sehgal, n.21, pp.141-149.
45. Chhina, n.19, p. 78. No squadron was allocated with number 5 and 11 since RAF squadrons with those numbers were stationed in India.

9

Human Element of Airlift Operations

Ashok K. Chordia

Airlift and Human Element

The success of airlift operations depends on the well-coordinated actions of a long and diverse human chain. Starting from the technicians who prepare the aircraft for missions; the aircrew who fly the mission; the controllers who provide guidance; the fighter escorts who give the safety cover; the parachute riggers who maintain and pack the parachutes; the dispatchers who assist in the exit of the *deliverables*; and the troops themselves, comprise the human element that contributes to mission success. This paper focusses on the hands that are specific to aerial delivery – aircrew, paratroopers, parachute jump instructors and the riggers.

Except when undertaken as a relief operation during disasters or natural calamities, or when resorted to in aid to civil administration, aerial delivery may necessitate flying through the enemy area. The aircraft used for aerial delivery provide relatively slow moving easy targets to the enemy ground and air defence and expose the aircrew and the passengers to exclusive risks. On the part of the paratroopers, it entails exceptional courage to abandon the comfort of a perfectly well flying aircraft.

Technological innovations tend to replace human beings. Unmanned Aerial Vehicles (UCAVs) and cruise missiles are now being used effectively to strike targets accurately. Beyond Visual Range (BVR) capability enables strikes from standoff distances, keeping the aircraft and the pilot out of reach of enemy air defence. Unmanned aircraft may be a reality in the future. Yet, in the foreseeable future, the need to deliver men and material by air shall remain a necessity and, hence, the importance of the human element associated with it.

Victory is still measured by foot.

— Indian Army[1]

And, aerial delivery is the fastest means of being anywhere. It is the only hope of an army formation awaiting resupply or a pilot who ejects behind the enemy lines. Therefore, the human element, associated with aerial delivery, continues to draw the attention of military thinkers. Predicting human behaviour is a difficult exercise. The responses of individuals to situations depend on the perception and cognition. The reactions of people, even to similar situations, may vary from time to time and situation to situation. Individuals are known to behave differently in groups. Even the most timid people rise to the occasion as members of a team.

Human Element Over The Years

Aerial delivery operations came to prominence in World War II. The German airborne assault on Fort Eben Emael (Belgium, May 10, 1940) was a grand success. In a daring pre-dawn raid, nine flimsy fabric covered gliders landed 71 German paratroopers at Eben Emael and overpowered the Belgian troops in just over 30 minutes. This raid opened the gateway for the Germans to enter Belgium and France. The very next year, in May 1941, they suffered heavy losses in Crete. According to some estimates, there were 2,124 dead, 1,917 missing, 2,640 wounded and 17 captured and evacuated to Egypt[2]. The German experience was traumatic. In an immediate response, they decided to give up on airborne operations. Hereafter, during the rest of the war, Fallschirmjäger, the German parachute rangers, were used as normal infantry. The Allied forces comprising British, Australian, New Zealand and Greek soldiers too suffered heavy losses—3,990 dead, 1,925 wounded and 17,090 captured. Despite the heavy losses, the British embraced the concept of airborne operations. It is paradoxical that the two sides perceived their own losses so differently. The Germans chose to give up, and the British pursued, the concept. It appears that the British saw the losses in isolation and attributed them to the effectiveness of the German airborne assault. The British and the Americans trained a large number of pilots and paratroopers to raise a formidable airborne force.

At the outbreak of World War II, 6,000 young Americans volunteered to fly large unarmed cargo gliders.[3] It was perhaps the euphoria of war that encouraged them to risk their lives repeatedly and land troops and equipment in enemy territory. They had no motors, no parachutes and no second chance. After landing their gliders, they even fought as combat infantrymen. As per some accounts, they were fearless, adventurous beings who lacked military discipline and were always eager to fight. They resisted attempts to be chastened and guided by superiors[4]. This attribute of a combatant is conspicuous by its absence in the aircrew of today who exhibit much professionalism and discipline. But behind the façade of that negative attitude, the glider pilots had matchless e*spirit de corps*. They flew motor-less, fabric-covered gliders that bounced violently and jerked on nylon ropes behind the tow planes. Nervous glider infantrymen sat behind them, some vomiting, many in prayer, as they flew at tree-top levels, bullets and flak tearing through the gliders. They tried not to think about the explosives aboard. "It was like flying sticks of dynamite through the gates of hell"[5].

The pilots of the transport aircraft were equally keen fliers. According to a memoir, "Young fliers in those days were much like doctors. They were always eager to see new and different cases, and operate on them, if anybody would let them. They would fly anything—new or old, in good shape or bad. They knew very little about maintenance, and cared even less. They flew both for the sheer exhilaration of it, and to build up their flying time"[6]. This desire to log flying hours is a universal trait and cuts across countries and generations. Aircrew, even today, look forward to being posted in appointments that enable active flying to build hours. Lack of opportunity to fly, due to any reason, affects the performance of the pilots adversely. It is detrimental to operational preparedness and lowers the morale of its personnel.

The aircrew that flew missions during World War II empathised with the people for whom they were flying. During the Berlin Airlift, Gail Halvorsen, an American pilot, flew into Berlin during his off hours and pursued photography as a hobby. On one such visit, he became friendly with children near the airfield. During his mission sorties later, he dropped candies, using small parachutes made from handkerchiefs. Some other pilots joined in. Over three tons of candy was dropped on Berlin. The operation came to be known as Operation Little Vittles. The German children christened the candy-dropping aircraft Raisin Bombers. This connect with people became a propaganda success[7]. Similar actions by Indian pilots flying relief missions have earned them epithets like Flying Angels, Angels of the East and Saviours from the Skies.

Training, Education and Learning

Sow a thought and you reap an action; sow an act and you reap a habit; sow a habit and you reap a character; sow a character and you reap a destiny.

— Ralph Waldo Emerson[8]

Precision, timeliness and safety of the troops till they touch down are essential ingredients of successful aerial delivery missions. Training and education are the tools to achieve those ends. They are the two facets of learning. It may be difficult to tell the difference between them, especially in today's system, but there are certain subtle and perceptible differences. Their purpose and methodology are vastly different. Training is the action of teaching a person or animal a particular skill or type of behaviour e.g. in-service training for staff or taming a tiger cub in a circus. It imparts skills, attitude and knowledge for direct application to *a task or job*. It is a structured presentation with a specific purpose and may or may not be classroom-based. Education is the process of receiving or giving systematic instruction, especially at a school or university. It imparts *skills, attitude and knowledge for application to life*. Life here implies the environment and activities far beyond a mere task or job. Learning implies adoption of skills, attitude and knowledge that impacts future behaviour. Training, development and education are all a subset of "learning". Learning may occur with varying levels of structure and purpose.

On those counts, due to the requirements, learning in the Indian Air Force (IAF) is mainly training-based. It focusses on achieving a task or a job through repeated actions. Instructions and training are through well formulated syllabi. There are many exceptional instructors and trainers but fewer teachers and mentors in the real sense of those terms. The interaction is restricted to work hours. Such official proximity limits transfer of work ethos and culture from one generation of personnel to another. Socio-economic changes have aggravated aloofness. Informal teaching and mentoring takes place on a personal basis. Due to the similarity of risk faced by the paratroopers and the Parachute Jump Instructors (PJIs), the bond between them is strong. They share a special bonhomie. It was for this reason that the dispatchers of an AN-32, whose nose wheel had collapsed during the take-off run, walked out of the aircraft only after all the troops had deplaned safely under the lurking fear of the aircraft catching fire.

It is appropriate to stress the need for education as the basis for learning. But the importance of training must never be undermined. Thoroughly focussed training and motivation can build operational character in individuals and a culture which ensures an expected and prompt response to situations. Thus, the prompt release of a *hang-up*[9] during the paradrop at Tangail was the result of years of training and coordination between the aircrew and the PJIs.

In one of the most successfully handled aircraft emergencies of recent times, the crew of US Airways Flight 1549, an Airbus 320A, safely landed their bird hit aircraft on the Hudson river in New York. All the 155 passengers and the five crew members escaped safely. Its success illustrated the importance of training-based learning. Captain Chesely "Sully" Sullenberger attributed the success to the fact that the crew responded with *"what they were trained to do"*[10]. Training plays a vital role when dealing with repetitive actions and when time is at a premium. Leadership also plays a vital role in handling unforeseen situations and emergencies.

In matters of aerial delivery of personnel, mental conditioning is as important as physical training. When the Indo-Pak War (1971) broke out, one of the troopers had just undergone his probation as a paratrooper. He was yet to go through the basic ground training (12 days) when his unit was tasked to paradrop in Tangail. The trooper made his first parachute descent after highly abridged ground training and verbal briefing. Here, it would be incorrect to conclude that training is unnecessary. Such examples can only be used during training to reassure novices that paratrooping is a safe activity and to inspire them to make deliberate unassisted exits from the aircraft.

Practical freefall training requires committed aircraft, a Drop Zone (DZ) and expensive parachutes. The cost of flying per hour and the wear and tear of the parachutes render the cost per jump prohibitive. Besides, an actual freefall lasts a few seconds. Due to the distance of the DZ from the airfield (a few kilometres), it is difficult to log many freefall jumps in a day. This prolongs freefall training and hinders desirable continuity and assimilation. A vertical wind tunnel provides a much cheaper solution and ensures continuous realistic training, more useful than actual jumps. Five minutes of freefall in a vertical wind tunnel would be equal to more than five jumps involving five aircraft sorties of one-hour duration each involving the aircrew and the groundcrew. Besides, the time spent in the wind tunnel could be under the close supervision of the instructors. A very important fact is that the possibility of a fatal accident is reduced to zero level. Therefore, wind tunnels and similar apparatuses have become integral to effective training of combat freefallers at low costs.

In a rapidly changing environment, it is not humanly possible to have all the knowledge on all subjects. Learning and acquiring new skills and knowledge rapidly when the need arises, addresses this shortcoming.

> *Minds, like parachutes, function best when they are open.*
>
> — A quotation written on the wall of
> Paratroopers Training School, Agra

Assimilation of Lessons

Lessons of military operations and exercises can be sources of great learning. It often happens that lessons are discussed, analysed, written and almost always well documented, but are then consigned to the archives. Shortcomings are addressed sometimes but strengths are not always consolidated.

Those who do not learn from history are doomed to repeat it

— George Santayana[11]

Operation Ivory Coast, popularly known as the Son Tay Raid (Vietnam, 1970), was a special force operation to rescue 61 American prisoners held captive in a Vietnamese village. It was a well planned and executed operation in as much as the force reached the objective, inflicted heavy losses on the Vietnamese defenders and got away unscathed. But the mission was a failure because the prisoners had been moved to another location well before the raid due to the fear of flooding. An account of the operation states that the raid was allowed to take place regardless because those who had the correct intelligence information were not aware that someone was contemplating a Prisoner of War (POW) rescue[12]. As a result, despite tactical success, none of the prisoners could be rescued. A decade later, in April 1980, the US embarked on another mission, Operation Eagle Claw—to rescue Americans held hostage by Iranian students in Tehran. By then, the immaculateness of the planning and execution of the Son Tay Raid had been forgotten and the positives of the Entebbe Raid (Uganda, July 1976) had not been absorbed. The operation was a failure—none of the 52 hostages could be rescued.

Wise men learn by other men's mistakes, fools by their own.

— H. G. Bohn[13]

In the Indian context, growing piracy in the Indian Ocean, political flux in Somalia and *jihadi* activities of Al Shabaab have endangered the security of the Lakshadweep Islands. According to Gen Shankar Roychowdhury (Retd), the lessons of Operation Cactus (the Maldives, November 3, 1988) have acquired fresh relevance because of the incidents of piracy and the arrest of 11 Somali pirates on May 28, 2010. The lessons must not be lost sight of.[14]

On the dawn of May 10, 1940, the Germans captured one of the strongest and well-defended forts of Eben Emael by landing 71 paratroopers in nine flimsy fabric covered gliders. For them, it opened the gateway to Belgium and France. The Germans did not learn the positive lessons from this success. But they were quick to draw negative inference after the Pyrrhic victory in Crete (May 1940). Hitler decided never to undertake airborne operations. The same operation impressed Churchill immensely. In a letter to the military wing of the War Cabinet Secretariat, he emphasised the need to expedite the raising of an airborne division. He wrote:

> We ought to have a corps of at least 5,000 parachute troops. I hear something is being done already to form such a corps but only, I believe, on a very small scale. Advantage must be taken of the summer to train these forces who can nonetheless play their part meanwhile as shock troops in home defence.[15]

It is important to analyse the outcomes of the operations critically. Gains and losses must be seen in a proper perspective. Lessons drawn must be deliberated at length before implementing action. They must be revisited from time to time. Repeated analysis exposes new dimensions and adds value to future training and preparedness.

Building and Consolidation of Capability

It takes time and enormous effort to build capabilities. If left aside, these can be lost unnoticed. According to Air Chief Marshal Sir Stephen Dalton[16], in 1997, the Royal Air Force (RAF) thought that they would never operate from a dirt strip airfield ever again but history proved them wrong. Again, in 2005, they almost certainly gave up dropping supplies by parachute but now they find that accurate resupply using parachutes is vital. New capabilities in terms of aircraft, systems and skilled people must be acquired thoughtfully. They must be practised, refined and perfected.

India's security concerns extend from the Malacca Strait to the Persian Gulf and beyond. Going to distant locations with men and material in response to situations, and operating from faraway bases in support of friendly forces, is now a distinct possibility. There may be a need of raising and operating temporary air bases. It may not always be possible to position a hundred specialists to commence operations at remote bases. There is a need to build teams of multi-skilled men who could move at the shortest notice, live off the ground and support operations under difficult conditions. They could be innovative men who could be familiar with the languages and cultures of the countries of interest.[17]

Psychology of a Paratrooper

It is important to study the mind of a paratrooper because he has to overcome tremendous pressures and fears to exit a flying aircraft. At that instant, even one refusal in a stick can jeopardise a mission. A typical Indian paratrooper is simple and God-fearing. He has faith in his superiors and instructors. He is trained to use his senses, skills and physical abilities optimally. It is enough for him if the instructor touches his parachute—he is assured of a perfect deployment of the canopy. Howsoever thrilling, adventurous and sporting it may appear, to a paratrooper, parachuting means tedious training. Preparation preceding an actual descent comes closer to being work. This tough life brings them close to each other. It establishes a unique bond among the jumpers. Strenuous training leads to camaraderie. It is because all of them—the officers and the men—face the danger together.[18]

Training for paratroopers goes beyond pure physical training. They experience physical injuries and, on rare occasions, witness fatalities. Otherwise oblivious of the lurking dangers, the troops become more aware and conscious immediately after an incident or an accident. These things bind men with a closer mutual understanding, which is a much sought after attribute in groups. Informally though, a paratrooper learns deep lessons in human psychology which other followers of the military profession must often learn only in the heat of battle. They are extremely proud of their organisations. The maroon beret, the parachute brevet and the proficiency badges mean much more than mere ceremonial paraphernalia placed on the uniform. These are earned through blood, sweat and tears and are revered and respected by those who understand the ethos. They are the symbols of undisputed courage and daredevilry.

The Fear Factor

Human beings are born with just two basic fears. One is the fear of loud noises. The other is the fear of falling. All other fears must be learned.

— Ronald Rood[19]

Fears are the result of cognition. Knowledge and learning through life generates new fears. Like any skill or ability, a fear can be acquired. Through appropriate and adequate training, fears can be unlearnt, too. But it takes enormous effort to overcome the basic fears. They cannot be eliminated but may be suppressed. Despite the best of training, these suppressed feelings surface sometimes. If, and when, the fear of falling comes up, paratroopers are known to refuse to jump. A refusal has a devastating effect on the morale of those in the vicinity or those following an unwilling trooper. During operations, a refusal can be disastrous.

The fear manifests in many ways. Charles Darwin provided a vivid description of the manifestations of fear in his book, *The Expression of the Emotions in Man and Animals*[20]. According to him, fear is often preceded by astonishment, and is so far akin to it, that both lead to the senses of sight and hearing being instantly aroused. In both cases, the eyes and mouth are wide open, and the eyebrows are raised. The frightened man at first stands like a statue, motionless and breathless, or crouches down as if instinctively to escape observation. The heart beats quickly and violently, so that it palpitates or knocks against the ribs. That the skin is much affected under the sense of great fear, we see in the marvellous manner in which perspiration immediately exudes from it. The hair on the skin stand erect and the superficial muscles shiver. In connection with the disturbed action of the heart, the breathing is hurried. The salivary glands act imperfectly; the mouth becomes dry, and is often opened and shut. Similar symptoms are visible among the jumpers and troops embarking on Special Heliborne Operations (SHBO). In the case of parajumpers, the fear of death and the fear of the unknown emanate from the basic fear of falling. Feigning sickness or reporting faults in the equipment are simple ways of deferring the issue. Such behaviour affects operations very adversely. A jumper refusing to bail out at the time of exit can jeopardise an entire exercise.

While perfecting the drills, training aims at allaying anxiety. A demonstration of how a parachute is packed and a display of the opening-sequence in slow motion instil great confidence. Statements like "It is safer than crossing a road in Delhi," "Even NCC girls can do it," and *"Paltan ki izzat ka sawaal hai,"* keep the fears suppressed. A pat on the parachute by a PJI reassures the paratroopers that everything is hunky-dory.

Effect of Accidents

Accidents have a ruinous effect on morale. In 1943, when para training had just begun in India, there was one fatal parachute accident every 500 jumps and, in the course of 15,000 descents, 17 men were killed[21]. The accident figures from No. 3 Paratroopers Training School, considered *low* in those times, are summarised here:

Table 1: Consolidated Accident Statistics (January 1944 – June 1945)

Number of Pupils	Number of Descents	Death	Death Rate	Minor Injuries	Injury Rate	Incapacitating Injuries (more than 7 days)
11,898	66,408	12	1:5534 (0.018%)	178	1:373 1.26%	113

Compare these statistics with the data for a recent 9-year period for static-line jumps at the Paratroopers Training School (PTS), Agra.

Table 2: Consolidated Accident Statistics (July 2001 – June 2010)

Number of Pupils	Number of Descents	Death	Death Rate	Minor Injuries	Injury Rate	Incapacitating Injuries (more than 7 days)
1,04,000	2,77,354	1	1:2,77,354 (0.0000036%)	205	1:1353 0.073913%	66

This marked improvement in the current safety figures over those of 1945 is due to the following reasons:

- Much improved parachutes. In the 1940s, the jumpers used X-type parachutes, which did not have vents at the apex for excess air to escape. As a result, the air used to *spill* from the periphery, causing the canopy to oscillate violently, resulting in landing injuries. The PTRM parachute, in use now, is larger in size, with a vent on top. It has a lower rate of descent and does not oscillate.
- Use of a reserve parachute. Initially, all jumps were carried out without a reserve parachute. Reserve parachutes were introduced much after World War II. It gave a second chance of survival in the case of failure of the main parachute. But, it had a distinct disadvantage. It reduced the capacity of a paratrooper to carry ammunition.
- Improved aircraft. The AN-32 and IL-76 provide better jumper comfort than the Dakota and Packet aircraft. Besides an aft end exit is less prone to parachute emergencies. The C-130J and C-17 Globemaster are way ahead in terms of human comfort.
- Better maintained drop zone surface. In the 1940s, the drop zones were uneven and not ploughed. Now an even and well-ploughed drop zone ensures softer landings and lesser instances of injuries.
- Refined training methods and Standard Operating Procedures (SOPs). The ground training and aircraft drills have been refined for safer jumps and landings.
- Better understanding of the jump process. Socio-economic changes and higher educational levels of troops have led to their better understanding of the jump techniques, thereby reducing landing injuries.

Now compare these numbers with the reported road accidents in Delhi. Nearly 120 people were killed and 3,300 injured in road accidents in Delhi in less than a year (from January 01, 2010 to August 17, 2010)[22]. Looking at these numbers, it is incorrect to draw the conclusion that parachute jumping at the Paratroopers Training School (PTS) is safer than walking on roads in Delhi. It is inappropriate to compare these data because the number of people using the roads and the number of moving vehicles has not been taken into account. Nonetheless, this analogy is used repeatedly during ground training of the paratroopers, and with positive impact. Another glance at the above data indicates a very high level of safety. This fact could be used to improve operational capability. A deliberate action could be taken to jump without reserve parachute during operations. This may not lower safety but will enable a paratrooper to carry more ammunition on his person.

The Morale Raisers

As said earlier, it takes phenomenal courage to exit a perfectly well flying aircraft at a thousand feet above ground level. There are different motivators and morale raisers or boosters that facilitate jumps. Some of these are self-generated, others indulged in as a group activity. Among such efforts, battle cries are a well known means of overcoming the jump anxiety.

The troops of the 501st Parachute Infantry Regiment yell '*Geronimo!*' when they exit an aircraft. There is a legend behind this battle cry. '*Geronimo*' was a Native American leader who fought against Mexico and the United States and their expansion into tribal lands during the Apache Wars. The story goes that in 1940, the troops of the 501st Parachute Infantry Regiment had undergone ground training and were ready for their first mass jump. The night before the jump, they watched a 1939 film, *Geronimo*, in which the actor playing *Geronimo* yells his name as he leaps from a high cliff into a river. Among others, Sergeant Aubrey Eberhardt, drew motivation from the film. Next day, when the troops were walking to the hangar to emplane for the jump, one of the trainees expressed his fears to Eberhardt saying that he would be scared of the jump and may faint on seeing the ground. In a measured response, Eberhardt told the other jumpers that if he felt comfortable, he would shout out, *'Geronimo!'* while exiting the airplane. Eberhardt did jump confidently and his '*Geronimo*' was heard by the troops. Thus, '*Geronimo*!' became the motto and the slogan of the regiment. The trend has since caught on elsewhere, becoming widely associated with any sort of high jump in popular culture. Over the years '*Geronimo*' has assumed several meanings: "*Hell! I am not scared*" and "*Let's show how it is done!*" Some have even stopped counting "*1000 – 2000 – 3000* ..." after bailing out. They would rather shout a slow, "*Gero-ni-mo!*" instead[23].

In the Indian context, the fact that the life of a jumper depends on the successful deployment and functioning of the parachute is emphasised repeatedly during training. A jumper learns to take extreme care of it. He reveres the canopy as a Mother Goddess—addressing it as *Chhatri Mata* (Mother Parachute). As a mark of respect, he avoids staining the fabric. He does not touch it with his feet. This reverence for the parachute manifests itself when the jumpers line up at the aircraft door, to exit the aircraft in flight. "*Chhatri Mata ki Jai*," is a cry that instills courage and keeps nervousness at bay. Hailed in chorus, this jump cry also generates camaraderie.

Badges and insignia worn proudly on the uniform give the paratroopers a different identity—a matter of pride for the wearer and a source of envy for others. According to them, "A *maroon beret* and a *paratrooper's brevet* cannot be exchanged for anything in the world."

Working Behind the Scenes: The Riggers

To begin with, the paratroopers were trained to pack their own parachutes. This prolonged their training with no useful outcome. Self-packing was, therefore, discontinued. The Safety Equipment Workers (SEWs) are now responsible for servicing and packing parachutes to be used by the paratroopers and the aircrew. In the Indian Air Force, till lately, the SEW trade belonged to Group 4. In the reorganised structure, they fall in Group 2 by default. On the quality of their output depend the lives of the jumpers. They are very well trained and supervised.

Innovativeness

Standard Operating Procedures (SOPs) are laid down for all envisaged activities leading to smooth aerial delivery of personnel and equipment. Yet situations arise that are not covered in the books of rules. The innovativeness and ingenuity of the men enables solutions. At the height of the 1962 India-China War, a need arose to airlift two troops of ANX tanks from Chandigarh to Chushul. It wasn't possible to load the tanks in the AN-12 aircraft because the metal ramp was too steep and smooth. The IAF technicians and the Army engineers overcame the problem by immediately constructing a ramp and placing wooden planks on the floor. Further, the Army representatives did not concede the IAF request to remove the turrets to lower the weight. So the pilots took off with less fuel, offloaded the tanks in 15 minutes (with engines still running) and returned immediately. The innovativeness of the ground and aircrew ensured successful airlift of the tanks[24].

During the 1962 Indo-China War, the Dakotas and Packets of the IAF operated in the Himalayas, in defiance of nature as well as the designed technical capabilities of their machines. The fact that these operations were carried out is a tribute to the skill, dedication to duty and innovativeness of the pilots and engineers of the transport fleets of the IAF and Kalinga Airlines.[25]

Soon after the failure of Operation Eagle Claw (Iran Hostage Rescue, April 24-25, 1980), the Americans embarked on another rescue mission codenamed "Operation Credible Sport." The US military made radical modifications to the Hercules aircraft to make it take off and land almost like a helicopter. The aircraft was fitted with several rockets so that it could take off and land in little more than its own length. The plane was equipped with lift rockets slanting downward, slowdown rockets facing forward, missile motors facing backward, and still more rockets to stabilise the plane as it touched down, in a Tehran soccer stadium. The first modified plane, created in just a couple of months, crashed on the runway after a rocket went off prematurely and ripped off one of the plane's wings. The engineers never got the chance to use the second modified plane they were working on, because before it could be tried, Iran announced plans to free the hostages. "Credible Sport" stayed in the test phase.[26] Such innovative spirit of men spells the difference between success and failure.

Ram air parachutes used with aircraft like the C-130J Super Hercules or the C-17 Globemaster can achieve a Circular Error of Probability (CEP) of 10 metres from standoff distances of 40 km by day and night. Today's technology can address most conceived needs of aerial delivery. It has even been possible to deliver a jumper from one flying aircraft to another. Pick-up of a soldier from the ground by an airborne fixed-wing aircraft has also been attempted successfully. Documentaries telecast by the Discovery and National Geographic channels often bring out the limitlessness of human imagination. Given today's technology and capability of people, in the future, imagination alone will limit innovativeness.

Conclusion

The ability of the armed forces in general and the air forces in particular to deliver men and material through the air has been in existence for over seven decades. Aircraft and delivery systems apart, the human element plays a vital role in the success of aerial deliveries. Undisciplined yet spirited aircrew and daring paratroopers started the legacy of aerial delivery that continues to this day. The Germans and the Allied forces exploited air power to deliver personnel and supplies. They viewed the outcomes of those operations differently. Several failed missions and accidents marked aerial deliveries of yesteryears. In the years between World War II and the Gulf War, aerial delivery was used sparingly with some spectacular and some unappealing results. Better parachute and aircraft designs have improved the means of delivery. Refined training has made operations much safer.

Aerial delivery of personnel develops strong bonds between troops. During training, this raises morale and fosters the much-desired camaraderie. Accidents have an adverse effect on morale. Education-based training reduces accidents and possible refusals. Drawing accurate lessons from the outcomes of campaigns and exercises is vital for further exploitation of aerial delivery systems. Considering the existing geo-political environment of the Indian Ocean Region (IOC) and the rising security concerns, it is important to revisit and refresh the lessons of Operation Cactus. The existing capabilities of men must be revalidated and reviewed. There is also a need to reinvest time, resources and energies in raising multi-skilled teams to meet future challenges.

Personal daring and innovativeness will limit the future employment of air power in aerial delivery. Lessons must be learnt from past experiences. They must lead to preparation of doctrines and SOPs, which must be revalidated and perfected through training. Training of personnel, their morale and innovativeness are the keys. Aerial delivery bestows the power of literal omnipresence on the force that uses it. This fact too, must be exploited for safe conduct of operations.

Notes

1. An Indian Army quote, available at http://forums.military.com/ eve/ forums/ a/ tpc/ f/ 3321924461/ m/ 9710085942001, accessed on January 12, 2011.
2. "Battle of Crete," available at http://en.wikipedia.org/wiki/ Battle _of _Crete, accessed November 23, 2010.
3. "Silent Wings: The American Glider Pilots of WWII," available at http: //www. janson.com / rights/2010/07/26/silent-wings-the-american-glider-pilots-of-wwii/ accessed on November 14, 2010.
4. "George 'Pete' Buckley, Glider Pilots*: 1942-45*," an article published in *USA Airborne: 50th Anniversary* by Bart Hagerman, available at http://books. google. co. in/ books/ frontcover/ usaairborne 50 anniversary, accessed on November 13, 2010.
5. From the memoir of a glider pilot of World War II. Available at http:// untoldvalor.blogspot.com /2007/ 08/ world-war -two-glider-pilots-rare-breed.html, accessed on November 14, 2010.
6. An article by a transport pilot titled, "Early Days," in a book by William H. Tunner in *Over the Hump* (USAF Warrier Studies, 1985), p. 3.
7. "Berlin Blockade," Wikipedia, available at http://en.wikipedia.org/wiki/Berlin_Blockade, accessed November 23, 2010.
8. http:// www.quotecosmos.com/ quotes/ 10741/ view, accessed on January 12, 2011.
9. *Hang-up*: This is a condition in which a trooper trails behind an aircraft after exiting for a static-line jump. Additional parachutes are connected to the static-line and the troop is released. Swift coordinated action among the aircrew and the PJIs is necessary for successful hang-up release.
10. Eduardo Salas and Dan Maurino, *Human Factors in Aviation*, Second Edition (Burlington, USA: Academic Press, 2010), p. 250.
11. George Santayana (1905) *Reason in Common Sense*, Vol. 1 of *The Life of Reason* available at http:// en .wikipedia .org/ wiki/ George _Santayana # cite _ note-0, accessed on January 12, 2011.
12. "Operation Ivory Coast," available at //en.wikipedia.org /wiki /Operation_ Ivory_ Coast, accessed November 21,2010.
13. "Thoughts on the Business of Life," available at http:// thoughts. forbes. com/ thoughts/ mistakes-h-g-brown-wise-men-learn, accessed on January 12, 2011.
14. Gen Shankar Roychowdhury, *The Pirates' Ally* (online edition of *The Asian Age*, September 21, 2010), accessed on November 21, 2010.
15. Official site of 5th Battalion, the Parachute Regiment, available at https:// www.4para.co.uk/ index.php?Itemid=119&option=com_content, accessed January 12, 2011.
16. Speech at Centre for Air Power Studies on November 3, 2010.

17. The allusion is to the aircrew of World War II who could jump into the cockpit of different aircraft and undertake missions; the glider pilots who fought as infantry soldiers after landing their gliders and the Israeli pilots who are known to learn Arabic to dodge the controllers of the neighbouring Arab countries.
18. Lt Gen William P. Yarborough, "The New Doughbouys," an article published in *USA Airborne: 50th Anniversary,* by Bart Hagerman, available at http://books.google.co.in/books/frontcover/ usaairborne 50 anniversary, accessed on November 13, 2010.
19. Quote from Ronald Rood, an American naturalist, author and radio commentator (1920-2001), available at http:// thinkexist .com /quotation /human –beings –are -born –with –just –two –basic -fears/ 763163.html; accessed on November 21, 2010.
20. M. Munger, *The History of Psychology* (New York: Oxford University Press), p. 221, available at http://en.wikipedia.org/wiki/Fear, accessed on November 15, 2010.
21. Col F.G. Neild L/RAMC (Retd), "Hazards of Early Parachuting in India (1941-43)", a first person account published in Maj Gen Afsar Karim, AVSM (Retd), *The Story of the Indian Airborne Troops* (New Delhi: Lancer International, 1993), p. 17.
22. NDTV data available at http://www.ndtv.com/article/cities/delhi-1-200-deaths-in-road-accident-so-far-45164, accessed on November 21, 2010.
23. http:// en.wikipedia.org/ wiki/ Geronimo, accessed on October 16, 2010.
24. Dr. B.P. Singh and Col A.A. Athale, *History of the Conflict with China 1962* (History Division, Government of India, 1992) p. 350. Available at http: //www. bharat-rakshak. Com /LAND-FORCES / Army /History /1962War /PDF/ 1962 Chapter08.pdf, accessed on October 18, 2010.
25. Ibid.
26. Richard Blystone, *How Many Rockets can Make a Plane Land like a Chopper? Jane's Reveals Iran Hostage Crisis Engineering Feat* (March 3, 1997), available at: http: //www. theaviationzone. Com /factsheets /documents /CredibleSport.pdf, accessed on November 22, 2010.

10

Fukushima and the Future of Nuclear Power

Manpreet Sethi

In September 2006, the ninth plenary meeting of the International Atomic Energy Agency (IAEA) adopted Resolution GC(50)/RES/13 that instructed the IAEA Secretariat to prepare, on a biennial basis starting from 2008, a comprehensive report on the status and prospects of nuclear power. Two such reports have since been provided – in 2008 and in 2010. Both corroborated a general sense of enthusiasm for nuclear power which had been evident for the last decade or so. This was manifest in the upward revision of projections of nuclear growth based on the start of ten new constructions in 2008, the most since 1987, and twelve in 2009.[1] This drift was largely sustained by ambitious plans for expansion of nuclear power programmes in China, India, Russia and South Korea, as well as spread of nuclear programmes to Southeast Asia and Middle East. Meanwhile, in the USA too, which had not seen a new plant in 30 years, plans for 24 new plants were submitted between 2007 and 2009. As a result of these developments, there was a general sense of a 'nuclear renaissance'. Projections during the period estimated that nuclear capacity would certainly double, even treble, by 2050.

The years 2009-10 also saw a number of conferences being held across the world on nuclear power. In April 2009, for instance, the International Ministerial Conference on Nuclear Energy in the 21st Century was held in Beijing which concluded that "nuclear energy, as a proven, clean, safe, competitive technology, will make an increasing contribution to the sustainable development of humankind throughout the 21st century and beyond."[2] Then, in March 2010, France, along with the Organisation of Economic Cooperation and Development (OECD), hosted an International Conference on Access to Civil Nuclear Energy. The conference deliberated upon bilateral and multilateral cooperation to help countries embark on nuclear power programmes. In the same month, an International Conference on Human Resource Development for Introducing and Expanding Nuclear Power Programmes was convened in Abu Dhabi. It focussed on the Human Resource (HR) requirements of a new nuclear nation and deliberated on how to meet the nuclear workforce requirements for the expanding nuclear industry. Meanwhile, in 2009, Japan had hosted an International Conference on Fast Reactors and Related Fuel Cycles, the first on this subject to be held in 18 years, and it indicated a growing interest in fast reactors.

As is evident, the nuclear mood was upbeat in 2008-10 as 441 nuclear power plants in 29 countries across the world provided 14 percent of the global electricity supply. At the end of 2010, 60 nuclear power plants were under construction, which was nearly double the number under construction in 2007. Consequently, it was projected that by the end of the 2020s, the contribution of nuclear power would marginally increase after having seen a dip in the nuclear generation owing to the rise in total electricity generation worldwide without an increase in nuclear generation as no new nuclear plant came online in 2008, and only two did so in 2009.

The evidently brightened prospects of nuclear power were attributed to three main factors—increasing electricity demand and fluctuating fortunes of oil and gas prices, growing environmental concerns owing to climate change from increased Green House Gases (GHG) emissions as a result of thermal-based power production, and increasing faith in nuclear power as a safe, reliable and environment friendly source of electricity. At the same time, even as the world was abuzz with talk of a nuclear renaissance, four challenges to the likelihood of it actually coming about were identifiable. These included issues related to the economics of nuclear power, nuclear safety, waste management and risk of proliferation. It was evident that any major development in any of these would have an impact on the prospects of nuclear growth.

This was put to the test in March 2011 on the issue of nuclear safety when an unprecedented natural disaster affected the safe operation of the Fukushima nuclear power station in Japan. The last major mishap in this field had occurred in 1986 in Chernobyl in Ukraine. This was blamed on faulty designing of the reactor, aggravated by human error. The nuclear industry drew several lessons from this accident and since then, reactor designs and operations have undergone several revisions to confidently rule out a repeat of a Chernobyl type of nuclear accident. Indeed, from 1986 to 2011, the world did see a largely accident free period of 25 years, which is unique compared to any other fuel used for electricity production!

On March 11, 2011, an earthquake and a tsunami—both of unprecedented magnitude[3]—struck the nuclear power station at Fukushima. Failure of the emergency core cooling system led to the dreaded loss of coolant accident, causing varying degrees of partial meltdown of three reactors at the same site. Expectedly, this shook public confidence in safety of nuclear power generation.

Through 2011, therefore, nuclear safety has remained the focus of attention. Public scepticism, especially since governments and the nuclear establishments have functioned in a largely closed manner, seems to have had a sobering impact on the nuclear enthusiasm so evident prior to March 2011. What will the future hold for nuclear power? How much impact will Fukushima have on nuclear power programmes across the world? Which will be the key nuclear areas demanding special attention? This paper examines these questions in some detail.

Abandonment, Reaffirmations and Deferments

Different countries, irrespective of the current status of their nuclear programme, have responded individually to Fukushima. For instance, while Germany, which has been generating 22 percent of its total electricity from nuclear reactors, has found it prudent to give up nuclear power, countries like China and India that get no more than 2 percent and 3 percent respectively of their total electricity share from nuclear power, have reaffirmed their nuclear plans. The reasons for these varied responses merit a deeper examination.

Countries Abandoning Nuclear Power

Let us look first at the case of Germany which has opted to abandon nuclear energy. In 2001, the German government comprising a coalition of the Social Democratic Party (SDP) and the Green Party that were opposed to nuclear energy had legislated a phase-out of the operating nuclear reactors. But, once the Christian Democratic Union (CDU) led by Angela Merkel came to power, she announced a reversal of the nuclear phase-out decision and decided to allow the operating reactors to continue to run as long as they could meet the safety criteria. Post-Fukushima, however, Merkel suspended her decision on continuance of nuclear reactors for three months and also called for an immediate shutdown of nuclear power plants set up before 1980. These steps were obviously taken in response to the public mood that seemed to have swung after Fukushima and which was being exploited by the Green Party with an eye on the pivotal parliamentary elections that were due in Baden-Wurttemberg, a state that had been ruled by the CDU for over 50 years without interruption. But, despite Merkel's deferment of the decision on nuclear power in Germany, the ruling party lost the election. Taking the electoral result as a clear reflection of the public sentiment on nuclear energy, the German Cabinet approved the amendments to the Atomic Energy Act in June 2011, which will facilitate the termination of nuclear power generation in Germany by 2022.

Besides the politics involved over nuclear power in Germany, several other factors pushed the country into abandoning nuclear energy. These include its socio-economic realities such as a stable population, a mature electricity market and a per capita energy availability of 7,030 kWh. The country foresees an electricity increase of no more than 1.1 percent per annum and has, in fact, been an exporter of electricity to the tune of nearly 15 billion kWh. In order to make up for the shortfall in electricity owing to the immediate shutdown of older reactors, Germany has decided to import more coal from Poland, more gas from Russia and nuclear generated electricity from France and Czechoslovakia, with the nuclear plants in the latter country being of even older vintage than the ones that Germany is phasing out.[4]

Meanwhile, it is also pertinent to note that there was a fair amount of scepticism in Germany on nuclear energy even before Fukushima. For example, a study commissioned by the German Federal Office for Radiation Protection gave its report in September 2009 after analysing the possibility of a worldwide expansion of nuclear energy based on the plans of the nuclear industry and the various scenarios painted by the Nuclear Energy Agency and the OECD. It identified several challenges that would hamper the realisation of a nuclear renaissance and concluded that nuclear energy would become less important by 2030 as ambitious plans fail to materialise.[5] Evidently then, nuclear power was anyway not very popular in Germany. The same situation also applies to Switzerland. While not taking as radical a decision of phase-out as Germany, Geneva nevertheless has decided to retire its five reactors as and when their licences expire between 2019 and 2034. Italy too has no enthusiasm for nuclear power.

Countries Reaffirming Nuclear Plans

A comparison of the case of Germany with that of India yields a completely contrasting picture. An emerging economy with an annual growth rate of 8-9 percent and a projected population increase of 1.58 percent, with a per capita electricity availability of only 631 kWh[6] and the highest projected annual electricity demand of 5.7 percent, India stands out as a nation with a huge electricity deficit. In such a scenario, the country can ill afford to rule out nuclear energy from its electricity mix since it needs to tap every watt of energy from wherever it can, including by emphasising and promoting energy efficiency and conservation. This is even more important since the addition to energy generation must meet the environmental criteria of GHG reductions. When measured by its carbon footprint, nuclear power is believed to be on par with solar, hydro, wind, biomass and geothermal, but it races ahead of the others in terms of its viability as a source of large scale base load power. Also, being a dense source of electricity, the land requirements of nuclear energy are only a fraction of the other sources. For instance, it has been calculated that "for a 1,000 MW power plant, nuclear requires about one square mile of space, compared with 50 square miles for solar, 250 for wind and 2,600 for biomass."[7]

Therefore, the Indian case is illustrative of the fact that countries with a large electricity demand, growing populations and limited alternative power sources that are also under pressure for reduction in national GHG emissions will continue to find nuclear power attractive for diversifying their energy mix. Not surprisingly, South Korea, China, Russia, France, Poland, the UK, South Africa, Turkey and Vietnam are some of the other countries that have ambitious nuclear plans and have reaffirmed these even in the wake of Fukushima.

The USA too considers nuclear power as an important part of its energy mix, especially for its environmental benefits. It was, in fact, President Bush who had initiated the favourable mood on nuclear energy. The US Energy Policy Act of 2005 promised loan guarantees and tax credits for up to $18.5 billion for the first 6 GW of nuclear power plants that would come on line by 2020. These were subsequently extended by the Energy Policy Act (EPA) of 2007 to $54.5 billion. Obama announced in 2010 that the first six plants would be eligible to receive several hundreds of millions of dollars in federal funds to reimburse them for any breakdown in regulatory processes or litigation. These measures did generate some enthusiasm, which led to 30 new reactors being announced, 20 of them at existing sites, to obviate public opposition to new acquisitions. However, even before the accident at Fukushima, there never was much expectation of all these plans reaching fruition, given the difficulty in raising capital in a recession-hit economy. Post-Fukushima, it will prove to be even more difficult and even the best estimates hope to see only 4-5 new reactors over the next decade or so. Nevertheless, the US has not lost its appetite for nuclear power and the 104 existing nuclear plants face no threat of premature shut down, even though the Nuclear Regulatory Commission (NRC) can be expected to be far more stringent in its oversight and licensing life extensions.

Amongst the major nuclear programmes in Asia, the Republic of Korea stands out for its rapid march in this field. Starting with its first nuclear power plant in 1978 with less than 600 MW, it has today a total nuclear generating capacity of 18,500 MW from 21 reactors representing 29.5 percent of the country's total power generation. The goal of Seoul is to increase the share of nuclear power to 56 pecent by bringing 11 more reactors online by 2021.[8] The country has also emerged as an aggressive nuclear exporter. It trumped the well established France to win its first contract for nuclear reactors in the

UAE in 2009 and has set itself an ambitious target of exporting as many as 80 nuclear plants in the coming decade.

Meanwhile, amongst the first timers, Vietnam has reaffirmed its commitment to nuclear power. It was in 2010 that the country had decided to build 13 nuclear power plants with a combined capacity of 16,000 MW by 2030. It had entered into a cooperation agreement with Russia for its first plant, Ninh Than 1, the construction of which was due to begin in 2014 after the conduct of the feasibility study, also to be funded by Russia. Moscow has recently announced that it will provide a loan of $ 9 billion for the construction of this first plant.[9] In another significant move, Vietnam has gone ahead and signed another agreement with none other than Japan to build two Boiling Water Reactors (BWRs) in southern Vietnam because it felt the "necessity of nuclear energy for securing energy supply".[10] Construction is set to start in 2013 and the plant is likely to be operational by 2020.

The Asian country with the most aggressive nuclear expansion policy is, of course, China. With 27 new plants under construction, it accounts for more than 40 percent of the global total of new reactor build. If completed successfully, this would double the world's nuclear capacity by 2030. Since the direction that China's nuclear programme takes would have such a huge impact on the global prospects of nuclear power, it would be worthwhile to examine China's response to Fukushima.

Projected as an important component of Beijing's plan to decarbonise China's economy, nuclear generating capacity is projected to rise from the current 11.3 GW to over 80 GW by 2020, making it the world's biggest reactor building programme. In the wake of Fukushima, China announced a temporary suspension of approvals for new projects until a review of the safety of existing ones could be concluded. But there is every indication that China will resume planned projects once that happens. As the nuclear safety Director of China's Environmental Protection Ministry said, "We're not going to stop eating for fear of choking."[11]

Yet, there is little doubt that Fukushima, as well as the high speed train collision in China, will have a sobering influence on the nuclear programme that earlier seemed to be proceeding at breakneck speed. Fortunately, the temporary slowdown will allow greater attention to be paid to the critical building blocks of nuclear safety, such as adequate training of operators and inspectors, formulation and implementation of independent and effective regulatory mechanisms and procedures, as well as reconsideration of future reactor technology. This is especially important since China has been considering large scale construction of indigenous CPR-1000 reactors designed in the 1990s, which are cheaper than the American AP 1000 or the French European Pressurised Reactor (EPR), but of second-generation vintage with an emergency cooling system dependent on electricity. After the Fukushima experience, the inherent safety of reactors with a passive cooling system has obviously grown and this will influence China's choice of reactor. It has also been reported that China would spend $ 23 million on nuclear safety, including radiation monitoring and technical support for supervising the civilian nuclear facilities and the safety of nuclear works.[12]

Countries Deferring Nuclear Decisions

As of 2009, the IAEA had reported having received an expression of interest in setting up nuclear power plants from as many as 65 new timers. The agency's technical cooperation projects had increased from 13 in 2007-08 to 35 in 2009-10 and as many as 58 countries were listed as participating in national or regional projects related to introduction of nuclear power through the agency's TC programme.[13] The major nuclear newcomers include Bangladesh, Egypt, Jordan, Mongolia, Saudi Arabia, Uruguay, UAE, as well as several countries of Southeast Asia.

Amongst these, countries have indicated varying levels of interest in nuclear power. A table prepared by the IAEA, and reproduced below, is indicative of this:

Table 1

Description of Group	**Number of Countries**
Not planning to introduce nuclear power plants, but interested in considering issues associated with a nuclear power programme.	31
Considering a nuclear power programme to meet identified energy needs, with a strong indication of intention to proceed.	14
Active preparation for a possible nuclear power programme with no final decision.	7
Decided to introduce nuclear power and started preparing the apt infrastructure.	10
New nuclear power plant ordered.	2
New nuclear power plant under construction.	1

As is evident from the above, a majority of these countries, even pre-Fukushima, had expressed an interest in learning more about nuclear power. Only a dozen countries had indicated a serious intent and were preparing the infrastructure for the purpose. For the time being, therefore, it seems likely that the countries that will persist with their nuclear plans will be the ones that already have an existing programme and/or those that are faced with large electricity demands and no easy alternatives. Others that were simply enthused by the 'nuclear renaissance' or wanting to make a national statement or garner domestic/international prestige by embarking on nuclear projects, would hold back, at least for the next few years.

For instance, Indonesia certainly identified with the natural disaster that hit Fukushima given that its islands are vulnerable to a similar phenomenon. As Prime Minister Yudhiyono stated, "National geological conditions render nuclear infrastructure vulnerable to damage" and he opined that the country should "explore ways to use other energy sources before building nuclear power plants."[14] Philippines, Peru, and Singapore could also be deterred since they were anyway more curious about, than committed to, nuclear power.

Meanwhile, countries like Thailand and Malaysia that had in place concrete plans have also opted for postponement of decisions. Thailand had planned for five 1,000 MW plants, with the first scheduled to become operational in 2020. But in May 2011, Bangkok decided to delay the programme by another three years to 2023. [15] It may be recalled that Thailand had first started a nuclear project in 1966 which was approved by the IAEA in 1970. But after selection of the site, the project was shelved in 1978 after natural gas was found in the Gulf of Thailand. Given its domestic energy resources, there obviously is no urgent compulsion for Thailand to opt for nuclear energy and the deferment of the decision is indicative of this.

Malaysia's Nuclear Power Corporation too had plans to start nuclear construction soon, but it has decided to reconsider its decision based on the mandate of the public. The national nuclear organisation is going to spend this time in raising domestic support to make the country nuclear-ready by 2013.

The Curious Case of Japan

The country that actually suffered the nuclear accident at Fukushima faces a dilemma on its nuclear energy programme. Before the disaster in March 2011, 54 nuclear reactors were providing 30 percent of Japan's electricity. The Japanese government had planned on increasing that amount to 50 percent by 2030. Two new reactors were under construction, 12 more were planned, and a waste management strategy that included recycling spent fuel was in the near-final stage of implementation. Today, only 11 reactors remain in operation, with work halted on other projects. Only one reactor has been restarted since

Japan began shutting down nuclear plants for regular maintenance and post-Fukushima inspections. Japan's remaining operating reactors are all scheduled to be shut down for regular maintenance by the next summer. Unless the reactors are also allowed to be restarted, Japan will be without nuclear power next year.

Interestingly, Japan chose nuclear energy in the 1970s after suffering the brunt of the oil crisis and with the clear aim of minimising reliance on imports of natural gas, coal, and oil. While it successfully managed to do so, in the process, Japan substantially increased its reliance on nuclear power. In the current scenario, when power plants have gone offline, Japan's vulnerability owing to its excessive dependence on one source of energy is evident. Meanwhile, public concern inhibits start-up of existing plants and casts a shadow on approval of the earlier nuclear plans. This uncertainty has huge economic implications by way of adding to the costs of fuel imports at a time when the country is struggling to cope with the costs of the devastating earthquake and tsunami. According to the Japan Centre of Economic Research, shutting down all Japan's nuclear plants over the next year will cause $ 94 billion or a 1.2 percent annual loss of the Gross Domestic Product (GDP). The Japanese government estimates that such an occurrence would result in a 10 percent power shortage and a 20 percent increase in electricity costs. Given that the Japanese industry accounts for 40 percent of the country's electricity use, such increases would be harmful for the industry, the consumers and the economy.

A recent report prepared by the committee under the government's National Policy Unit has calculated that additional safety measures such as emergency power generators and improved external sources of electricity as well as radiation protection gear for plant workers would cost $ 252 million per reactor.[16] This would amount to an increase of 5 percent in the cost of building a new reactor and thereby have an impact on nuclear energy not remaining the cheapest power source which it was in Japan before Fukushima. [17]

The country, therefore, faces a huge dilemma on nuclear power. While the public mood is obviously sceptical, Prime Minister Noda has expressed support for it in order to sustain the country's energy situation. It is also to be noted that Japan is a major nuclear supplier, especially of large sized reactor forgings. With a renewed focus on nuclear safety and regulatory processes, it is likely that Japan will return to restarting the existing nuclear plants, but that its long-term strategy would be to explore other options for energy generation.

Areas of Special Emphasis post Fukushima

The nuclear power sector has been faced with many challenges since the commercial use of nuclear energy first started. These issues have evoked varying amounts of interest, depending on the immediacy of the times. Post Fukushima, it would be useful to highlight three areas that will demand greater attention in the coming years if nuclear power has to make a meaningful contribution to the global electricity mix.

Restoration of Public Confidence

The faith of the public in nuclear energy has obviously been hugely dented after Fukushima. In fact, the information revolution enabled people in countries far and wide from Japan to view and live the horror of those in the vicinity of the nuclear plant. Consequently, public support for nuclear power obviously took a beating. A global study of 24 countries shows that a quarter of the people had changed their mind on nuclear power after Fukushima. Even in France, which has the highest contribution of nuclear energy in the world, 75 percent of the people expressed support for a slow phase-out of nuclear power.[18]

A big change in the coming times could be that people who earlier constituted the silent entity in nuclear decision-making could emerge as a powerful voice. Democratic or not, officialdom everywhere can no longer afford to ignore public sentiment and if nuclear plants are to be built in the future, then public confidence will have to be restored. Fukushima has raised the necessity of engaging with the populations and the nuclear establishment will have to proactively explain its case for nuclear energy and justify it in comparison to other alternatives, in order to win back public support. Two issues require special attention in the conduct of this exercise.

The first of these is the issue of regulatory independence and effective oversight. A preliminary report prepared by an IAEA fact-finding mission to Japan in May 2011 concluded that the accident was "a failure of regulation and design, not of operation". The tsunami hazard had been underestimated and the National Institute of Safety Assessment (NISA) was unable to perform its primary responsibility of safety since it was part of the ministry responsible for promoting nuclear energy. The most obvious lesson that stands out from Fukushima, and which has a resonance in all countries operating nuclear power plants, is the need for regulatory independence.

India has taken this seriously and the government has since taken several measures to rectify some of the institutional deficiencies. The Nuclear Safety Regulatory Authority Bill 2011 was introduced in Parliament earlier this year. It provides for the creation of a Council for Nuclear Safety to be headed by the Prime Minister to oversee and review policies relating to radiation safety. Meanwhile, the Nuclear Safety Review Committee appointed by the Atomic Energy Regulatory Board has recommended some 'back steps' at some nuclear power plants to raise safety standards. For example, in the case of the Tarapur Atomic Power Station (TAPS) 1 and 2, which are BWRs like at Fukushima, the committee has suggested back-up water to the emergency condenser for uninterrupted cooling of the reactor in case of a station blackout. Another pertinent suggestion is to set up additional air cooling generators and portable generators at all reactors.[19]

The second requirement stems from the need for increasing public awareness on the necessity of nuclear power in the electricity mix of nations that have to add new generation capacities while reducing GHG emissions. Unless these come from renewables, removing nuclear from the basket would lead to an increase in global Carbon Dioxide (CO2) emissions. According to one estimate put out by the Institute of Energy Economy of Japan, "Global carbon dioxide emissions may rise by 7 percent by 2035 should the Fukushima nuclear disaster slow the pace of expansion in atomic power generation."[20] From the environmental point of view then, there is a role for nuclear energy and this must be adequately highlighted so that the general public can make a cost benefit calculation.

Focus on HR Training

In 2008-10, the shortage of qualified and trained personnel for the projected expansion of nuclear power had been identified as a major area demanding special measures. Countries expanding their domestic programmes were faced with the challenge of having to scale up their existing education and training infrastructure even as nuclear exporting nations had also to ensure transfer of education and training capacities for construction, licensing and operation of power plants in first timer nuclear nations. Governments, industry, utilities and universities were identified as the instruments to undertake recruitment, retention, training and improvements of the nuclear workforce. At the Abu Dhabi HR conference in 2010, it was decided that the IAEA and other nuclear related organisations would undertake the following activities on a global scale: a survey of HR at existing power plants, a survey of demand and supply of HR for nuclear regulatory bodies, a survey of educational organisations and programmes that support nuclear power, development of workforce planning tools for new nuclear nations.

Post-Fukushima, the need for adequate training at all levels of activity in the nuclear sector will be even more critically felt. This is an area in which no compromises can be made. In fact, it must be considered a basic prerequisite for every new plant that is planned. Even where the reactor is to be constructed by an outside supplier, the HR requirements, including assistance in training, must be incorporated as an essential component of the exercise.

Addressing Waste Management Concerns

Management of radioactive waste and decommissioning of power plants has generated concerns and raised questions on the viability of nuclear power production. No country has yet designated a national site as a deep geological repository for high level waste. The USA, in fact, which had travelled a fair distance towards building and operating a waste storage facility at the Yucca Mountain, abandoned the plan in 2009 and has since appointed a Blue Ribbon Commission to provide recommendations for developing a safe long-term solution to the problem.

On June 19, 2011, the 27 European Union (EU) member states issued a directive on management of radioactive waste and spent fuel management. It creates a European framework of binding standards for final repositories for waste and requires states to present a detailed programme to the commission by 2015. Each state is also tasked to set up a regulatory body for managing spent fuel and publishing information on this so as to give an opportunity to the public to participate in the decisions on the subject. The member states are also obliged to submit periodically to an international peer review to exchange their experiences.[21]

Meanwhile, countries like India, France, Japan and Russia have adopted closed fuel cycles that allow them to recycle spent fuel, thereby reducing the amount of high level waste. Even in the case of Light Water Reactors (LWRs), new aqueous and non-aqueous spent fuel reprocessing technologies are being investigated to significantly decrease the waste generation. Of course, the final end product has to be disposed of but in most countries it is stored in interim storage sites. For final disposal, development work is being undertaken to investigate suitable sites and engineering of barriers to enhance safety of the site.

As far as decommissioning of nuclear power plants is concerned, experience in the area is slowly building up since 15 reactors have been dismantled and 51 more are in the process of being dismantled. The technology for decommissioning has matured and radiation hazards based on amount and type of wastes are well understood. Safe practices on the subject are also established. However, there is obviously ample scope for sharing best practices and building a data bank on the processes and procedures involved.

Conclusion

In 1979, when the first major nuclear accident at Three Mile Island occurred, a total of 233 nuclear power plants had been under construction. Even though this incident was placed at 3 on the International Nuclear Event Scale (INES), it did have an impact on the future of nuclear power worldwide. An even greater blow was felt when only seven years later, the accident at Chernobyl, rated 7 on the INES and the worst that the world has seen, rocked the nuclear industry. It took the world a good part of a quarter century to recover from that accident. It had a huge impact on reactor designing, operations and emergency preparedness.

The nuclear industry saw no other major nuclear mishap after 1986 until 2011 when an accident at Fukushima was triggered not by human error or faulty reactor operations or design, but because of the unprecedented scale and combination of a natural disaster. To its credit, the operating nuclear reactor did shutdown. But the failure of the emergency core cooling systems led to the huge complications that the world witnessed. Yet, no human life was lost as a result of radiation at the plant. In fact, the World Nuclear Association asserts that apart from Chernobyl, it is "not aware of a single radiation fatality that has occurred in the entire history of nuclear power, spanning some 14,500 reactor-years of nuclear electricity generation in some 30 nations worldwide". Public perception of nuclear safety, however, tends to assume otherwise.

Fukushima has compelled an analysis of the risk and benefits of nuclear energy, especially vis-a-vis other sources of electricity. Obviously, each country is arriving at its own assessment of the risks and acceptable tradeoffs. Countries that have access to oil or gas, or those developed nations which do not envisage a high energy demand, can reconsider the need for nuclear energy in their electricity mix. But, emerging economies that face a huge domestic electricity demand and have limited domestic fuel availability cannot find it prudent to rule out nuclear energy in their electricity mix. Therefore, the decision of each country to abandon or retain a nuclear power programme will be determined by its energy scenario, electricity availability and demand projections, as also the political constitution of the governments.

The IAEA has brought out two projections for the world's nuclear power generating capacity – the low projection estimates a growth from 367 GWe today to 501 GWe in 2030 through an addition of 90 new reactors. Compared to its pre-Fukushima assessment of the growth projection, this indicates a decline of 8 percent. The high projection, on the other hand, also indicates a similar decline of 7 percent as the nuclear electricity grows to 746 GWe from 350 new reactors.[22] Most of this growth would be in countries already operating nuclear power plants and mostly in Asia and the Far East. In fact, Western Europe shows the biggest difference between high and low projections, with the low scenario indicating a drop in nuclear generation capacity from the present 123 GWe to 83 GWe and, in the high scenario, though the figure rises to 141 GWe, it would still be 17 GWe below the growth projected last year. The only region where nuclear power projection in both the high and low scenario shows only slightly lower levels than projected last year is Eastern Europe which includes Russia, the Middle East and South Asia.

The predominant trends in the future of nuclear power post-Fukushima can be encapsulated as follows:

- In countries where the long-term drivers of nuclear energy are high electricity demand based on population and economic growth, nuclear energy will remain a part of the national energy mix.
- In countries which were venturing into nuclear energy with prestige as the main motive rather than energy security, there could be a pullback on nuclear energy.
- Countries that need to raise capital for building new reactors will find it difficult to do so at sufficiently attractive rates. The US faces this situation despite the offer of loan guarantees from the federal government.
- Extension of licences for existing power plants will come under scrutiny. This was routinely being done in most countries. It is a fact that most nuclear power plants are today running beyond the number of years for which they had first been licensed. For instance, nearly two-third of the American 104 nuclear power plants have had their original 40-year licences extended by 20 years. The United States Nuclear Regulatory Commission (US NRC) has never been known to have turned down a request for the life extension of a reactor. While this has been great for the economics of nuclear power, it is likely that post-Fukushima, the regulatory agencies would apply far more stringent criteria for extensions of plant lives.
- Environmental concerns, especially climate change, will compel implementation of stringent policies at reducing GHG emissions which will, in turn, compel inclusion of nuclear power in the energy basket of countries that envisage a rapid expansion of electricity production.
- Public support for nuclear power will have to be painstakingly built through proactive efforts aimed at the transparency and approachability of nuclear power for the ordinary man.
- Strengthening, including through revamping of regulatory processes and licensing procedures, will be seen across the countries as one way of restoring public confidence.
- Safe operation of nuclear reactors is as much a responsibility of the supplier as of the recipient. Therefore, supplier nations will have to temper their rush to bag new contracts to ensure that the highest levels of safety and regulation are available in the recipient nation before nuclear operations begin.
- Finally, while nuclear safety is a national responsibility, it must be performed in

compliance with international safety standards and practices. The experience of Fukushima – all that went wrong and all that functioned well– needs to be transparently shared for others to learn and imbibe.

Fukushima will have a sobering influence on nuclear enthusiasm. This, however, is not a totally unwelcome development. Given the nature of the technology, it is critical that national programmes grant nuclear safety the attention and the courtesy it deserves, especially if the world has to reap the full potential of this source of energy.

Notes

1. The last time such an aggressive reactor build was seen was in France when it commissioned 50 new reactors between 1977-90; 15 of these became operational in 1980-81.
2. Report by IAEA Director General, *International Status and Prospects of Nuclear Power*, GOV/INF/2010/12-GC(54)/INF/5
3. The earthquake has been placed as being of 9.0 magnitude on the Richter scale while the tsunami scaled a gigantic height of 46 feet.
4. Interestingly, the Czechs have drawn up a proposal for a national energy strategy which will increase focus on nuclear energy with the possibility of the share of nuclear contribution going up to 80 percent by 2060 compared to the current 32 percent. "Czech Strategy May Boost Nuclear Power Focus, Minister Says", http://www.bloomberg.com, September 8, 2011.
5. See Matthias Deutsch et al, "A Renaissance of Nuclear Energy?", Report prepared by Prognos AG, September 2009.
6. According to the Human Development Index, per capita electricity availability of at least 4,000 kWh annually is the dividing line between developing and advanced countries.
7. "US Energy Policy After Japan: If not Nuclear, then What?", http://www.knowledge.wharton.upenn.edu. March 30, 2011, accessed on April 21, 2011.
8. "Thailand's Looming Nuclear Question", *Bangkok Post*, August 29, 2011
9. "Russia to Lend Viet Nam $ 9 billion for First Nuclear Power Plant", http://www.bloomberg.com, November 22, 2011.
10. Alex Martin, "Vietnam Reactor Deal Advances", *Japan Times*, November 1, 2011.
11. "The Fukushima Accident – Three Months In", Interview of James Acton and Mark Hibbs at http://www.carnegieendowment.org/2011/06/10/fukushima-accident, downloaded on November 2, 2011.
12. "China to Spend $ 23 million on Nuclear Safety", *Economic Times*, May 15, 2011.
13. IAEA report, p. 10.
14. Andrea Berger, "Renaissance on Hold: Public Opinion and Nuclear Energy in Southeast Asia", *RUSI Journal*, accessed at http://www.rusi.org, on October 21, 2011.
15. "Thailand Delays First Nuclear Power Plant to 2023", *Reuters*, April 27, 2011
16. "Japan Nuclear Safety Steps May Cost 19 Billion Yen per Reactor", *Business Week*, November 15, 2011.
17. According to the Federation of Electric Power Companies of Japan (a group of 10 power utilities), the cost of atomic power in 2004 stood at 5.3 yen per kWh compared to coal at 5.7 yen, gas at 6.2 yen, oil at 10.7 yen and hydro at 11.9 yen. Ibid.

18. Mycle Schneider, "Nuclear Power in a post Fukushima World", *The Bulletin of Atomic Scientists*, July-August 2011.
19. "NSRC Proposes Back-up Measures to Enhance Nuclear Safety", *Economic Times*, September 4, 2011.
20. Aaron Sheldrick, "Global CO2 Emissions May Rise 7% After Fukushima Nuclear Crisis", http://www.bloomberg.com, OctOBER 28, 2011.
21. "EU has New Rules for Radioactive Waste Management", http://www.europolitics.info, July 19, 2011, accessed on July 30, 2011.
22. Alan McDonald and Holger Rogner, "IAEA Projects Slow Nuclear Growth After Fukushima", http://www.iaea.org/newscenter/news/2011, downloaded on November 2, 2011.